REF: 658.5

Operations Management

Operations Management

A Personal Skills Handbook

D. T. Johns

H. A. Harding

Gower Technical

Published by
Gower Technical
Gower Publishing Company Limited
Gower House
Croft Road
Aldershot
Hants GU11 3HR
England

Gower Publishing Company
Old Post Road
Brookfield
Vermont 05036
USA

British Library Cataloguing in Publication Data
Johns, D.T. *1948–*
   Operations management
   1. Manufacturing industries. Management
   I. Title II. Harding, H.A. *1927–*
   658.5

ISBN 0 566 09011 2

Contents

Part III   TECHNICAL SPECIALIZATIONS: A NEED TO KNOW

Part IV   MANAGING PEOPLE: IMPLEMENTING THE CHANGES

The conduct of negotiations – Personal development task
no. 16 – Chapter summary points – References – Audit
checklist

Illustrations

Figures

Tables

Acknowledgments

We would both like to acknowledge the assistance provided by colleagues at Sundridge Park Management Centre. In particular the help given by Will Newbold in providing structure and material for the section on negotiations proved invaluable.

Thanks also go to the consideration given by our families during this project.

Part I
INTRODUCTION: THE RATIONALE

1 The job of the operations manager

Introduction: the operations environment

The modern operations manager is intimately involved in the management of change. Now, more than ever, the person who will gain advantage for themselves and their organization will be the individual who manages the change process most successfully.

Figure 1.1 illustrates how the Operations Manager is centrally placed to manage change in the operations environment. All of the areas illustrated are in the process of rapid and almost continuous change and, to be effective, an Operations Manager must keep abreast and take account of all of them.

The dimensions of the *marketplace* are changing, both in size and location. The increasing opportunities to capitalize on the ability to segment markets mean that the organization, including the operations area, must get closer to the customer. This can involve substantial and risky changes, but time is of the essence.

The *competition* have not been standing still – indeed many are way down the track, restructuring their operations to provide better service to their customers. And the competitive advantage is not necessarily derived from a lower unit cost basis but more on the ability to deliver on time a repeatedly good product – benefits which the customer values and may be prepared to pay more for. In short, competition has been developed through 'excellence' in the operations area, supporting customer-sensitive and targeted product development.

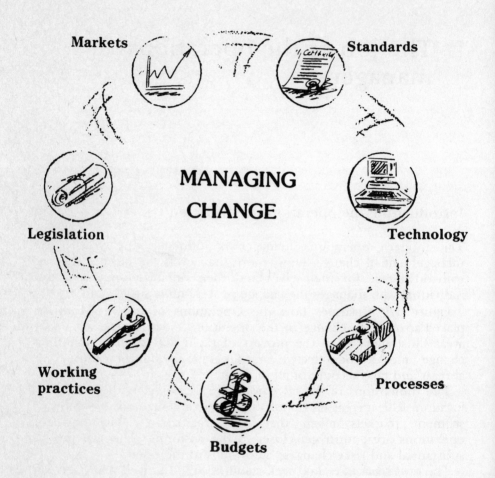

Figure 1.1 Managing change in the operations environment

Threatening as this may be, there are still opportunities to catch up by harnessing the substantial potential offered by the *technologies*.

Investments in *process technology* can revolutionize an industry's competitive structure, but that investment needs to be implemented in such a way that its full potential is realized. This may involve complementary organizational or system changes far removed from those visualized for the actual equipment hardware itself; changes which, if they are not effected, could prejudice the whole project viability.

Information technology offers a tremendous opportunity to learn more about customer needs, to integrate activities and to control operational performance more effectively, all features which can be translated into competitive advantage. But how often do system changes not quite reach their potential? In their early days, MRP (Material Requirement Planning Systems) systems were notorious for not delivering expected benefits! Often, non-delivery was not a fault of the system itself but rather because the far-reaching demands and effects of the change were not recognized in the implementation process.

The role of the operations manager with reference to new technology is to ensure that genuine benefits are highlighted, valued and delivered. This is made all the more difficult when we consider the constraints within which he or she operates.

The annual *budgeting* process in the operations environment has traditionally emphasized the 'cost sink' view of the area, and targets tend to be set in the cost-saving arena without considering the true role that can be played by the function. Instances abound where short-term cost savings have been realized at the price of flexibility and operational responsiveness, both factors which could be fundamental to winning orders in the marketplace. The ultimate price paid is, of course, long-term non-competitiveness and ultimate decline.

The problem is further compounded when we consider the link between achievement of budgeted results and the organizational reward structure. Emphasis on short-term results conditions managers to consider expediences which may not be in the best longer-term interests of their function or of the organization as a whole. Further reinforcement of this view can be evidenced in the capital expenditure budgeting process which in itself can be prejudiced against the longer-term, integrated, 'character-changing' type of project in favour of the faster-return 'satisficer'. The danger of this approach is that over a period of time the operational capability loses touch with the needs of the marketplace.

The operations manager's role in this area must be to persuade and influence others so that the appropriate performance measures are set, and to ensure that appropriate investment opportunities are highlighted and implemented to maintain an operational capability which matches the needs of the future marketplace.

The ability to persuade and influence also extends into the sphere of employee relations, where the need for change in operational effectiveness places pressure on existing *working practices*. A lack of skill or emphasis in this area can nullify any potential benefits to be gained from capital investment. Indeed, many investments or changes in operational capability require complete attitudinal changes if they are to succeed – a fact seldom recognized let alone effected.

A further constraining influence is the effect of *legislation* within which the operations manager has to operate. Recent times have witnessed changes in the application of legislation in the operations arena, and the successful firm will be the one that is able to work within these changes and still achieve demanding objectives.

This changing and challenging operating environment will either be seen as a threat or an opportunity, depending on one's approach to the management of change. The winners in this scenario will be those individuals and organizations who harness the potential of people, technologies and vision to get closer to their customers and service their needs most effectively.

Roles in the change process

Everybody has a role to play in this change process, as illustrated in Figure 1.2. Broadly, the individual contribution can be split into two aspects:

- Deciding the actual changes required
- Effectively implementing the desired changes

Both aspects are complementary, and the existence of either one without the other will negate any chance of effectively managing the process.

The emphasis on each aspect will depend on the nature of the change and the level of the individual within the organization. In general, operations strategy is formulated at the higher levels of the organization, albeit with input and stimulus from below. By contrast, the implementation of the desired changes tends to be intimately involved with the lower levels, albeit within the planning guidelines established from above. A general guideline for involvement in the change process is given in Figure 1.3.

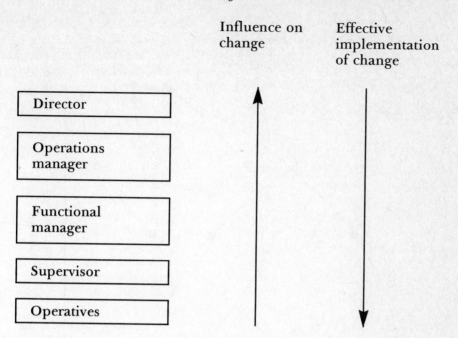

Figure 1.2   Roles in the change process

The skills needed to manage the process

The skills needed by the individual, if he or she is successfully to manage change, reflect the two aspects of the process: namely, deciding what is required and then successfully implementing those changes. In Figure 1.4, the first two headings reflect the first part of the process and are concerned with gaining a perspective on the necessary changes through an appreciation of operations strategy, and then understanding how the individual technical specializations can support that strategy to give the organization a competitive edge in · the marketplace. The second two headings reflect the implementation aspect of the change process, since all changes have to be implemented by people through people. They are concerned with managing others on an individual or team basis and, as a prerequisite, developing the ability to manage oneself.

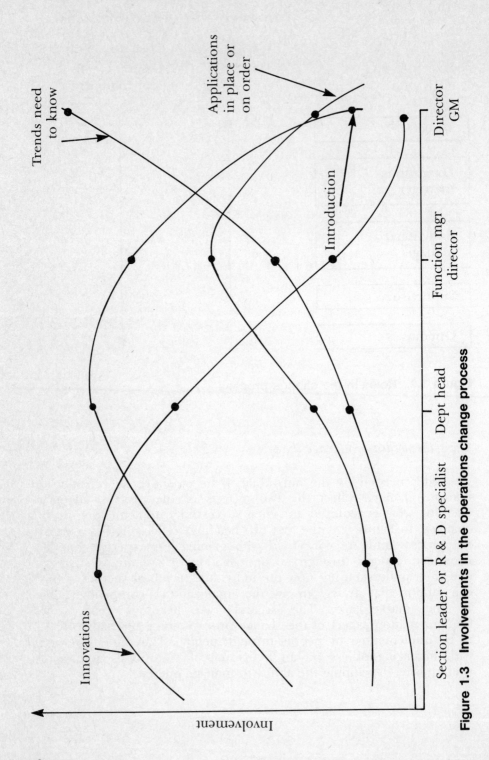

Figure 1.3 Involvements in the operations change process

Involvement

Innovations

Trends need to know

Applications in place or on order

Introduction

Section leader or R & D specialist   Dept head   Function mgr director   Director GM

8

The complete Operations Manager needs to have developed competence in all of these areas.

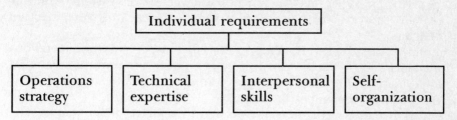

Figure 1.4   Skills needed to manage change

The book

The rationale for this book follows very closely the framework discussed above. It is intended to be a guide to the complete range of skills which the practising operations manager needs to succeed in today's rapidly changing world. As such, it is aimed at practising operations managers or functional managers in an operations environment.

The book is probably unique in that it does not just concentrate on the technical requirements of the job, nor does it present a range of behavioural skill techniques without setting them in a context that the operations manager would recognize. Instead, it acknowledges the intricate and complementary balance of technical and behavioural skills required and presents them in a format that the manager can apply to his or her job.

Structure

Part I provides an understanding of what changes are required in order to service the customer better and provides a framework that can be used to restructure the operation to that end. It is the 'outward-looking' view of the operations area and serves as a vocabulary that can be used to highlight the pitfalls and benefits of various strategies to non-operations individuals.

Part II considers each of the technical areas under the operations manager's control on a 'need-to-know' basis. It is not intended to give a detailed theoretical discussion of the variety of techniques involved, but rather to highlight the appropriateness of the application to particular operating environments in order to illustrate typical benefits and to consider any key issues posed by the application in practice. Checklists are used to aid this process. Since the development of a strategy can be considered as the accumulation of a series of incremental changes, it is important to ensure that changes proposed at the functional level are consistent with the overall strategy. This issue is covered in each of the relevant chapters.

Both Parts I and II refer to the first aspect of the operations manager's job – that of deciding what changes are required. Parts III and IV refer to developing the complement of behavioural skills necessary to implement the changes.

Part III deals with the skills needed to manage other people. The first approach is on an individual or one-to-one basis, since it is at this stage that the influence of motivational techniques and persuasion and influencing skills becomes apparent. The second approach reflects the increasing need to use a team approach to manage what are often multidisciplinary change problems. It considers the techniques needed to generate and manage an effective team, both in a formal and informal setting.

Part IV recognizes that it is difficult effectively to manage other people until you have learnt to manage yourself. This is particularly relevant for the operations manager as there are never-ending demands on his or her time. It is important that a system for categorizing and prioritizing work is developed and used, and these chapters provide a framework that can be used to this end.

The final Part of the book provides a view of the expected future demands on the operations manager. There is no doubt that the accelerating rate of change is going to place very great pressures on the operations area to achieve significant targets. This challenge presents a great opportunity both for the operations function and the operations manager to raise their corporate profile and demonstrate their ability to make real contributions to competitive advantage.

Methodology

The reader is invited to 'dip' in to the book as required, but it is important to remember that a balance between the technical and behavioural skills is required to function effectively in the job. To help, checklists are included at appropriate points in the text. These summarize the principles involved and form a practical guide which the reader can use to evaluate his own or his firm's performance. Self-help tasks are suggested where appropriate to focus the application to the reader's own environment. These are relevant tasks which can be used to test understanding, evaluate performance and direct further action. A recommended reading list is given at the end of each chapter.

Personal development task no. 1

1   Use the personal audit checklist on page 12 to audit your own performance as an operations manager, and highlight your strengths and weaknesses against the dimensions shown.

2   Use this as a guideline to read the book, concentrating on eliminating weaknesses and then building on strengths. Note that specific checklists which cover each area in detail are given at the appropriate point in the book.

Chapter summary points

● Operations management is intimately involved with the management of change.
● To be successful at managing change, individuals need a combination of both technical and behavioural skills.
● The book reflects this skill balance in its format.
● In the technical area, individual changes need to fit in with the strategy for operations.
● It is important to have the ability to manage yourself before trying to manage others.

Further reading

Lockyer, K. G., Oakland, J. S. and Sohal, A., *The Career Development of the Production Manager in British Industry,* British Institute of Management, 1987.

Personal audit checklist

Area: Operations Management

Topic: Personal Audit

Subject	Findings

1. List your strengths and weaknesses in
    individual performance against the following
    headings:

–   **Operations Strategy**

    –   definition of the key task
    –   interface with the business needs
    –   ability to make structural trade-offs with
        operators:

        –   process choice
        –   facilities
        –   organization structure
        –   systems
        –   linkages with suppliers and customers

–   **Technical Knowledge
    Planning and Controlling the Operation:**

    –   understanding the role of inventory
    –   approaches to reduce the inventory
        holding
    –   planning and controlling the flow:

        –   production planning and control
        –   just in time philosophy
        –   finite scheduling procedure

–   **Managing the Facilities**

    –   the concept of a facilities strategy
    –   facility trade-off decisions
    –   the acquisition process:

        –   financial appraisal
        –   required rates of return

12

Personal audit checklist cont'd

Area: Operations Management

Topic: Personal Audit

Subject	Findings

- – maintaining the fixed asset base
- – current issues in maintenance management

- **Managing Quality**

  - – the principles of total quality management
  - – the total costs of quality
  - – quality control systems and procedures

- **Managing the Finances:**

  - – the financial planning process
  - – the budgeting and performance reporting process
  - – the financial consequences of quality decisions:

    - – product mix
    - – pricing
    - – limiting factor
    - – break-even point

- **Managing People**

  Managing the Individual

  - – the impact of personality on motivation
  - – theories and approaches to motivation

  Managing the Team

  - – techniques for generating effective teams
  - – techniques for managing teams
  - – the skills and practice of negotiation

Personal audit checklist cont'd

Area: Operations Management

Topic: Personal Audit

Subject	Findings
Managing Yourself – the concept of accountabilities – the ability to set adequate objectives for self and staff – personal planning and agenda setting – principles of time management	

Part II
OPERATIONS STRATEGY: GAINING A PERSPECTIVE

Introduction

This part of the book is concerned with linking the capability of the operation to the needs of the marketplace. The emphasis is on focusing the performance of the operation to achieving competitive advantage for the firm.

The methodology followed is to consider the possible bases for deriving competitive advantage, translate these into a meaningful objective for operations, and to investigate the structural decisions that need to be made if advantage is to be derived. This analysis utilizes a variety of frameworks that build on previous work in this field –principally that of Porter, Skinner, New and Hill.

The end result of following this strategic approach is an operation which is focused on the needs of the customer, both now and in the future, with the potential to support and enhance the firm's competitive strategy.

2 Operations strategy: linking the operation to the needs of the marketplace

Introduction

A strategy developed for the operations area should ensure that *operations capability supports the firm's desired competitive advantage in its marketplace*. For example, if the firm is operating in a price-sensitive marketplace and pursuing a cost leadership strategy, then the key task for operations will be to become the lowest-cost operator. By this means the firm will derive, or maintain, a competitive advantage that can be exploited in its market. Failure to pursue this low-cost strategy in operations facilities, linkages and infrastructure decision-making will mean that the operation fails to make its fullest contribution towards the firm's competitive position. Indeed, the firm could be vulnerable to a competitor that has focused its efforts in this way.

Operations strategy reflects the outward-looking approach to operations decision-making, focusing on market and customer needs, with a view to enhancing the firm's chosen competitive position, both now and in the future. The desire is to provide a range of operations capabilities which can be exploited for commercial gain.

There are several implications of this approach. First, the firm must lay its cards on the table and declare its desired competitive position. Failure to do this will result in the setting of diffuse or conflicting objectives and a corresponding lack of commercial performance. Experience has shown that firms that do not actively position themselves in the marketplace, but instead adopt an 'all things to all men' approach are constrained to mediocre or below par performance.

Second, the chosen basis for competitive advantage must be communicated within the firm, in order to allow functional areas to focus on supporting that strategy by making individual, but consistent, decisions. For example, if the firm is following the cost leadership strategy mentioned earlier, it is very important that the purchasing department set up the appropriate lowest-cost linkages with its suppliers. This may involve arranging regular small batch deliveries from flexible suppliers using the firm's own transport – a policy which could minimize the total resourcing cost to the firm. Without the effective communication of the basis for competitive advantage, this policy may well be ruled out as inappropriate.

Third, and linked to the above, the firm must have a very clear idea of how it will measure operations performance. That is, the concept of operations productivity must very strongly support the direction taken by the firm's competitive strategy. Operations can be 'productive' in a number of ways, not just in the labour or machine-hour measures traditionally used. For example, an operation can be very 'productive' in the rapid introduction of new products to the marketplace. In a fast-moving consumer goods market which is fashion- and not price-sensitive, this concept of productivity is far more appropriate than any labour productivity measure. In fact, rigid adherence to traditional measures can focus an operation's efforts away from sustaining the firm's competitive advantage in the marketplace by failing to support the reasons why customers buy its products. The message is that failure to use appropriate measures of performance will rapidly encourage the decoupling of operations capability from the market needs.

Fourth, it must be accepted that corresponding structural decisions need to be made in the operations area. Operations cannot be all things to all men: for example, if the firm is pursuing a differentiation strategy, then, in supporting that target, operations will very rarely also be the lowest-cost operator (unless it has a supreme technological advantage). Under these circumstances, a more realistic objective for operations is to fully support the differentiation strategy whilst maintaining a cost proximity to other firms operating in the market.

In supporting the desired objective, the Operations Manager has to make structural decisions in three main areas:

1 Facilities capability
2 Supporting operations infrastructure
3 Internal and external linkages or interfaces

The test of a successful strategy implementation is whether there is consistency of decision-making within these three structural areas to support the desired competitive advantage.

In summary, the achievement of goal congruence or focus in the operations area, and the potential to translate that into competitive advantage, requires the formulation of an operations strategy, its communication and effective implementation. These tasks form part of the role of the operations manager.

In order to develop this concept further, the remainder of this chapter considers:

1 ways of developing competitive advantage for the firm;
2 methods for communicating that message to the operations area;
3 a framework for evaluating structural decisions in the light of competitive operations capability.

Competitive advantage for the firm

Firms need to decide on what basis they will compete within their industry. The objective is to earn greater returns for their efforts by advantageous positioning of the firm relative to its competitors. The degree of success achieved will depend on the characteristics of the industry, together with the viability of the chosen competitive strategy.

Porter[1] has shown that competitive advantage may be derived from either a cost leadership or differentiation strategy – an advantage that may be achieved on an industry-wide or focused sector basis.

If the firm decides to pursue a *cost leadership strategy* its objective is to provide a range of goods or services comparable to its competitors, but at lower cost. This strategy will allow it, if it so wishes, to follow aggressive pricing policies whilst maintaining greater margins than its competitors. This can sometimes lead to the achievement of a greater market share as others are driven from the marketplace. The pursuit of such a strategy has great implications within the firm, not least in the operations area. It will certainly impact on the acceptance criteria for investment decisions, on attitudes towards recruitment and remuneration, the linkages developed with suppliers and so on. All these decisions will need to be focused on minimizing the firm's total operating costs and, if this strategy has been established for some time, then the decision-making process will be embedded in the firm's 'minimum cost' culture.

The other option is for the firm to follow a *differentiation strategy*. In this instance its objective is to provide a range of products or services which are different from its competitors and where the differences are perceived by potential customers to be of such additional benefit that they would be prepared to pay a price premium for them. In providing this capability, the firm would aim to maintain a cost base proximity to its non-differentiated competitors, thereby ensuring that the price premium charged outweighs the costs associated with the differentiation and therefore generates enhanced profitability.

In practical terms, the perceived benefits will be valued if they either lower the customers' costs of use or enhance their performance. For example, opportunities exist for a differentiation strategy if a firm uses a manufacturing process that can hold closer product specification tolerances than its competitors. However, the viability of applying that strategy will depend on whether customer applications could use the enhanced product specification either to reduce their own operating costs or to provide extra real performance gains to their customers (in this case the consumer). If neither of these gains apply, then the original manufacturer's ability to use the differentiation strategy is limited. Indeed, if the close tolerance process in question is more expensive to run than the competitors' processes, it could even become a millstone around the Operations Manager's neck, delivering an expensive capability that is not valued by the marketplace and which also precludes the effective adoption of a cost leadership strategy.

As with the previous strategy, a differentiation strategy will impact on the structural decisions made by the firm. However, as illustrated by the example, opportunities to differentiate only exist if the corresponding benefits are valued by the marketplace. This is a case for ensuring that all investment decisions are related to deriving real competitive advantage in the marketplace, that research and development (R and D) activity is focused on truly-valued product or process improvements, and that infrastructure decisions support the particular basis for differentiation within the industry.

However, a fact common to each strategy is that the firm needs to make the choice of how it will compete, for it will not be able to service all options simultaneously. Attempting to take the latter approach will result both in a below-par commercial performance and the erosion of any previous competitive position held by the firm.

In making the choice between strategies, the firm will need to consider industry prospects and its own ability to support a continued and economically viable position within that industry. For example, if the firm chooses the cost leadership option does it realistically possess the R and D effort to sustain the process technology development work necessary to ensure that it maintains its low-cost competitive advantage. If funding is not available to support the continued efforts needed in that direction then it is questionable whether such a strategy is tenable in the long term. Certainly, if the process development work is not funded, rivalry amongst competitors or new entrants will eventually eliminate the initial low-cost advantage.

What the firm is looking for is the ability to establish long-term viable competitive advantage in its industry. This will result in either a cost leadership or differentiation strategy which will need to be supported by operations. In particular, the decision will need to be communicated to the operations area in a way that will encourage the appropriate operations decisions to be taken.

The link between competitive advantage and operations capability

If the operations area is to support the firm's competitive advantage then it needs to reflect the chosen basis for advantage in its decision-making. The task is to develop the characteristics of the operations area in line with the market needs. Thus, if the marketplace opportunity exists to win business by rapid delivery of customized products or services, then structural and operating decisions made in the operations area should all be designed to foster volume and variety flexibility. By adopting this approach, the firm will be able to win business over competitors who do not exhibit this degree of focus in their decision-making process, or who may be following a misplaced minimum cost strategy.

If firms are to make the linkage between competitive advantage in their industry and operational capability, then they will need to define and communicate optimum operational performance. This can be done through the context of what Skinner[2] has called the 'key operations task' – that is, a focused objective for the operations area which will directly support the desired competitive advantage.

The key task is the unique linkage between operational capability and competitive advantage. It answers the question: 'What does operations have to do really well if we are to succeed in the marketplace?' As such, it can have a number of dimensions, relating to the characteristics of the industry or marketplace and the firm's chosen basis for competitive advantage. It is against these dimensions that operations decisions are taken and subsequent performance measured.

The first set of dimensions relate to *industry or market characteristics,* which set the competitive scope for operations. They relate to such factors as the scale of operation, linkages with suppliers and customers, competitor performance and so on. Typical market characteristics would include:

- Volume
    - scale:
    large
    small
    - demand pattern:
    stable
    erratic
    seasonal
    - typical order size:
    large
    small
- Variety
    - product range:
    wide
    narrow
    - frequency of new product introduction:
    high
    low
- Competition
    - basis:
    product
    process
- Customer and supplier linkages
    - established, integrated
    - embrionic
- Barriers to entry
    - scale or capital requirements
    - technology or learning curve
    - proprietary interests
    - established linkages
    - cost of changeover

Within the constraints of the industry dimensions, the key task will take on the *competitive strategy characteristics* as defined below:

● Cost leadership

● Differentiation
  - specification:
    uniqueness
    reliability and consistency
    performance
    customization
  - delivery performance:
    availability
    extended reliable lead times

Each of these market characteristics is considered in more detail below.

Market Characteristics

Volume The volume characteristics of the marketplace can be expressed against a number of dimensions.

A traditional approach has been to refer to the scale of the operation as 'large' or 'small', referring to the absolute level of operating volume involved. Therefore, two firms could be operating in the same industry but, because of differing market strategies, one could be involved in a large-scale operation whereas the other could focus on achieving success with small-scale production. An example is the volume car manufacturer versus the specialist. In this case the criterion for success for operations is totally different, reflecting the different market needs and hence a different key task. The volume scale dimension is closely related to the firm's chosen scope of operation in its industry and will be reflected in the structural decisions made within operations.

Within the scale of operation the pattern of demand takes on an important dimension. Traditionally, the response to a seasonal demand pattern has been to size the plants to deliver annual demand on a stable monthly rate, and to insulate the plant from its market by finished goods stock. In other words, it is recognized that the plant does not possess the inherent volume flexibility necessary economically to adjust its output to match the specific month's requirements. However, the result of this assumption is to accept the cost of holding stock, and it may be that an alternative approach may prove serviceable and more economic when the total cost of production, including stockholding, is taken into account. For instance, the operation could be structured to be deliberately labour-intensive and could be located in an area where there is a sufficiently large pool of suitable labour who can be employed on an ad hoc basis to flex the volume of output to suit the market requirements. Provided care is taken to 'error-proof' the operation, this could prove to be a suitable alternative. The appropriate choice will depend on the definition of the key operations task.

A stable demand pattern would make the position correspondingly easier.

The typical order size is principally of importance when the firm is operating in a 'make to order' situation. If in this case the firm is operating in a market which is characterized by a small number of large orders; then one of its key concerns will be to manage its' capacity effectively. Here, it may be expedient to structure a low fixed cost operation to avoid the cost penalty of low utilization. This can be achieved using a small homebase facility concentrating on 'core technology', with significant use of subcontract activity for the routine work. Again, with regard to the key operations task, the approach chosen will reflect the definition of 'what business are we in?'

Variety The variety dimension will influence the degree of flexibility that is structured into the facility. Note that this will not only be confined to the equipment, but also to the organizational structure and supporting systems.

If the firm is operating in a limited product range environment, then there is the opportunity to dedicate facilities and so derive additional cost efficiencies. However, where the industry is characterized by either wide product variety through customization or rapid new product introductions due to technological improvements, then a key operations consideration will be to engineer flexibility into the operation.

This can be achieved through reducing machine changeover times, encouraging responsiveness in the organization structure, and by developing flexible planning systems. If these actions are not taken, the operation will not be able to compete successfully in its marketplace.

Competition The basis for competition will colour the attitude taken within the firm towards product and process development. If the main competitive thrust is through new product development, then the emphasis within the operations area will be in developing the ability to take an engineering design and rapidly translate that into a viable, manufacturable product with the appropriate facilities. If the basis for competition is process-based – that is, using and building on expertise already developed for certain process technology, the emphasis within manufacturing will be to consolidate and further enhance that process expertise.

In the first case, the process technology expertise is the derived item, relating to the new product development, whereas in the second instance it is the product development that is the derived item, relating to current expertise and market advantage in a possibly unique process technology.

Customer and supplier linkages The key task for operations will also be influenced by the stage of development of customer and supplier linkages. One of the prerequisites for a flexible operation is to develop responsive linkages with both customers and suppliers. If these linkages are not present, many of the benefits developed by engineering flexibility within the operation will not accrue. For example, the ability to run small batch sizes within the firm will not develop a sustainable competitive advantage within the industry unless the distribution system is in place to deliver those small batches to the customer, and unless the supplier relationships exist to encourage frequent, small-quantity deliveries.

Where a firm's competitive position hinges on flexibility of response to its marketplace, the development of the appropriate customer and supplier linkages could be a key task for operations.

Barriers to entry There are several barriers to market entry existing within an industry. They could relate to the degree of capital funding needed to break in and become established as a presence within the industry, or they may be related to the need to break down and reinstate the appropriate customer and supplier linkages that exist. Other types of barriers have been listed in the previous section.

Whatever barriers exist may well colour the operations task of firms that are already part of the industry, as well as those that are trying to break in. Those already established in the industry will be concentrating on reinforcing the barriers and making it even harder for potential competitors to enter – for example, by getting closer to suppliers through long-term supply agreements, by enhancing their lead in specific process technology and so making it more difficult for competitors to climb the learning curve and so on. Those firms trying to break into the industry will attempt to develop the appropriate linkages, engineer a lower capital intensity into the process or look for alternative ways of skirting the existing barriers to entry.

Both sets of firms will have their key operations task significantly influenced by the effects of the barriers to entry.

Thus, the first set of characteristics that influences the key operations task relates to the industry that the firm operates in. The second set of characteristics relates to how it decides to compete within that industry.

Competitive strategy characteristics

Cost leadership If the firm chooses to compete through a cost leadership strategy, then this must be reflected in the definition of the key operations task. All structural decisions in the operations area must be made with a view to reducing costs, as this will be totally in concert with the firm's position within its industry.

Plant and equipment will therefore be chosen with cost-saving as a major consideration; an organization structure will be chosen that avoids duplication and is cost-effective; operating systems will be chosen that can be managed to drive out costs; and both process and information technology will be used to gain competitive advantage through cost-saving. If the operations area makes a concerted and consistent effort against all these dimensions, it will develop an internal culture supporting the key operations task of structuring the lowest-cost operations facility in the industry. If that objective is achieved, real competitive advantage will accrue to the firm through operations performance.

Differentiation The firm may choose to compete through a differentiation strategy and, in this instance, the key operations task must be to structure the operation to support and enhance the chosen basis for differentiation. For example, if the firm competes through the achievement of a product specification that cannot be attained by the competition, then a key task for operations is to maintain the process capability of hitting and (if the market warrants it) improving that specification.

If the chosen basis for competition is superior delivery performance, then the key task for operations is to structure the most flexible operation in the industry, with the appropriate customer and supplier linkages. Failure to achieve this task means that the operation is not effectively supporting the firm's chosen basis for competition, and may render the whole firm vulnerable to a competitor who targets his competitive basis on superior delivery performance.

27

The critical activity for the operations manager must be to structure the operation to support the firm's chosen basis for competition, and to capitalize on the market or industry characteristics as appropriate. By this means, operations becomes an important member of the corporate team with a direct influence on the organization's success.

Responsibility for defining the key operations task

By defining the key task in these terms, the operations manager has the basis for structuring and measuring operations performance. However, this is not just his or her responsibility alone. In fact, whilst the operations environment can provide an assessment of current capability, it is not best placed to evaluate desired future capability, since this relates to market conditions and competitive stance. Therefore, a joint approach involving both operations and marketing is best as, between them, they can evolve an operations strategy which will support the desired competitive thrust in the marketplace and which will realistically be within the capability of the operation to achieve and sustain.

That is not to say that the operations manager should not be adopting a positive, pro-active stance in this matter. Indeed, the initiative will probably rest with the operations manager to present potential competitive opportunities through operations capability to other non-operations managers. It is through this approach that the operations contribution will be truly recognized.

Typical key tasks for the operation include:

- To manufacture a narrow product range in high volume on a make-to-stock basis, where the competitive strategy is low cost. In this instance, delivery performance and the achievement of a product specification on a par with customer expectations and competitor achievements is a qualifier to be in the market at all.

OR

- To manufacture a wide product range in low volumes on a make-to-order basis, where the competitive strategy is one of differentiation, based on rapid delivery performance. In this instance, quality or the achievement of product specification is a qualifier to be in the business at all.

OR

- To manufacture a range of products in narrow volumes where the product technology is subject to rapid change. Here, the strategy followed by the firm is that of differentiation, based on product innovation. The key operations task needs to reflect that.

Once the key operations task has been defined against these dimensions, the appropriate operations decisions need to be made to support its achievement.

Structural choices in the operations area

Since the implementation of strategy can be witnessed through the range of incremental decisions made in the operations area, it is very important that each individual decision supports the firm's competitive position.

For example, are the negotiations surrounding the proposed bonus scheme focusing on the flexibility required by the firm's differentiation strategy or will they build in a degree of rigidity which will hinder and eventually preclude the effective pursuit of that competitive advantage?

In order to achieve consistency in decision-making, individual decisions should be made within the context of an overall framework. This gives the advantage that each decision can relate to the key operations task, and also that any interrelationships can be highlighted.

A framework is highlighted in Figure 2.1 which illustrates the nature of the strategic decision-making process within the firm.

We start with an industry focus and at this stage the firm's task is to decide the basis for competitive advantage and the scope of that advantage. As previously discussed, this takes the form of either a cost leadership or differentiation strategy over an industry-wide or focused sector target.

Having established the basis for competition, the task becomes one of communicating that basis within the firm in order to set the emphasis for decision-making. The communication link to the operations area is via the key operations task which defines those critical characteristics of operations performance that will support the firm's desired competitive advantage.

In order to translate this into a reality, the operations manager will need to make relevant choices in each of three areas: facilities, infrastructure, and the corresponding linkages with suppliers and

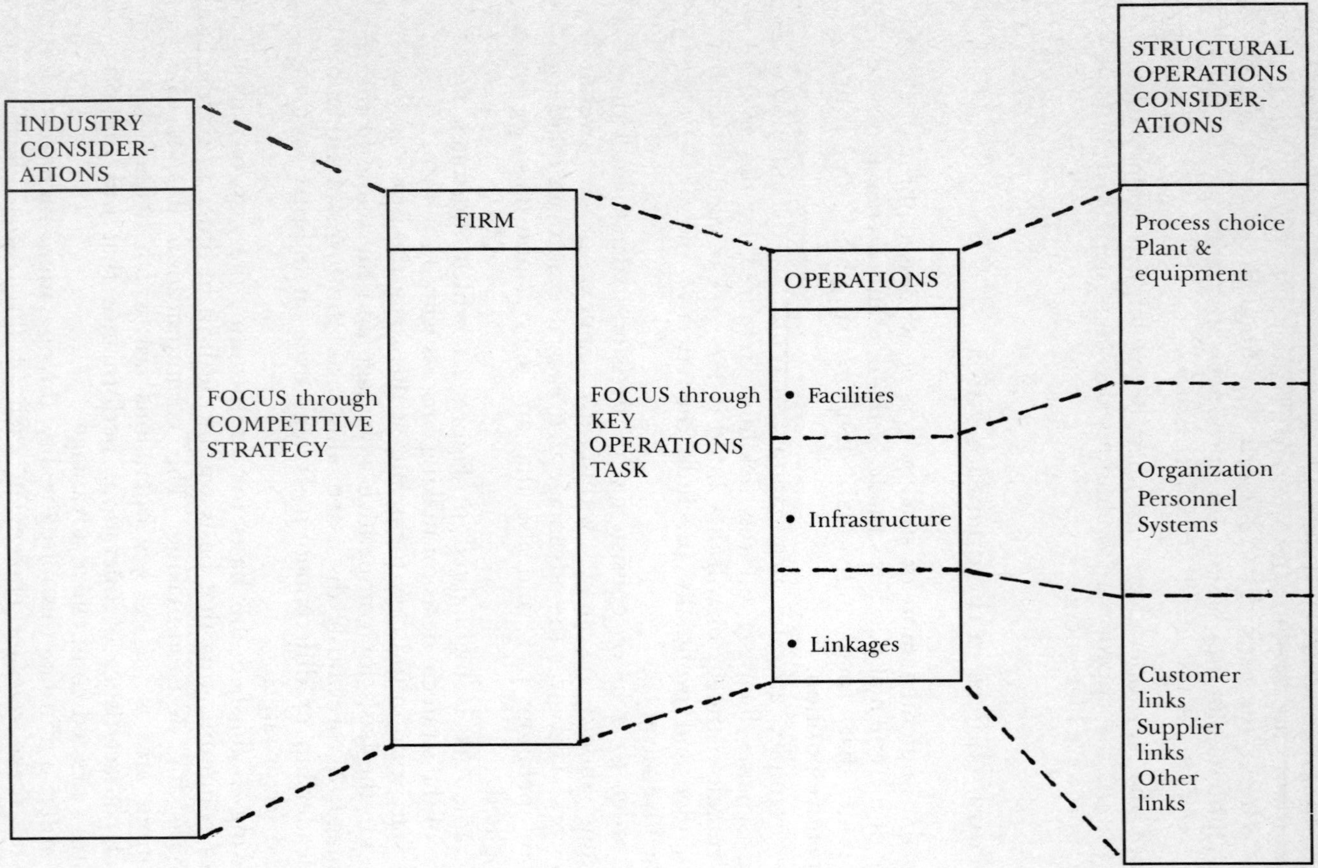

STRUCTURAL OPERATIONS CONSIDER-ATIONS	OPERATIONS	FIRM	INDUSTRY CONSIDER-ATIONS
Process choice Plant & equipment	• Facilities		
Organization Personnel Systems	• Infrastructure		
Customer links Supplier links Other links	• Linkages		
	FOCUS through KEY OPERATIONS TASK	FOCUS through COMPETITIVE STRATEGY	

Figure 2.1 The strategic decision-making process

customers. The detail of the choices and the implicit trade-offs are covered in Chapter 3.

Personal development task no. 2.

1 Using the key task checklist on page 28 develop the key task for your operation.
2 Does this correspond to your present operational competence?
3 What mechanisms exist to track the way market characteristics are moving and hence modifying the key task?
4 How involved do you get in setting and supporting the firm's competitive strategy?

Chapter summary points

- Operations capability supports the firm's desired competitive advantage in its marketplace.
- The key operations task is the link between the operation and the marketplace. It answers the question; 'What does operations have to do well if we are to succeed in the marketplace?'
- The key task has dimensions that relate to the firm's industry and its chosen competitive strategy.

References and essential reading

1 Porter, M. E., *Competitive Advantage,* New York; Free Press, 1985.
2 Skinner, W., *Manufacturing: the formidable competitive weapon,* New York: Wiley, 1985.

Audit checklist

Area: Operations Strategy

Topic: Key Operations Task

Subject	Findings

1. Specify the characteristics of the key operations task against the following dimensions:

   Volume

scale	:	(large or small)
demand pattern	:	(stable, seasonal or erratic)
typical order size	:	(large or small)

   Variety

product range	:	(wide or narrow)
new product introduction	:	(frequent or infrequent)

Competitive Direction	:	(product or process)
Linkages	:	(supplier or customer)

   Competitive Strategy

   Cost Leadership
   Differentiation:

   - specification
   - delivery performance
     - rapid
     - extended but reliable

2. Formulate the key task assigning priority to the various dimensions alone (ie distinguishing between criteria that are qualified to be in the market and other criteria that win orders)

3 Structuring the operation and implementing the strategy

Introduction

The link between the operation and competitive advantage in the marketplace is the key operations task. This chapter considers the structural decisions that need to be made if the operation is to perform effectively against that key task. For it is against this measure that operations performance should be assessed, as it is through this process that operations can give the firm a competitive advantage in its marketplace.

Operations decisions can be grouped under the following categories:

- Facilities:
  - Process choice
  - Equipment characteristics and selection
- Infrastructure:
  - Organization
  - Personnel
  - Systems
  - Procedures
- Linkages:
  - Customer
  - Supplier
  - Other

Note that although decisions are shown in the above discrete groupings, they will in reality be interrelated. For example, a change made in the process choice area will have an effect on the systems needed to schedule that equipment as well as the type of organization and personnel needed to support the new process. Failure to recognize this interrelationship and to make the appropriate changes will normally result in a failure to realize the full benefits of the process choice change.

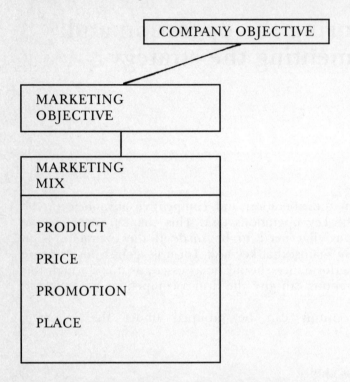

Figure 3.1   The translation of company objective into marketing mix

The marketing mix

An analogy can be drawn with the marketing mix framework, and this is illustrated in Figure 3.1. In this instance, the organization highlights its corporate objective, which is generally expressed in financial terms, and the link is made to the corresponding marketing objectives. In other words, the marketing objectives, if achieved, become the means by which marketing makes its contribution to the corporate goals. For these functional objectives to be meaningful they must relate to the corporate requirements, be realistic and achievable.

Typical focused marketing objectives include 'the marketing and selling of these products into these markets at these margins' or 'the introduction of this new product range into this market consuming these resources'.

Once the objectives have been defined they are achieved using the elements of the 'marketing mix' – that is product, price, promotion and place. The intention is to devleop or use the right product to satisfy the customer needs, price it with the appropriate pricing policy, promote it accordingly and get it in the right place at the right time using the appropriate channels of distribution. If these actions are carried out effectively, the marketing objective will be achieved, and hence the corporate objectives can be attained.

The significant points about this approach are:

1   The use of a marketing objective to focus marketing efforts on achieving corporate goals – that is, the equivalent of the operations key task.
2   The use of the marketing mix elements to achieve the marketing objective – that is, the equivalent of the operations structural decisions mentioned earlier.
3   The interrelationship of the marketing mix elements. If one element is changed there will nearly always be the need to change another element, as they are interrelated. A product change could easily result in the need to change the channels of distribution, or the need for a pricing policy change. Another noteworthy point is that 'product' tends to be the marketing mix element that predominates and is supported by the other three.
4   Not only does the marketing mix framework provide a structure for coordinating efforts, it also acts as a vocabulary for discussion of the options and merits of various strategies.

The marketing mix framework has therefore a very important role to play in focusing and coordinating marketing efforts to the corporate needs.

New, Hill and others have worked on developing an equivalent framework for operations, giving rise to the concept of an operations mix.

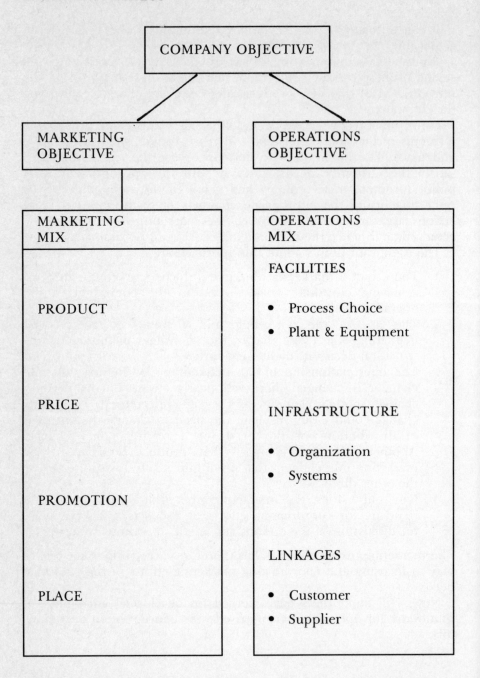

Figure 3.2   The translation of company objective into operations mix

The operations mix

Figure 3.2 demonstrates how the link to the corporate objective is through the operations objective, which is the equivalent of Skinner's key task. This represents the focused, achievable objective against which operations performance will be measured. For this to be meaningful, it must be related to both the characteristics of the industry in which the firm operates and to the competitive strategy chosen by the firm. In other words, it defines the operations 'productivity' that is required if the firm is to achieve competitive advantage in its marketplace.

The operation achieves this objective by structural and tactical decisions in three areas: facilities, supporting infrastructure and the appropriate internal and external linkages. These areas constitute the elements of the *operations mix.*

Before considering each of these categories in turn it is worth noting that, just as applied to the marketing mix, each of these elements is interrelated. Thus, if a change is effected to any one of them then supporting changes will be required in at least one of the other three elements. For example, the introduction of a significant system change will normally necessitate corresponding changes in the organization structure. If these supporting changes are not made, it is doubtful whether the full system benefits will accrue. Similarly, the installation of a new piece of equipment which incorporates new technology will not yield full benefits to the firm unless the new personnel and system requirements to support that new technology (for example, maintenance activity) are met.

A related point is that a firm desiring a competitive advantage in its industry must focus each of the operations mix elements on achieving the same key task. In order words, if the firm is following a 'lowest cost' strategy, then it is very important that all elements of the operations mix are also focused on achieving that low-cost strategy. This has implications for the equipment purchased, the organization structure developed, the systems used, and the linkages developed outside the company.

By pursuing this approach, the firm is likely to see the benefits of synergy in its operations capability, as opposed to fragmentation as the differing mix elements pull the operation in opposing directions. Of course, it goes without saying that it is very important to define the key task correctly in the first place!

Structuring the operation

Once the key has been defined, the critical activity for the operations manager is to make the appropriate decisions in each of the operations mix elements. The test of whether a coherent strategy is being followed is to examine the consistency of decision-making both amongst the individual mix elements, and in how they relate to each other.

Of all the mix elements under consideration, the process choice element is the one that has traditionally predominated, as it is this element that links the operation characteristics through the key task to its marketplace. The following section examines each of the mix elements in turn.

The facilities mix element

Process choice

The traditional operations process choice options fall into the following categories:

- Project
  Jobbing or 'one-off'
  Batch
  Flowline:
  - Assembly line
  - Continuous process

Each of these process choices possesses a set of traditional characteristics that either helps or hinders the achievement of the key operations task. In other words there is no universally acceptable process choice that allows the operation to interract successfully with every industry situation and every choice of competitive position. A decision will need to be made to use the process choice that best matches the present and future needs of the firm. This concept of compromise has directed significant technological effort into modifying the traditional characteristics of particular process choices. For example, as will be discussed later, much effort has been directed towards employing flexible automation with flowline processes in order to achieve both the benefits of scale and the ability to handle variety. However, at this juncture, it is appropriate to concentrate on the traditional characteristics found with different process choices.

Project The 'project' type of process choice is typically associated with the more complex type of product or service. These could range from the specification, design, manufacture and commissioning of large capital plant such as a rolling mill to the provision of complex consultancy assignments. Certainly, the method is traditionally associated with complexity.

With this type of process choice, control is normally exerted through some system of 'milestones', which form part of the overall planning and control system. The scope of the task has prompted the use of computers to coordinate the wide-ranging set of activities.

Jobbing or 'one-off' The 'jobbing' process choice involves the manufacture of goods or services to customer specification on a one-off basis. The product itself tends to be of a simpler nature than the 'project' type of product or service. Examples of this type of process choice include the manufacture of prototype equipment, where the design may be specified by the customer, or the provision of a tailored service which exactly matches a customer requirement.

With this type of process choice, the flow of the individual products or services through the factory or facilities will be related to the requirements of that particular product, and will differ from other products being manufactured at the same time. Again a key consideration is the management of this complexity in order to deliver the product on time, whilst minimizing the levels of work in process.

Batch The 'batch' process choice has similarities with the above since, again, there will be differing process flows through the factory, although this time they will be associated with different groups or batches of products and services. Whereas the 'jobbing' process choice is associated with the 'make-to-order' environment, the batch process could well include elements of 'make-to-stock', the batch size having been influenced not only by the market demand but also by the characteristics of the equipment (for example, by the desire to maintain a certain set-up to run time ratio).

One of the critical activities in this environment is the management of the complexity of the process flows to achieve desired output targets with minimum work in process.

Flowline Processes There are two types of flowline processes: assembly line and continuous process.

The *assembly line* environment is associated with a limited range of products following a predetermined flow path through the facilities, with set operations being carried out at each work station. In this instance, the equipment used has traditionally been dedicated to the narrow range of products or services produced, and a key consideration has been to maintain high line speeds and high equipment utilization.

Typical products produced in this environment include motor cars and 'white goods' type products where there is little variation in product specification and where a critical consideration is to reduce manufacturing costs by taking advantage of the benefits of specialization offered by the line.

With *continuous process*, the product again passes through a predetermined flow path, with successive operations being carried out at each stage. Unlike the line environment there is no assembly operation involved, but rather the further conversion of the product at each stage. Typical examples of this process choice include certain chemical industry processes and paper production.

Again, a key consideration for the operations manager is to maintain high equipment utilization in order to amortize the normally high equipment capital costs associated with this type of process.

A fundamental choice for the operations manager is to decide which type of process choice best matches the needs of the business. As mentioned earlier, this is best effected by linking in to the key operations task.

Each of the process choices described above has a series of traditional characteristics that it imposes on the operation, and the critical activity is to capitalize on those characteristics that help the firm compete in its marketplace and to minimize the effect of those characteristics that hinder its performance. Technology plays a significant role in adapting the traditional characteristics of process choices to build on their strengths and minimize their weaknesses – for example, by engineering variety flexibility into an assembly line process without prejudicing its traditional low unit cost benefits.

We shall first consider the traditional characteristics of process choice in order to link them to the key task, and then see how technology and other external influences are modifying the basic rules.

The process choice link to the key operations task From the previous chapter, it was seen that the key operations task is specified against two dimensions: market characteristics and competitive strategy characteristics. It is important that the process choice made reflects the needs of both sets of characteristics, and Table 3.1 highlights the dimensions of the key task characteristics and the traditional characteristics of the particular process choice. The table makes the link between process choice characteristics and the key operations task dimensions. For example, it can be seen that the inherent characteristics of the flowline process have made it traditionally suitable for high-volume operation, with a limited product variety of mature products in a make-to-stock environment, where the competitive strategy characteristic is that of cost leadership. Provided that this is the firm's desired basis for competitive advantage, then this process choice is appropriate. Any other process choice would be unable fully to support the market and the firm's competitive strategy posture, and would result in an operation that is out of focus with the needs of the business.

However, were the firm operating in an industry characterized by lower product volumes but with increased product variety and were the basis for competitive advantage a differentiation strategy, then a batch process choice would, on balance, supply the operations characteristics that most closely match the needs of the marketplace.

Note that the adoption of a differentiation strategy does not imply the disappearance of attention to product costs, since the firm will still need to maintain a price proximity to its competitors. Therefore, the appropriate solution for operations is to adopt the batch process choice which traditionally has the characteristics to match the market needs, and to use technology as a focus for cost reduction without prejudicing variety flexibility. A more radical approach would be to adopt a flowline process choice where technology has been successful in engineering the requisite degree of variety flexibility. In other words, although Table 3.1 is the starting-point to link the process choice to the marketplace, opportunities exist to change the rules using either process or information technology.

The first structural choice made by the operations manager is the process choice decision. The effects of this choice are far-reaching, as supporting structural choices will need to be made in the areas of facilities, infrastructure and industry linkages. If these complementary decisions are not made the operation as a whole will not be focusing on the needs of the customer, and will be vulnerable to any competitor who has targeted that same market sector for competition. It is necessary to consider each of these complementary areas in turn to develop the critical activities of the operations manager against these dimensions.

Table 3.1
Traditional characteristics of process choice

Characteristics	Project	Jobbing	Batch	Flowline
				Assembly Line Cont. Process

Market Characteristics

Volume
- Scale   Low ⟶ High
- Ease of handling erratic or seasonal pattern   Easier ⟶ Difficult

Variety
- Range   High ⟶ Low
- Ease of handling new product introductions   Easier ⟶ Difficult
- Typical order size   Small ⟶ Large (?)

Competition Basis

       Product ⟶ Process

Competitive Strategy Characteristics

       Differentiation ⟶ Cost ⟵ leadership

Note: Adapted from an approach by Hill and others

Equipment characteristics and the link to process choice

The first set of complementary decisions arises in the area of equipment characteristics. The type of equipment chosen greatly influences the limitations imposed by the process choice decision.

For example, the equipment selected to support the flowline process choice has traditionally been capital-intensive, with limited volume and variety flexibility. These limitations have been translated into process choice limitations. However, the application of process technology improvements in this area can remove some of the limitations, at a price. Therefore, a critical activity for the operations manager is to evaluate the requirements of the competitive strategy and to suggest areas where the impact of technology can enable the firm to eliminate the restrictions of traditional process choice, and to get closer to its customer requirements.

Table 3.2
Traditional equipment characteristics linked to process choice

Characteristics	Project Jobbing Batch	Flowline Assembly Line	Flowline Cont. Process
Scale			
• Relative capital cost	Low ⟶		High
• Intensity	Labour ⟶		Capital
• Scale economies	Low ⟶		High
• Span of manufacture	Wide ⟶		Narrow
Flexibility			
• Volume flexibility	Reasonable ⟶	Poor (after limit)	
• Variety flexibility	Good ⟶		Poor
General			
• Operating task	Bottleneck management ⟶	Plant utilization	
• Technology focus	Information technology ⟶ ⟵	Process technology	

Note: Adapted from an approach by Hill and others

A set of traditional equipment characteristics linked to the process choice are shown in Table 3.2. If we accept for a moment the traditional limitations normally imposed by the type of equipment associated with the different process choices, then certain *critical success factors* emerge with relation to the differing types of process choice.

For the *flowline* process the restrictions imposed by the equipment characteristics are that the equipment is dedicated to a narrow range of products, is relatively expensive and has limitations with regard to capacity increase or product change. Therefore, a critical operations activity must be to time and size the next capacity increment. In this case it is vital that close links are maintained with the market and the necessary internal linkages developed with marketing, forecasting and technology departments. If an error is made in this process then it will be very difficult to recover on a day-to-day basis. These issues are covered in Chapter 6.

Linked in to this process is the day-by-day requirement to maintain high equipment utilization. This is imposed by the expensive nature of the equipment and the competitive strategy of low-cost operation. Only by attaining high utilization levels will the equipment be able to amortize its purchase price over a sufficiently large base to support a low-cost operation. This means reducing non-value-added activities such as waiting-time, set-up or changeover time, and machine downtime. Thus, on a day-by-day basis, the critical activity for the operations manager must be to direct efforts at improving machine utilization through 'waste' reduction programmes, and to set up reduction programmes and preventative maintenance techniques. By concentrating efforts in this direction the operation will be focusing on a contribution that is of value in the marketplace. (An additional benefit of reducing changeover times is the opportunity to take advantage of the corresponding product variety flexibility. If the marketplace is moving towards greater variety, this can prove to be a key discriminator between the performance of rival firms.)

With regard to the *jobbing and batch* environments, the characteristics of the equipment imply a differing set of critical activities for the operations manager. In this instance, the emphasis is on managing the bottleneck workcentres to achieve throughput targets whilst operating in an environment of complexity and change. The equipment flexibility of this environment is necessary to accommodate the product variety involved, and the application of traditional batch sizing rules means that work-in-progress levels are normally high. With varying product mixes, the location of the bottleneck workcentres can vary, and therefore attention has been placed on using information technology to track bottleneck location, optimize the scheduling around these workcentres to achieve delivery targets whilst operating at the lowest corresponding cost base by limiting the levels of work in process. This tends to be the environment where the prime emphasis is on information technology to achieve this end, whereas the flowline environments tend to major on process technology improvements. That is not to say that the other technologies do not have an important role to play. For example, in the jobbing/batch environment, much process technology effort has been used successfully in eliminating the traditional complexity associated with this operation and thereby simplifying the information technology task. An example is the move towards 'cell' type operating environments.

The infrastructure mix element

The elements of the supporting operations infrastructure need to support the competitive advantage for the firm. Where the firm is following a differentiation strategy it is vital that the operations organization supports the chosen basis for differentiation and that the operating systems control the resulting 'productivity', as needed by the marketplace.

For example, if the firm differentiates its performance through a fast, responsive delivery performance, then the organization structure chosen for operations must encourage the fast entry of that customer order into the system and speedily carry out the tasks needed to convert that order to a shipped product or service. Therefore, the rigid functional organization structure found in a large number of firms may not be the answer, and a move to a more responsive matrix structure may be appropriate for certain areas of the company. Again, the concept of focusing on customer needs is paramount.

The planning and control systems used also influence the firm's performance, since what is needed in this last instance is a rapid order entry system together with a flexible planning and scheduling system to respond to the rapidly changing needs of the marketplace. Rigid systems can hinder the satisfaction of customer needs and possibly work against customer requirements in this environment.

Table 3.3
Organization structure linked to competitive strategy

Organization Focus	Differentiation Strategy		Cost Strategy	
	Project	Jobbing	Batch	Flowline
Key focus				
	Support basis for differentiation ——————————→			Low-cost operation
Structure				
•	Decentralized ——————————→			Centralized
•	Team (matrix?) ←————+————→			Functional
•	Narrow span of control ←——————→			Wide span of control
Personnel				
•	Entrepreneurial ——→		←———	Systematic
•	Wide skill range ←————+—→			Narrow skill range

Note: Adapted from an approach by Hill and others

Table 3.3 links the focus of the operations infrastructure to the competitive advantage sought by the firm and links organizational focus to the needs of the firm. Certain *critical success factors* emerge. For instance, if the firm is following a *cost leadership strategy* then it is critical that it pursues the cost benefits offered by centralizing organizational activities where this does not prejudice the relevant service level. For example, there are low-cost benefits that accrue through bulk purchasing activity which can be a centralized function in certain operation environments. A firm that is able to take advantage of this option will, all other things being equal, have a cost advantage over a competitor which has been unable to harness these benefits. A modifier to this is the use of information technology to gain the benefits of virtual centralization, without necessarily physically relocating departments. Either method will be in concert with the competitive advantage desired by the firm, and the deciding factors will rest with the degree of technology it presently employs and the cost-effectiveness of maintaining duplicate purchasing personnel.

Other areas which offer themselves for centralization, either physically or electronically, are longer-term production planning for multiple sites, finished goods and distribution planning and control, certain capital projects, maintenance tasks and so on. The deciding factor when the firm is pursuing a cost leadership strategy is the resultant cost savings set against any increased coordination or service-level problems.

In the cost leadership arena, the firm should also examine the number of levels in the management structure, and work at ways of increasing the span of control thereby reducing the layers of management. This has obvious cost advantages. Methods of achieving this objective could involve the use of systems to reduce the complexity of the management task, and the development of supporting policies to bring routine into the daily decision-making process.

A firm following a *differentiation strategy,* should ensure that the organization structure supports that strategy, and in this case a critical success factor for the operations manager is to develop the 'culture' within the organization to support the chosen basis for differentiation, whether that is delivery responsiveness, new product innovation or quality initiatives.

The next component of operations infrastructure, the systems element, is illustrated by Table 3.4 . In this instance, a critical activity is to ensure the presence of planning and control systems which support the needs of the business, and in particular how it chooses to compete in its marketplace. The table illustrates the emphasis that should be placed on system development and implementation to support the chosen competitive strategy and the inherent characteristics implied by the associated process choice.

With regard to the *low cost strategy* it can be seen that great emphasis should be placed on developing better processes and associated process control. With this type of operating environment a great deal of the resulting product cost is related to the process performance itself; thus, any improvements made there can result in real competitive advantage in the marketplace. This may be as a result of better material yields, less wastage, or by reducing the previously high capital equipment costs. Note that any advances made in the last direction not only change the basis for competition, but can also alter the characteristics of the industry by reducing the impact of previous barriers to entry. This could result in a change of industry emphasis from a large central single-plant environment to many smaller geographically dispersed facilities.

Other areas for system emphasis with the low cost strategy approach include finished goods and raw materials control.

47

Table 3.4
Systems focus linked to competitive strategy

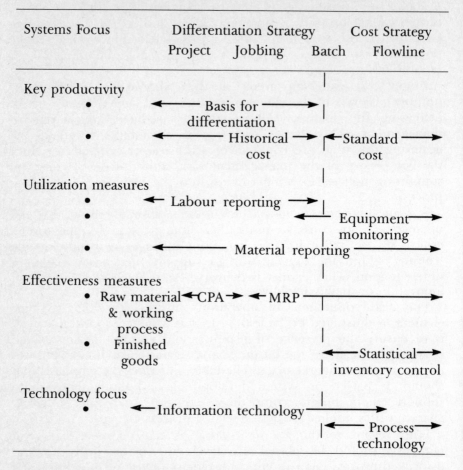

Systems Focus	Differentiation Strategy		Cost Strategy	
	Project	Jobbing	Batch	Flowline

Key productivity
- ←———— Basis for ————→ differentiation
- ←———— Historical → ←Standard ——→ cost cost

Utilization measures
- ← Labour reporting →
- ←— Equipment → monitoring
- ←———— Material reporting ————→

Effectiveness measures
- Raw material ←CPA→ ← MRP ———————→ & working process
- Finished ←—Statistical→ goods inventory control

Technology focus
- ←Information technology———→
- ←— Process→ technology

Note: Adapted from an approach by Hill and others

Traditionally, this strategy has been characterized by the holding of finished goods stock in order to isolate the poor flexibility of the flowline process from the needs of the marketplace. Any system improvements which can reduce the investment in stock whilst not prejudicing customer service can be translated into cost advantages. Such improvements can result from better forecasting methods, and more frequent and closer stock controls (such as real time systems). A more fundamental way of reducing the need for finished goods stock is to change the traditional limitations of the process itself through the application of more flexible technology – a point covered earlier.

Raw material stockholdings have sometimes been employed to buffer the operation from its suppliers. Technology can help eliminate the need for such buffers by providing better controls in this area. The methods for controlling dependent stock items are covered in Chapters 4 and 5 but, in addition, technology offers the chance to develop better linkages with suppliers and so reduce the reliance on stock buffers. Information technology can afford suppliers a better and earlier picture of their customer requirements in order to match their schedules. Such an early warning system can eliminate the uncertainty inherent on the demand side of the supply process and can eliminate a major reason for holding stock. Any firm that invests in these electronic linkages with its suppliers can translate them into real competitive advantage in its marketplace.

Obviously, since firms in this environment are pursuing a low cost strategy, it is vital that they have fast, accurate and timely cost information, and the supporting control systems are needed to evaluate the impact of every significant business decision along this dimension – the chosen basis for competitive advantage

A similar emphasis should be placed on firms that are following a *differentiation strategy* – namely that the appropriate systems are in place to support the chosen basis for differentiation. For example, if the firm is following a differentiation strategy based on delivery performance, then the focus of the associated control systems should highlight how successful the firm is at achieving the relevant aims. As mentioned earlier, the performance of any other support systems should also be oriented towards this end: that is, the order entry system should be speedy so that delivery lead time is not lost in this process, the scheduling and sequencing system must be responsive to changing customer requirements, and any progressing system must be attuned to actual customer requirements. Again, the use of flexible technology to enhance process capability with regard to delivery responsiveness has got to be a good thing.

Where the differentiation is based on 'quality', or more specifically on the consistent achievement of a specification product or on the achievement of a specification that the competition cannot match, then again the planning and control systems used should support the basis for differentiation. Obviously, in this instance, emphasis must be placed on maintaining the relevant processes under control, probably using computerized process control techniques.

The significant point with the infrastructure element is that it has as important a role to play as the traditional plant and equipment element in achieving competitive advantage for the firm. If the focal point of infrastructure decision-making is not aligned with the key operations task, dilution of operations capability will result, with a concomitant lack of competitiveness in the marketplace.

The operations linkages mix element

Normally, every operation involves the transformation of certain inputs into outputs, and whilst it is important to consider the elements of the operations mix that relate to the transformation process itself, it is also very important to consider the relationships between the transformation process and the suppliers of raw materials or between the transformation process and the customers themselves. Indeed, major discriminators in industrial competitive advantage can be the relationships or linkages developed between the operation and its customers and suppliers.

Table 3.5 illustrates the linkages involved in relation to competitive strategy.

Table 3.5
Operations linkages and competitive strategy

Linkages	Differentiation Strategy	Cost Strategy
Customer and Supplier Links:		
Focus	Support basis for differentiation	Low cost
Techniques	Good coordination and communication using IT. Develop flexible (variety and volume) linkages appropriate to the competitive strategy.	Price pressure, frequent low-quantity deliveries, no stockholding, use IT for schedule visibility etc.

For any firm that is following a *low cost strategy,* a critical activity in this area must be to develop the appropriate low-cost linkages. For example, it is advantageous to develop supplier links that permit the frequent delivery of small-quantity batches to minimize the costly holding of raw material stocks. This can be done by using suppliers that are in close proximity to the operation (or by encouraging them to move closer!), by setting up cheap transportation methods and so on. An example of the latter is where the operation itself runs a small transport fleet to collect small-quantity deliveries from the suppliers and so avoid the potential problems of partly full loads, for instance. Another trend is to develop closer linkages with fewer suppliers, thereby obtaining not only the benefits of bulk price discounts but also the advantages of closer supplier knowledge and liaison. These are advantages that can all be translated into cost competitiveness.

The use of technology to enhance the potential of supplier and customer linkages has already been discussed, but it is worth noting here that such linkages can be used as a barrier to entry both at the level of cementing relationships with customers and suppliers, and also at the industry level.

With regard to the *differentiation strategy,* the key linkage task is to support and enhance that strategy. For example, it is no use having a flexible and responsive production facility matched to the customer delivery expectations if it is not supported by a similar responsiveness in the distribution system. It is therefore important to look for flexibility in distribution, and this may be achieved by structural decisions (for example, size of lorries, location of depots and so on) as well as the more day-to-day decisions relating to the operation of scheduling systems. The organization that succeeds in this direction will support its competitive position in the market.

Where the operation differentiates its performance through the 'quality' or product specification dimension, it is important that the customer and supplier linkages enhance that image. Packaging can affect performance to this end, as can the degree of operations or service back-up offered. Whatever the basis for differentiation, the operations manager and his or her peers will need to examine how the appropriate links should be developed to enhance the basic product offering. This is not a passive role, but rather a key influence on how customers perceive the firm's competitive stance. The creative use of information technology can greatly assist in differentiating one from another.

Key operations tasks within the organization

So far, the emphasis has been on deciding the key operations task for the operation as a whole. However, the concept of focusing on a critical task can be extended within the operation. The following examples illustrate the concepts of focus within the operation.

Example no. 1

In this instance the firm operates in a marketplace with a wide product range, but is having difficulty in servicing the requirements of each market sector. A Pareto product distribution applies, with 80 per cent of the volume being associated with only 20 per cent of the product range, this part of the range being sold at low price. Conversely the remaining 80 per cent of the product range accounts for only 20 per cent of the volume, and is being sold via a differentiation strategy.

The appropriate solution here is to set up two focused facilities within the factory, the first servicing the high-volume (80 per cent) low-variety sector (20 per cent), and the second serving the low-volume (20 per cent) high-variety (80 per cent) sector. The operations mix elements would need to be different to service the two differing requirements, since any attempt to service both requirements with common facilities would constitute a compromise vulnerable to targeting by a correctly focused competitor.

This situation is illustrated by Figure 3.3 which shows the concept of focus applied along the direction of process flow:

Process stages

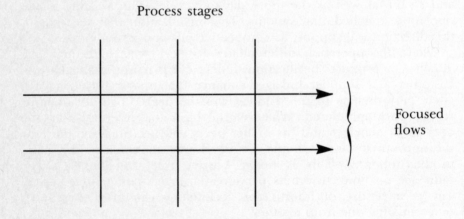

Figure 3.3 Focus applied along process flow

Example no. 2

In this case the firm is functioning with two major stages in its operation – a 'making' stage followed by a 'conversion' stage. The 'making' stage is characterized by high volumes with a limited product range, whilst the 'conversion' stage comprises the conversion of standard product to customer requirements with specific packaging and bottling requirements – that is, high variety and smaller volumes in a market where the customer is delivery-sensitive.

The appropriate focused approach here is to recognize the different tasks and to split the plant according to the processes involved. Therefore, the 'making' stage will be one focused facility and the conversion stage another focused facility, with differing key tasks and supporting operations mix elements. This will give the opportunity to take manufacturing costs out in the early process stages and to engineer flexibility into the later stages to handle the rapid delivery requirements. A stock buffer can be used to separate the characteristics of the two stages, although the flexibility of the conversion stage and the use of early visibility ordering systems can keep this to a minimum. A critical activity for the operations manager will be managing this interface.

The operation is illustrated by Figure 3.4. The concept of focusing the facilities, both as a whole and within the plant or operation, is a fundamental basis for achieving an operation that is attuned to serving the customer needs, and provides a basic building block in achieving competitive advantage through operations.

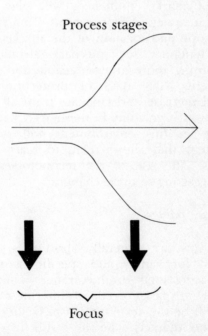

Figure 3.4   Focus applied at different stages along the process flow

Audit checklists for the application of operations strategy can be found at the end of the chapter.

Influences on operations stategy

The classic stages of development of a strategy for operations are, first, the development of the key operations task, the linking of the operations characteristics to that task through the appropriate choice of manufacturing process, and the reinforcement of those characteristics by focusing the operations infrastructure and linkages to achieve the same end.

Since, in this area, we are considering structural decisions with relatively lengthy implementation timescales, it is important that the operation is not only matched to the needs of the business as it is today, but also to the needs of the business as these are perceived for tomorrow. Therefore, any significant environmental influences will need to be anticipated and taken into account.

Market influences

The industry of market influences will play a key part in the development of a strategy for operations. Trends in this area include the changing scope and location of the marketplace where there is an increasing tendency for internationalization, with individual customers becoming more knowledgeable and more demanding in their requirements. The days of protectionism are gone, and competition will increase and emanate from all quarters. There is a distinct trend towards volatility in the marketplace and the successful firms operating in this environment will need to develop an operations strategy that allows them to react quickly to changing customer needs. The use of the technologies will be critical in identifying and reacting to these changes.

Product and service influences

Product life cycles are generally shortening in response to the customers' need for variety and specific tailored solutions. Most firms are increasing their product range. The operation needs to accommodate the disparate needs of differing markets, and a critical success factor will be the development of facilities focused on serving the various 'niche' markets. The successful firm will be the one that predicts market segmentation and develops operational capability to service the specific segments, where the order-winning criteria are all different.

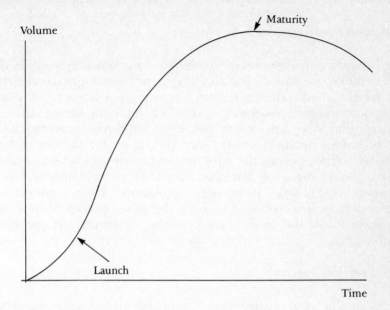

Figure 3.5   Stages in a typical product life cycle

This can be illustrated by reference to Figure 3.5 which illustrates the stages in the typical product life cycle. At each stage in its life cycle the product features and order-winning criteria are different, and hence the key operations task will be different and will need to be supported by different operations capabilities. For example, at the 'maturity' stage, the product is characterized by a high-volume, low-variety operation where the order-winning criterion is normally low price. This is characteristic of a low cost strategy for operations and is traditionally achieved by a flowline operation with supporting infrastructure and linkages. However, at the 'launch' stage, the product features are characterized by a high-variety, low-volume operation and it is the intrinsic qualities of the products themselves that win the order. In this instance, the correct operations response is to follow the appropriate differentiation strategy, with the supporting structural decisions. It therefore comes as no surprise to realize that operations which have traditionally operated with mature products have operational difficulties when confronted with a need to introduce many new products in response to market pressure.

The pressure on product life cycles illustrates the need for a continual audit on operations strategy to ensure that the operations capability still matches the needs of the new marketplace.

Resource influences

The resource environment includes raw materials and other consumables, personnel and funding. Any viable operations strategy will need to take future resource trends into account if it is to contribute towards the future success of the firm. For example, any strategy that does not reflect trends in employee expectations will not be successful. In a similar way, the rapid developments in new material science permit the adoption of creative operations strategies which can change the basis or scope of competition within the industry. Certainly, technology advances have redrawn the boundaries of low-cost operation by the development of new, more efficient materials and corresponding advances in processing technologies.

Technology influences

Technology advances offer what is probably the greatest potential for new competitive advantage. The rapid rates of change in operations capabilities offered by information and process technology pose one of the most serious challenges to the operations manager. The firm that is successful will be the one that develops an operations strategy which anticipates the needs of the marketplace, and uses the potential of new technology developments to service them. Any strategy that does not take the advances of new technology into account must be severely limited and vulnerable to competitive attack.

Examples abound where technology has improved process capability, changed the rules regarding process characteristics, radically altered organization structure and focus, and provided an innovative approach to the development of new operations linkages. This will be a key discriminator in the firm's future competitive performance.

Audit checklists on product technology, process technology and information technology can be found at the end of the chapter.

Implementation of the strategy

Having formulated a strategy, the next stage is to implement it. Chapter 1 illustrated that everybody has a role to play in this process, and there are certain key issues that must be considered if the implementation is to be a success:

The need to create the correct climate

A critical task of the operations manager is to create the correct climate to ensure the success of the strategy. This entails the involvement of the right people at the right time in the formulation of the strategy, its communication upwards, downwards and sideways in the organization, and the selling of the benefits.

Formal (and informal) communication of the strategy develops a common vocabulary and can help promote ownership of the key tasks in strategy implementation.

The need to develop 'champions'

Since there are a wide range of tasks permeating the operation, the implementation of a strategy can be greatly assisted by the development of 'champions' to handle certain of its aspects. Successful champions should be opinion-leaders in the organization, see a real benefit for themselves in the successful implementation of the strategy and should be able successfully to represent the views of the operations organization.

The need to structure the implementation

The classical structure for strategic development is first to develop the *strategy,* develop the organization *structure* to support it and then to develop the *skills* and *staff* to implement it, taking care to establish a system of *shared values.*

In order to succeed, the operations manager will need a wide range of interpersonal skills as well as the self-discipline to succeed. These aspects are covered in the last two sections of the book.

Personal development task no. 3

1 Develop the operations mix capability required by your firm to achieve its key task

2 Audit the actual operation to assess your present capability against these dimensions
3 Prepare a list of strengths and weaknesses against the operations mix elements
4 Consider the future environmental influences that will impact on the organization and influence the future key operations task. What are the corresponding threats and weaknesses?
5 Develop an action plan to eliminate present weaknesses and build on present strengths, as well as capitalize on future opportunities whilst minimizing threats.
6 Prepare an implementation plan.

Chapter summary points

- The key operations task links the operation and competitive advantage in the marketplace.
- Operations decisions can be considered under three groupings:
  - Facilities
  - Infrastructure
  - Linkages
- These decisions are interrelated.
- A wide range of environmental factors impact on the viable operations strategy, including market factors, product and service influences, resource influences and the impact of technology.
- Successful strategy implementation involves:
  - The correct climate
  - The development of 'champions'
  - A structured approach.

Essential reading

Constable, C. J. and New, C. C., *Operations Management,* London: Wiley, 1976.

Hill, T., *Manufacturing Strategy,* London: Macmillan Educational Ltd, 1985.

Porter, M. E., *Competitive Advantage,* New York: Free Press, 1985.

Skinner, W., *Manufacturing: the formidable competitive weapon,* New York: Wiley, 1985.

Audit checklist

Area: Operations

Topic: Operations Strategy

Subject	Findings

1. **Strategy**

   Is there a defined operations strategy in existence for the business unit?

   How does it relate to the business needs and how frequently is it reviewed?

2. **Product Features and Focused Objective**

   What product features affect operating performance?

   e.g.   Volume
          Variety
          Make to order/stock
          Order winning criteria
             cost
             delivery
             quality

   What is the expected future trend in these features and how will it affect operating performance?

   Is the operations objective or key task defined, focused and realistic?

3. **Operating Mix Elements**

   In what ways do the chosen elements of the operating mix give the company a competitive edge in the marketplace?

   What about future requirements?

Audit checklist cont'd

Area: Operations

Topic: Operations Strategy

Subject	Findings

i. Process Choice
 	
Are the following process features in line with the needs of the business:
 	
Process technology?
Automation?
Control systems?
etc
 	
ii. Plant and Equipment
 	
How are the following features linked to future business needs:
 	
Capacity increments?
  – Timing
  – Size
Flexibility?
Maintenance systems?
etc
 	
iii Organization
 	
Is the operating organization in line with the future needs of the organization?
 	
Centralization/decentralization
Matrix/hierarchy
Skill requirements
Integration
Supplier linkages
Customer/distribution linkages
etc	

Audit checklist cont'd

Area: Operations

Topic: Operations Strategy

Subject	Findings
iv **Systems** Are the correct control systems in place (now and in the future)? e.g. Finished Goods WIP Raw Materials Productivity – Labour – Plant – Materials etc Do the reward systems match Company requirements? Do the Capital Expenditure Control Systems match business needs? What is the likely impact of future legislation on the firm?	

Audit checklist

Area: Technology

Topic: Impact on Product Technology

Subject	Findings

1. What mechanisms exist to focus R&T product technology developments on the future needs of the market place?

    –   skills needed and resources

2. What criteria are used to rank and resource projects faced with conflicting requirements:

    –   are these appropriate to business needs?
    –   how often are the criteria reviewed?

3. What vehicles are used for communication across the following interfaces with R&T:

    –   Customer
    –   Marketing
    –   Production
    –   Finance
    –   External research bodies
    –   Suppliers?

    Are they appropriate for the needs of business now and in the future? Is the planning horizon realistic to protect the long-term future?

4. How are the projects audited to ensure:

    a) Compliance with deadlines?
    b) Original objectives achieved?

Audit checklist cont'd

Area: Technology

Topic: Impact on Product Technology

Subject	Findings

5. What mechanisms are used to gain knowledge of:
 	
   – competitor developments
   – marketplace developments
 	
in the product technology area?
 	
6. What mechanisms exist to predict future skills and facility requirements in this area? Are they focused on the needs of the business?	

Audit checklist

Area: Technology

Topic: Impact on Process Technology

Subject	Findings

1. How are current operating processes
    appraised in terms of their life cycle and
    appropriateness to business needs?

2. What linkages exist to ensure that process
    technology developments are focused on
    meeting current and future business
    requirements?

    e.g. flexibility
          process capability
          quality and product consistency
          dependability
          cost
          raw material availability

3. What vehicles are used for communication
    across the following interfaces with R&T:

    -   Customer
    -   Marketing
    -   Production
    -   Finance
    -   External research bodies
    -   Suppliers?

    Are they appropriate for the needs of the
    business now and in the future? Is the
    planning horizon realistic to protect the
    long-term future?

4. How are projects audited to ensure:

    a) Compliance with deadlines?
    b) Original objectives achieved?

Audit checklist cont'd

Area: Technology

Topic: Impact on Process Technology

Subject	Findings

5. What mechanisms are used to gain knowledge of competitor developments?
 	
      how do we measure in terms of:
 	
            cost
            quality
            flexibility
            dependability/consistency
            etc
 	
      marketplace developments
 	
      environmental development and legislation
 	
      process control developments in the process technology area
 	
6. What mechanisms exist to predict future skill and facility requirements in this area? Are they focused on the need of the businessman?
 	
7. How are downstream/upstream process integration issues handled? Are the methods used appropriate?	

Audit checklist

Area: Technology

Topic: Impact of Information Technology on the Business

Subject	Findings

1. **Marketplace**

    i   How will technology affect the following
         features of the marketplace:

             Size?
             Location?
             Segmentation?
             Volatility?
             Responsiveness?
             Competitiveness?

    ii   How can technology be used to my
         company's advantage in the marketplace?

2. **Product/Services**

    i   How will technology affect the company
         range of products and services?

         e.g.   Life cycle
                Differentiation
                Service enhancements
                Variety
                Customer compliance
                etc

3. **Resources**

    i   How will technology affect the resources
         needed by the business?

             Personnel and their skill level
             Materials
             Energy
             Finance
             Equipment and Processes
             etc

Audit checklist cont'd

Area: Technology

Topic: Impact of Information Technology on the Business

Subject	Findings

ii How will technology affect the way the company interfaces with its:
 	
    Personnel?
    Suppliers?
    •Suppliers and capital?
    etc
 	
What linkages can be developed?	

4. Organization
 	
i How will the shape and form of organization structure change as a result of new technology?
 	
    e.g.   Integration of activities
           Centralization/decentralization
           Rank/role
           Matrix/hierarchy
           Skilled/unskilled
           etc	

5. Control
 	
i How will the way business is run be affected by new technology?
 	
    e.g.   real time
           decision-making
           control systems
 	
ii How will technology affect financial performance criteria?
 	
    e.g.   Short-term hurdle rates
           etc	

Audit checklist cont'd

Area: Technology

Topic: Impact of Information Technology on the Business

Subject	Findings
6. Environment	

6. **Environment**

    i   How will technology affect the firm's external environment?

        e.g. Legislation
              Centralized control

    ii How will technology affect the firm's internal environment?

        e.g. Individual aspirations and perceptions
              Need for freedom

Part III

TECHNICAL SPECIALIZATIONS: A NEED TO KNOW

Introduction

This Part considers the technical areas under the operations manager's control.

The intention is not to give a detailed theoretical discussion of the areas involved, but rather to highlight the techniques involved and to indicate their applicability to different operating environments. Since the implementation of a strategy for operations involves the actioning of a series of discrete decisions in the technique area, linkages have been made wherever possible to show how the individual techniques support a particular strategy.

Checklists are used throughout Part III to allow the reader to audit their own operating environment and to structure actions to improve performance.

4 Planning and controlling the operation: the role of inventory

Introduction

Inventory is an important investment decision and, as such, should be subject to formal scrutiny.

It is interesting to note the Japanese philosophy, which regards inventory as 'waste' since it adds cost, but not value to the product. Their intention is to reduce this waste by a systematic process, and so improve the effectiveness of their production operation. Therefore any decision to hold inventory should be seen in this light, and an appropriate cost–benefit analysis carried out.

In order to consider the issues involved in this analysis it will be necessary to consider the types of inventory involved, the functions which they serve and the corresponding costs involved. It is then important to consider the techniques that are available to improve the cost–benefit trade-off.

Types of inventory

The principal types of inventory found in a typical manufacturing operation include:

- finished goods
- work in process
- raw materials

As discussed in Chapter 3, different process choices will place the inventory emphasis in different positions due to the inherent nature of the process choice itself. However, it is appropriate at this point to consider the different functions served by the differing types of inventory. A summary is given below.

- Finished goods
  - provide rapid customer service
  - smooth output fluctuations
  - help cope with seasonal demands
  - provide an insurance against breakdowns and strikes
- Work in process
  - decouples production stages
  - allows flexibility in scheduling
  - allows for improvement in plant utilization
- Raw materials
  - decouples the firm from its suppliers
  - allows firms to take advantage of quantity discounts
  - provides a hedge for inflation
  - provides strategic stocks of sensitive items

A fundamental reason for holding inventory is to decouple sequential stages in the operations chain, and the justification for this requirement varies according to the inventory type.

Finished goods inventory is used to decouple the factory from the customer or consumer. This is an overt acceptance that the productive capability provided does not match the market requirements.

For example, it may be that the *customer needs rapid delivery* which the factory in its present form is incapable of providing. A reason for this could be the large batch sizes scheduled for the factory in order to optimize the set-up to run-time ratio on significant items of plant. In other words, the factory does not have the inherent flexibility required by the marketplace. The conventional answer to this mismatch has been to use stock as a buffer and so isolate the characteristics of the factory from the needs of the marketplace. A more correct approach would be to tackle the root cause of the problem and try to engineer flexibility into the factory through a formal programme of set-up reduction, thereby eliminating the need to hold significant finished goods stocks.

It may be that the reason to decouple the factory from the customer relates to *geographic location,* and this is one of the issues covered in Chapter 6 under the heading 'Facilities strategy'. Certainly this highlights the issues of where to locate plants, single versus multiple plant set-ups and also the role of finished goods warehouses in the logistics chain. Structural choices made in this area can radically affect the amount of finished goods stock held in the total operations chain.

Another rationale for holding finished goods stock is to *decouple the productive rate of the factory* from the rate of demand in the marketplace. For example, if the product has a strong seasonal demand then conventional practice has been to size the plant to achieve the appropriate annual requirements on a uniform monthly rate, and to use stock to smooth out the peaks and troughs of the seasonal demand pattern. Whilst in some circumstances this may be the only viable alternative, consideration should also be given to attempting to engineer volume flexibility into the facilities so that the unit can respond flexibly to the varying volume demands in the marketplace, and so eliminate the need to hold finished goods stock. This could be achieved by selecting the appropriate process choice and using a flexible labour force (for example, outworkers) and recruitment policy to match the seasonal demands of the market. Obviously, much will depend on the type of product as to whether such an approach is viable, but there could well be significant cost advantages if the total costs of holding inventory are taken into account.

Further techniques for smoothing the output fluctuations of the facility will be considered in Chapter 5 when we look at the 'just in time' philosophy for running a factory.

As well as the decoupling reasons for holding finished goods inventory, there may well be *structural reasons* associated with labour relations. For example, in certain industries with a long history of poor labour relations, a decision is made to hold a level of finished goods stock as an insurance against strikes. The holding costs incurred are therefore the price of poor relationships and, whilst it may appear simplistic, a more correct approach would be to place an emphasis on improving the industrial relations situation and so eliminate the costly alternative of holding stock. This is all the more urgent now that firms are operating on a world stage where not all the players are subject to the same constraints.

A similar set of reasons are given for the holding of *work in process stock*, in this instance stressing the need to decouple sequential stages in the production process itself. The benefits cited are improvements in plant utilization and flexibility in plant scheduling.

Again, the basic rationale needs to be questioned. What is there about the stages in the process that make them incompatible with each other, so much so that we have to hold stock? Certainly, if there is a *change in process choice* from, say, batch to line then the differing characteristics of the processes could support the reasoning for holding stock. However, the advent of new technology incorporating flexibility on to the line has changed the rules and characteristics of the process choice decision. There is a trend towards obtaining the benefits of the flowline without relinquishing the different benefits of the batch process. The effect of this has been severely to question the rationale for holding interim stock buffers. Indeed philosophies such as 'just in time' production have the benefit of dramatically reducing the levels of inventory held at all stages in the production process.

It is only by questioning the basic assumptions underlying our premises in this area of stock control that we will begin to achieve the benefits of 'stockless' production.

The decisions in this area are not isolated from other aspects of the production scenario; we have already seen how they impact on process choice issues by highlighting the need to direct automation into certain plant areas. But there are other fundamental items that need to be addressed.

One of the benefits highlighted for holding work in process stock was to permit *flexibility in scheduling*. In itself, this is a worthy objective, but what is there that prevents us obtaining this as a matter of course? Again, the basic inflexibility of the production facilities causes us to have to buy ourselves a solution by investing in stock. A more satisfactory approach would be to find ways of making the plant items more flexible and so eliminate this need.

A further benefit cited for holding work in process stock has been the *gain in plant utilization*. How relevant is this as a plant effectiveness measure? Certainly, if we are in the batch environment, particular items of plant will be bottleneck workcentres whereas others will be non-bottlenecks. Exactly which machines will play which role will depend on the product mix going through the factory. However, the significant point is that, if the plant is fully loaded, all the bottleneck machines will be fully occupied but, by definition, the non-bottleneck machines will have spare capacity. Therefore, whilst it is correct to run the bottleneck machines flat out, it is inappropriate to run the non-bottleneck machines continuously, because they have spare capacity. The effect of attempting to run all machines all the time at high utilization levels will be to create additional work in process stock by using up the spare non-bottleneck capacity. Therefore are we wastefully investing in stock in order to derive a benefit (high total machine utilization) which is not really a benefit at all?

The same set of fundamental questions need to be posed when we consider the holding of *raw material* stock. In this instance, stock is conventionally held in order to *decouple the production unit* from the vagaries of the material and component supply situation. Typical justifications quoted include an intermittent supplier delivery performance, wrong quantities delivered or poor quality and hence high potential reject rates.

Again, the tacit acceptance of this situation must be brought into question. Why are we prepared to accept *non-conformance performance* from our suppliers and then further compound the sin by incurring even more costs by holding stock to circumvent the problem? A more successful solution could be achieved if we set out to improve the supplier performance record. Certainly, many firms are taking up this banner and expecting assured quality and delivery performance from their suppliers – witness the growth in quality assurance programmes, supplier education programmes and so on. But this is a joint responsibility and, to be successful, the suppliers and the supplied need to get together, to understand each other's perspective and problems, and to work at achieving a mutually beneficial solution. An indicative trend of the changing supplier–supplied relationship is the reduction in the number of suppliers per major industrial customer. Concurrent with this is the changing role of the purchasing department who are no longer encouraged to purchase solely on price, but rather to evaluate the total supplier performance including the ability to deliver regularly in small batch sizes, with repeatable quality and reliability.

Again, by taking action along these dimensions, firms are able to reduce their reliance on raw materials stocks and so reduce their total manufacturing costs.

Another favourite reason for investing in such stockholdings is to reduce the reliance on one supplier – for example, if we are *single-sourced* on a sensitive item. Whilst this is understandable, the question must still be raised as to whether we can get closer to the supplier in order to anticipate problems before they occur and so reduce the reliance on what could be an expensive stockholding.

In inflationary times, or for certain types of commodity products, a decision is made to invest in order to provide a *hedge for potential price increases.* In order to fully analyse the benefits of this approach, the true costs of holding stock should be included and conventional investment appraisal techniques applied.

The message of this section is that, whilst there are tangible benefits to holding stock, they really need to be evaluated against the needs of the business. Wherever possible, the basic rationale for stock investment needs to be questioned and radical, alternative approaches devised which will eliminate the need to hold stock at all. If we fail to adopt this radical approach then we cannot hope to be competitive in the future world market.

Costs of holding inventory

Typical costs associated with carrying inventory, are illustrated below:

Cost of capital	10–20%
Obsolescence, shrinkage	2–5%
Storage space	1–3%
Insurance	1–2%
TOTAL	14–30%

Cost of capital could refer to the costs of funding the inventory directly through bank loans and so on, or more correctly to the opportunity cost foregone. That is, when the decision was made to invest £1 million in inventory, by implication the decision was also made not to allocate the scarce capital resource to a new item of equipment which could have offered, say, a 20 per cent return. In other words, the opportunity cost of investing in inventory is the rate of return possible on competing investment decisions which do not go ahead because the funds have already been allocated to inventory.

Obsolescence occurs when inventory becomes outdated through product changes and modifications, poor demand and so on. The effect is that it cannot be used at full value, and so the associated 'losses' are included as part of the cost of holding inventory. There is a great likelihood of this occurring within a fast-moving marketplace with products of short life cycles. In this case, these costs can become quite significant. Shrinkage occurs through pilferage of inventory.

Storage space costs include the charge for the space itself, and again the concept of opportunity cost applies. If space in the facilities is in short supply then at some stage the decision was made to allocate that space to inventory rather than to equipment which could be producing, and hence generating, contribution. That represents the opportunity foregone. In addition to the space charge there are costs for inventory control staff, supporting organization amongst others.

A final cost category is that of *insurance* which is self-explanatory.

If we are to measure the effectiveness of inventory in supporting the firm's objectives then, as mentioned earlier, it will be necessary to carry out a cost–benefit analysis. How well are the various categories of inventory carrying out their function and at what cost? Wherever possible we should be devising solutions which are designed to eliminate the need for inventory and avoid the associated cost penalty. Certainly, the costs of holding inventory are high and, where there is no alternative solution, we are duty-bound to ensure that such inventory holding should be subject to management control.

Inventory control objective

This brings us to the *objective* of any inventory control system: *To minimize the investment in inventory, consistent with providing the required levels of service.*

This definition highlights the trade-off involved in ensuring that inventory effectively services the function for which it was intended, but also in a very cost-effective way. The basic assumption again is that inventory is needed in the first place!

Inventory control system

In order to ensure that an inventory control system is effective, three basic questions must be successfully answered:

1. WHAT to control
2. WHEN to re-order
3. HOW MANY to re-order

Whilst there may be a high degree of sophistication in how the optimum solution is derived, the basic questions remain. Figure 4.1 illustrates the application of these principles to different classifications of inventory. We shall now consider each of these decisions in turn.

What to control

The first decision relates to the class of inventory in question. An effective way to control inventory relates to the ABC or Pareto classification of stocks. This is a way of separating inventory into three classes based on their annual usage value.

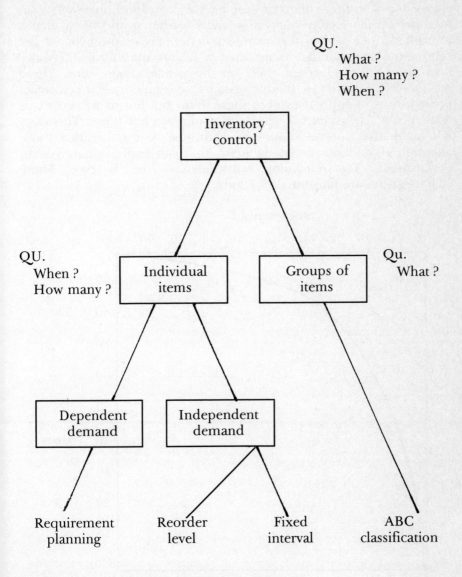

Figure 4.1   Methods of controlling inventory

A typical analysis would reveal that 75 per cent of annual usage value of inventory is represented by just 15 per cent of the inventory items. These represent the 'A' class items – that is, the relatively few items which account for a large proportion of the total annual usage value. If we are to manage inventory effectively, we need to apply close control to these items as they have a disproportionate effect on total performance. Carrying the analysis further would reveal that a possible 60 per cent of the inventory items only account for 10 per cent of the annual usage value; that is, a large number of inventory lines have little individual effect on the annual usage value. These are the 'C' class items. In this instance, effective inventory control procedure is to apply control to these items but not so stringently as with the 'A' class items, since the pay-offs are not there. This does not mean that control should be abdicated, but rather that more attention should be placed on items that can really impact system performance. The remaining items fall into the 'B' class. These characteristics are illustrated in Figure 4.2.

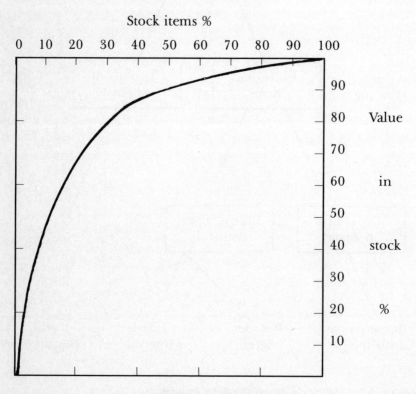

Figure 4.2   Pareto classification of stocks

ABC CODE	STOCK NUMBER	DESCRIPTION	PROD GROUP	UOM	STANDARD COST	ROL	ROQ	STOCK ON-HAND	ALLO-CATED	ISSUES LST YR	ISSUES Y-T-D	STOCK MTHS USAGE	ANNUAL USAGE VALUE	CUM % VALUE
A	C200 2100-000	Junior Roadster 20in	2000	EA	56.255	250	500	50	1220	2500	2500	0.2	153422.72	14
A	WA 1000-000	WHEEL ASSEMBLY (26in)	1100	EA	28.340	500	1000	628		3750	4120	1.8	121655.89	26
A	R2600 1000-000	ROADSTER 1000 26in	2000	EA	135.550	500	250	20	1510	600	970	0.3	116080.10	37
A	FA 1100-000	FRAME (26in)	1000	EA	35.000	450	1000	180		2500	2140	0.9	88581.82	46
A	FR 2000-000	FRAME ASSY (Jun. Roadster)	1000	EA	50.000	75	150	100		1200	1150	0.9	64000.91	52
A	FR 1000-000	FRAME ASSY (R1000)	1000	EA	54.700	100	250	260		850	1235	2.7	62208.82	58
A	SA 1300-000	SEAT ASSEMBLY	1300	EA	7.500	600	1400	435	100	0	4400	1.0	39600.00	62
A	FR 2100-000	FRAME (20in)	1000	EA	30.250	200	500	150		1250	1148	1.4	39567.00	66
A	WA 2000-000	WHEEL ASSY (20in)	1100	EA	25.600	200	500	125		985	1520	1.1	34978.91	69
A	AC 1000-410	TOOLKIT CASE (Leather)	5000	EA	2.850	500	1000	650		12255	9562	0.7	33915.52	72
A	WR 2400-000	WHEEL RIM (20in)	1100	EA	3.750	125	250	100		8525	7564	0.1	32909.32	76
A	OT 1100-100	OUTER TYRE (26in)	1100	EA	4.350	250	2000	1100		7500	6180	1.8	32458.91	79
B	IT 1100-200	INNER TUBE (26in)	1100	EA	3.150	500	1100	475	0	9816	8097	0.6	30777.79	82
B	TA 1100-000	TYRE ASSEMBLY	1100	EA	12.000	500	1000	715	100	1735	2005	4.2	24480.00	84
B	PA 1400-000	PEDAL ASSEMBLY	1400	EA	4.150	500	1200	200	0	5028	4225	0.5	20945.43	86
B	HB 1200-000	HANDLEBAR ASSEMBLY	1200	EA	8.050	150	350	65	0	2605	2084	0.3	20588.97	88
B	HB 1200-100	HANDLEBAR	1200	EA	6.750	100	250	40	0	2100	1835	0.2	14487.95	90
B	AC 1000-500	SADDLEBAG	5000	EA	5.850	250	800	575	0	1755	1593	3.8	10683.16	91
B	HA 1200-000	HUB ASSEMBLY	1100	EA	5.800	500	1000	600	0	0	1400	4.3	9744.00	92
B	AC 1000-400	TOOLKIT	5000	EA	4.500	250	800	325	0	2083	1743	1.9	9391.09	92
B	PB 1400-100	PEDAL BODY	1400	EA	2.500	150	500	3	0	3642	3151	0.0	9263.18	93
B	SA 2300-000	SEAT	1300	EA	7.250	100	250	85	0	925	854	1.1	7035.14	94
B	OT 2100-100	OUTER TYRE (20in)	1100	EA	4.500	300	600	354	0	1200	1556	2.8	6764.73	95
B	VA 1100-300	VALVE ASSEMBLY	1100	EA	1.500	500	1500	125	100	4036	3813	0.4	6421.91	95
C	AC 1000-100	FRONT LIGHT	5000	EA	3.850	200	500	285	115	1250	1686	2.1	6165.60	96
C	FP 1400-200	RUBBER FOOT PAD	1400	EA	1.100	750	1500	465	35	5062	4123	1.1	5511.00	96
C	TA 2100-000	TYRE ASSY (20in)	1100	EA	4.850	100	250	125	0	850	750	1.7	4232.73	97
C	AC 1000-430	PUNCTURE REPAIR KIT	5000	EA	0.700	300	600	500	0	5648	4358	1.1	3820.47	97
C	AC 1000-200	REAR LIGHT (Red)	5000	EA	2.900	750	1500	456	50	1150	1201	4.3	3718.85	98
C	HG 1200-200	HANDLEBAR GRIP	1200	EA	0.650	750	1500	567	0	5438	4975	1.2	3691.88	98
C	AC 1000-300	REAR REFLECTOR (Red)	5000	EA	1.750	500	1000	300	100	1706	1354	2.2	2920.91	98
C	AC 1000-436	PATCHES	5000	EA	0.425	750	1500	560	0	6458	5884	1.0	2861.10	98
C	IT 2100-200	INNER TUBE (20in)	1100	EA	2.560	100	250	85	0	875	1025	1.0	2653.09	99
C	PR 1400-300	PEDAL REFLECTOR	1400	EA	0.550	550	1100	235	90	3546	2884	0.8	1929.00	99
C	WR 1400-000	WHEEL RIM (26in)	1100	EA	2.540	750	1500	1055	0	500	500	23.2	1385.45	99
C	AC 1000-420	SPANNER	5000	EA	0.950	500	1000	560	0	1254	1026	5.4	1181.45	99
C	AC 1000-432	CHALK (Powdered)	5000	EA	0.200	500	1000	750	0	5012	3055	2.0	880.04	99
C	SP 2300-000	SPOKES (10in)	1100	EA	0.450	150	300	125	0		1256	1.0	678.24	99
C	AC 1000-433	GLUE	5000	EA	0.100	250	500	180	0	5025	4365	0.4	512.18	99
C	SP 1300-000	SPOKES (13in)	1100	EA	0.250	3500	7500	5065	0	1000	2500	31.8	477.27	99
C	SP 1300-100	SPOKE WIRE	1100	IN	0.004	5000	7500	18525	0	98025	86124	2.2	401.78	99

Figure 4.3 ABC analysis of stock

The ABC analysis highlights the difference between effectiveness and effort. Using the analysis, it is possible to identify those items which really impact on the firm's inventory performance, and effective management would be to concentrate on those few items whilst not neglecting the others. Without the benefit of this analysis it would be possible to spend a great deal of effort attempting to manage all items with equal emphasis, and fail to be effective overall.

An example of an ABC analysis is given in Figure 4.3.

Independent and dependent items

Having considered inventory items on a group basis, the next two decisions – when and how many to re-order – relate to each individual item. Before proceeding, it is worth distinguishing between independent and dependent items.

Independent items are those where the demand for them does not relate to internal factors but rather to external factors, such as market conditions. This is the case with finished goods inventories where the demand is influenced primarily by customer needs.

Dependent items are those which relate to factors under the firm's control, such as the production schedule or the demand for 'parent' items.

If we take the example of a bicycle manufacturer, then the demand for bicycles generally falls outside the firm's direct control, relating instead to the strength of the marketplace. However, the demand for wheel assemblies will be totally under the firm's control since it relates directly to the final assembly schedule for bicycles – that is, it represents a derived demand. Therefore, in this instance, bicycles are independent items and wheels are dependent items.

We need to make this distinction between the two classes of inventory items because it has a great impact on the applied methods of control. For independent items, future demand has to be forecast, usually using some projection of past performance. For dependent items – for example, work in process and raw materials – the derived demand can be precisely calculated once production plans have been established.

With independent items we shall focus on the use of statistical inventory techniques, whereas with dependent items we shall use the techniques associated with requirements planning. This chapter concentrates on finished goods control using statistical inventory techniques.

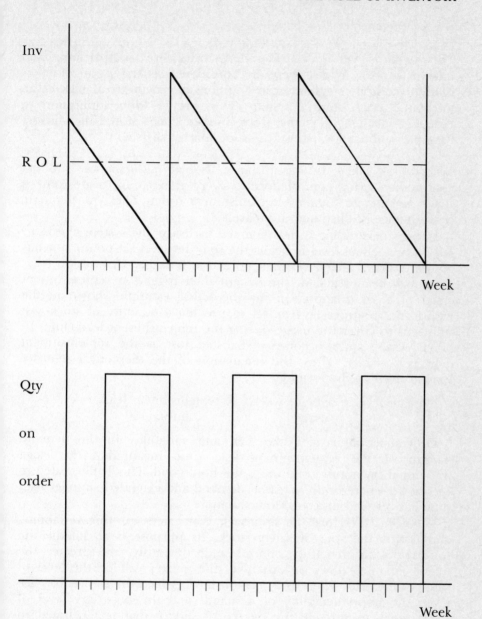

Figure 4.4   Re-order level control (a)

When to re-order

Two methods will be considered: re-order level control and fixed interval control. Whilst these are considered separately, in practice, modern computer systems can combine the methods as part of an integrated stock control system. They are of wide application to independent demand items, from finished goods stored in a factory location to goods located on the supermarket shelves.

Re-order level control In this instance, system performance is under continuous review and, following every transaction, a decision is made whether to trigger a replenishment order. The typical system performance is illustrated in Figure 4.4.

As the stockholding is decremented by usage, the system checks to see if the residual level is below the re-order level set-point. If it has not yet reached that level then no action is taken. If, however, that point has been reached, the system then triggers a replenishment order of a set quantity. In the theoretical example shown in the Figure, the re-order level is set to provide a quantity of stock just sufficient to cover the usage during the replenishment lead time. In other words, stock becomes exhausted just as the replenishment delivery is made. Thus, the calculation of the theoretical re-order level is given by the formula:

re-order level = average weekly × replenishment lead time
usage   (in weeks)

Of course life is not like that, and variability in the demand pattern or the replenishment lead time mean that the exact traditional saw-tooth graph does not hold good. This is illustrated in Figure 4.5 where both increased demand and extended supplier lead time has resulted in a stock-out situation.

We need, therefore, an approach that caters for this variability, and this is the role of safety stock. Its purpose is to handle the uncertainty in inventory control and, obviously, the greater the degree of uncertainty or variability the greater will be the level of safety stock held. There is a relationship between the desired service level, the unpredictability of demand, and the necessary level of safety stock to provide the degree of service that is illustrated in Figure 4.6.

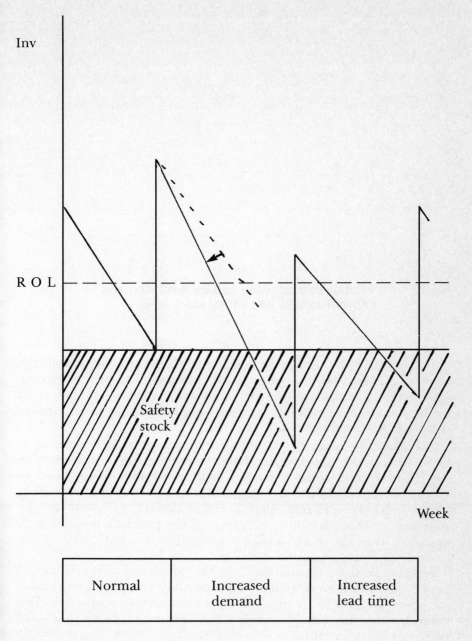

Figure 4.5   Re-order level control (b)

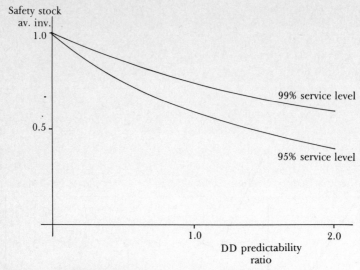

Figure 4.6 Relationship between service level, demand unpredictability and safety stock level

From this figure it can be seen that the more predictable the demand pattern the less safety stock is required to provide a high probability of servicing the market requirements. A similar chart could be drawn relating to the unpredictability of supplier replenishment lead time.

Therefore, the objective in the safety stock area must not just be to apply blindly the appropriate charts or nomographs to ensure that the requisite level of safety stock is held, but rather to get closer to the source of variability, to understand the nature of the underlying causes and to develop permanent solutions to remove that uncertainty. This way the root cause of the problem is eradicated, together with the corresponding investment in redundant safety stock.

Supplier lead time variability can be conquered by developing a better communication system with possibly fewer, more reliable suppliers and, in so doing, eliminating delivery 'surprises'. This could be just one part of a quality management initiative which can deliver startling benefits.

Uncertainty in the area of market demand can be checked by the appropriate application of statistical forecasting techniques in order to predict the future demand pattern more accurately. The application of these techniques are covered later in this chapter.

Where it is felt that safety stock is justified, there is a case for simulating the effect of a variety of re-order levels on system performance with a corresponding range of demand and replenishment lead time scenarios. A variety of software packages are available for this purpose, and their adoption for use on 'A' class items is recommended.

In summary, under re-order point or re-order level control, the decision of when to place an order rests on two separate factors. The first is the straight re-order level consideration, based on normal usage and replenishment values, and the second is the safety stock consideration, based on the degrees of uncertainty involved and the service level required. Since both need to be considered, re-ordering is triggered, with this method, when:

re-order level = average weekly × replenishment + safety
usage lead time (weeks) stock

Fixed interval control In this approach to controlling stock, the stockholding position is reviewed at fixed intervals, which could be daily or weekly, and a re-order quantity is triggered to bring the stock up to the desired level. This contrasts with the re-order level control system where performance was reviewed constantly and at

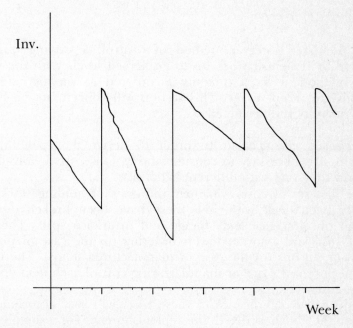

Figure 4.7   Fixed interval control

varying intervals, and where a fixed re-order quantity was ordered when the re-order point was triggered. With the fixed interval method, a varying re-order quantity (depending on actual usage) is ordered at fixed intervals as stock replenishment. The operation of a fixed interval system is illustrated in Figure 4.7. There is an enhanced version of this method which will only issue a replenishment order at the fixed interval time provided that the stock has fallen below a lower limit – the purpose being to limit the number of orders being placed for small quantities.

Obviously the more frequently the performance of the system is reviewed – that is, the shorter the fixed interval – the finer the control that will be exerted with this method. In this case, the appropriate interval will be influenced by the degree of volatility in market demand, the degree of control required and the trade-off the company is prepared to make with stockholding costs.

As mentioned earlier, with modern computerized inventory control systems it is possible to combine the performance of both the re-order point and fixed interval control systems and develop a system which scans the stockholding at regular fixed intervals, but also, by exception and as it occurs, flags any item that has triggered a re-order point.

How many to re-order

With the fixed interval method of control, a varying quantity is ordered to replenish stock up to an agreed level. With the re-order level method, a fixed quantity is ordered at varying intervals in response to recent usage. This section will concentrate on how that fixed quantity is determined.

The economic order quantity In order to derive the economic order quantity it is necessary to consider the various costs involved and to see how they vary with different batch sizes.

The first set of costs – namely the costs of holding stock – have already been dealt with, and these have been broken down into capital, obsolescence and storage and insurance costs. The second set of costs are associated with ordering (in the case of purchased items) or set-ups (in the case of manufactured items). The third set are the purchase price or manufacturing cost of each item (excluding set-up costs).

The relative significance of these costs will vary according to the size of the batch ordered for replenishment. For example, as the batch size grows so the relative importance of the set-up cost (for these purposes, effectively a fixed cost) diminishes on a per unit basis. However, as the batch size increases so the significance of the holding cost of a per unit basis increases. This is because the larger the batch, the longer we are likely to have them in stock before usage. These relationships are illustrated in Figure 4.8. The total cost curve is shown and represents the sum of the other three graphs. The lowest point of this curve represents the economic batch quantity and this would represent the optimum quantity to re-order when the re-order level system triggers – that is the re-order quantity that would result in the lowest unit product cost, taking into account the relevant costs and their relationship to batch size.

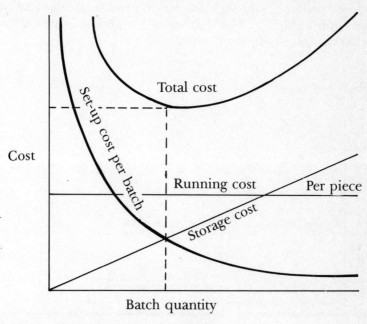

Figure 4.8 Economic order quantity

This can also be expressed in the following formula:

$$q = \sqrt{\frac{2\,e\,b}{c}}$$

where

q = economic order quantity
e = cost of ordering or set-up cost
b = annual usage value

c = holding costs
(Like units should be used throughout the formula.)

This formula has been in use for a number of years and has formed the basis of a large number of computerized re-order quantity calculations. However, in recent times, there has been much debate not into the mechanics or validity of the calculation, but rather into its application.

The formula is based on forecast usage, which is obviously subject to a margin of error, and also on assumptions concerning set-up times and holding costs. More and more individuals are questioning the necessity of having a set-up cost at all. As Figure 4.9 shows, as the set-up or ordering cost element approaches 0, so the economic batch size approaches 1. This has quite important implications in the purchasing and production control sphere.

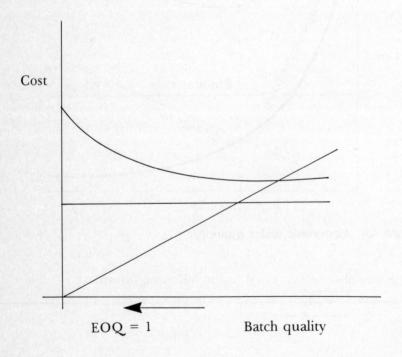

Figure 4.9 Economic order quantity where set-up is zero

The lack of set-up costs will result in reducing batch sizes but with more frequent issuing to the shopfloor, since production capacity is used more effectively not to make stock but rather to make for specific customer order requirements. The competitive edge potential is enormous through reduced stockholding, faster throughout times and enhanced customer service, but the appropriate supporting infrastructure will be necessary. What we are seeing is the move to make productive capacity more flexible and more attuned to the needs of the marketplace. This underlying flexibility is one of the key prerequisites for 'just in time' manufacture.

Similarly, with the ability to reduce ordering costs – for example, by using information technology – there is a drive towards more frequent small-quantity deliveries from suppliers. The benefits again are reduced inventory holdings, together with the corresponding potential for cost savings. Although this is not a new concept – the benefits of the 'call-off' order situation has been known for years – what is new is that this should be achieved without the supplier having to hold stock to service the customer requirements. In other words, it is achieved through the supplier becoming alerted early to the likely customer needs and then responding flexibly to deliver direct from production as and when required.

We are therefore again witnessing a radical reappraisal of the principles underlying stock control, with a questioning of old assumptions which until recently were regarded as truisms. This most recent investigation – that of questioning the rigidity of set-up times – has other interesting ramifications.

If we achieved our ideal state with perfect volume and variety flexibility in the plant, then the need for production forecasting is brought into question, since the plant will now be able to respond perfectly to any given market situation. Whilst we are unable to achieve our ideal, the recent developments in engineering flexibility into our processes, systems and organizations can have the effect of reducing our reliance on forecasts to manage the operations facility. That is, if we accept that the marketplace is volatile and difficult to predict, it is right that equal efforts go into nullifying the effect of that volatility as well as into trying to predict the volatility in advance, through statistical forecasting techniques.

That is not to say that forecasting techniques are not important, as they have a vital role to play in attempting to help manage the interface between productive capability and market requirements. A stock control audit check list is provided at page 97 and a matrix for the application of stock control principles is given in Figure 4.10.

DEMAND TYPE	ITEM CLASSIFICATION		
	A	B	C
Dependent demand	Requirements planning	Requirements planning	2 – Bin (R O L)
Independent demand	R O L FI	R O L FI	2 – Bin (R O L)

Figure 4.10 Inventory control matrix

Sales and production forecasting

Techniques

Time series forecasting uses past or historical data to predict future performance. This approach is appropriate where the historical pattern continues or if adjustments account for any future changes. However, the models neither attempt to explain the performance pattern nor to indicate what factors have the greatest influence on it. This is the role of regression analysis, which attempts to highlight the key controlling factors influencing the behaviour.

The purpose of this section is not to cover the various techniques in detail but rather to highlight their applicability to production-type situations. The decision tree shown in Figure 4.11 gives a broad illustration of when to apply a particular method.

In order to use the decision tree, the following definitions may be helpful:

Trend	A long-term change in level
Seasonality	Variations of a constant length that occur periodically
Winters' model	A model that calculates the level, trend and seasonality factors using exponential smoothing parameters to create a forecast of future performance
Moving average	The calculation of the average value of past data over the latest period – e.g. twelve-month moving average
Exponential smoothing	A weighted moving average that gives a greater weight to more recent data
Seasonally adjusted moving average	The multiplication of the forecast moving average value by a seasonal adjustment factor to obtain a seasonally adjusted moving average
Multiple linear regression	The identification of several key factors that affect performance and their relative significance

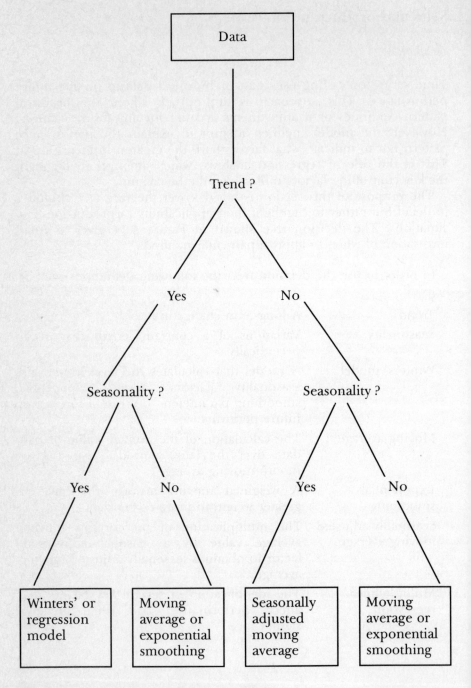

Figure 4.11 Forecast-method selection

The methodology for applying these techniques are given in a number of specialized publications (see essential reading list at the end of the chapter), but the statistical techniques involved are just one factor that influences the practical usefulness of forecasts.

Influencing factors

A key decision in any forecast is to decide what is the appropriate forecasting *horizon*. In some instances, it is appropriate to look five years ahead whereas in other circumstances it is more correct to confine ourselves to just the one year. The critical dimension is the nature of the decision that is to be made on the basis of the forecast and the necessary response time to decide and to implement that decision. For example, if we are using the forecast to make long-term capacity planning decisions, then a typical response time to evaluate, select and commission a new plant may well be three years. Therefore if we are not forecasting at least this far ahead we will always miss the market opportunity.

Related to the forecasting horizon is the *level of detail* that is required in the forecast. Again the simple maxim is that it should be related to the level of detail required to support the decision to be made, congruent with the ability to forecast requirements to a satisfactory level of accuracy.

The *review frequency* is another factor that can greatly influence the usefulness of forecasts to production personnel. If they are reviewed too infrequently they will fail to represent reality and fall into misuse. Again, if they are reviewed and issued too frequently there is a danger that the user may be unable to assimilate them. The correct review frequency will depend on the volatility of the subject-matter. For example, if we are dealing with a fast-moving high-technology market, characterized by short product life cycles, rapid technical changes and so forth, then we would need more frequent market forecasts than if we were operating in a slow-moving, stable mature product market. However, really to use the forecast information to the full would require the appropriate infrastructure set-up together with the ability to respond quickly within the plant. A forecasting audit checklist is provided at page 98.

Personal development task no. 4.1

1 Obtain an empirical analysis of where inventory is held in the firm.

2   Starting with the most significant inventory holding, determine the function performed by that inventory, and the associated stockholding costs.
3   Carry out a cost–benefit analysis and where appropriate suggest action plans either to carry out the function in an alternative manner or to reduce the stockholding without prejudicing service level.

Personal development task no. 4.2

1   Apply the following checklists to your operation to highlight relevant strengths and weaknesses:
    -   stock control (Ref. Audit Checklist (Stock Control), p. 97)
    -   forecasting (Ref. Figure 4.11, p. 97)
2   Develop action plans to eliminate weaknesses and build on strengths.
3   Implement the actions against an agreed timescale.

Chapter summary points

-   Inventory adds cost to product but not value.
-   There is a need to question why we hold inventory, and to see if that function can be performed more effectively by an alternative approach.
-   Inventory should be subjected to a cost–benefit analysis.
-   Where inventory is warranted it should be subjected to effective control:
    -   ABC analysis
    -   Statistical Control Techniques for independent items
    -   Requirements Planning for dependent items
    -   Appropriate forecasting techniques

Essential reading

Vollmann, T. E., Berry, W. L., and Whybark, D. C., *Manufacturing Planning and Control Systems,* Illinois: Irwin, 1984.
Cass, T., *Statistical Methods in Management,* London: Cassell, 1980.

Audit checklist

Application Area: Stock Control

Audit Objective

To establish that the stock control system (SC) provides the appropriate service level whilst maintaining the minimum investment in inventory.

Points to Consider

1. What is the stated stock control policy?
2. Are stock items grouped according to an ABC system?
3. Are independent stock items controlled using statistical inventory control techniques, e.g. re-order level or fixed interval method?
4. What assumptions underlie the establishment of re-order levels, i.e. forecast usage and safety stock calculation?
5. What assumptions underlie re-order quantities (ROQ)?
6. How are lead times determined?
7. How are stockholding, stock-out and re-ordering costs determined?
8. How is re-order interval determined?
9. Are dependent items controlled using requirements planning techniques ? (see MRP Checklist)
10. Are appropriate stock control procedures in force?

Detailed Tests

1. What service levels are desired and actually being achieved?
2. What is the frequency of stock-outs?
3. Selective sampling to confirm the accuracy of all assumptions mentioned in the section 'Points to Consider', above.

Audit checklist

Application Area: Sales Forecasting

Audit Objective

To establish whether accurate and appropriate sales forecasts are being produced for use in the master production schedule (MPS).

Points to Consider

1.   Is the forecasting horizon appropriate?
2.   Do the forecasting time periods relate to the MPS?
3.   Are the forecasting assumptions clearly stated?
4.   What use is made of statistical techniques for trend, seasonality factors, etc?
5.   Is the forecast based on the correct level of detail, i.e. end items or families of products?
6.   Is sales/marketing responsible for preparation and review of forecasts?
7.   Is there correct level of liaison with production?
8.   Data to be based on demand NOT sales.
9.   How often is actual performance compared with forecast?
10.   How are future changes and revisions incorporated?

Detailed Tests

1.   Review actual demand against forecast and investigate deviations.
2.   Establish the procedure for preparing forecasts and validate assumptions, accuracy of data and the application of statistical techniques.
3.   Establish the responsibility for preparation and review by interview.

5 Planning and controlling the operation: planning and controlling the flow

Introduction

The previous chapter considered the role of inventory in managing the operation. This chapter considers the techniques for planning and controlling the flow within the facilities. It is assumed for these purposes that the shape of the facilities is fixed within the short term, longer-term capacity planning having been considered as part of the facilities strategy outlined later in Chapter 6.

In particular, this chapter will consider the role of the master production schedule (MPS) the development of the capability to service the schedule using requirements planning techniques and the ways that the schedule can be translated into action using shop floor planning and control methods. Consideration will also be given to the just in time (JIT) and finite capacity scheduling philosophies.

Planning and control framework

An overall planning and control framework for operations is given in Figure 5.1 which illustrates the planning and control hierarchy within the operation.

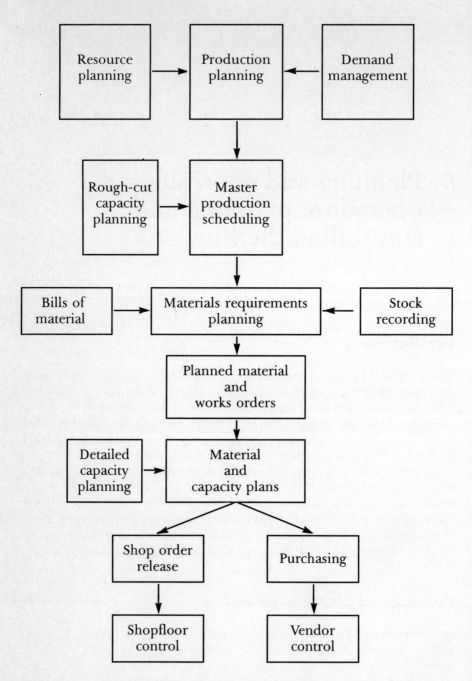

Figure 5.1 Manufacturing planning and control

The operation may be thought of as comprising three stages: demand management resulting in a viable MPS, master scheduling giving rise to planned material and works orders and, finally, the aspects of detailed production planning and shopfloor control. We shall consider each of these stages in turn.

Demand management and the master production schedule

Figure 5.2 illustrates the processes involved in producing the master production schedule. The components are discussed in detail below.

Resource Planning activity relates to the determination of the longer-term capacity requirements in order to service the future profile of the company's markets. It will need to take into account not just the size of the company's marketplace, but also its shape in terms of product variety and rate of new product introduction. There is a strong link between this stage and the development of a facilities strategy highlighted in Chapter 6.

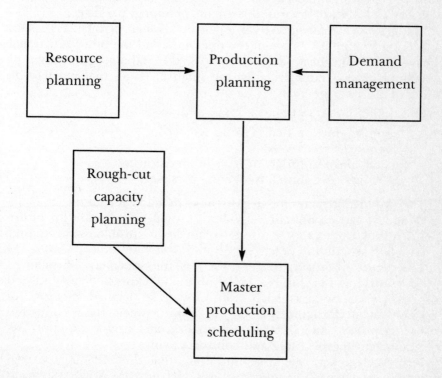

Figure 5.2 Input into the master production schedule

Demand Management includes the activities of demand forecasting and sales order entry.

An introduction to forecasting techniques was given in Chapter 4, together with the appropriate audit checklist. It is important that production planning activities are related to this forecast, which should include all relevant information (that is, finished goods in the appropriate level of detail, spares categories and so on) to allow a realistic plant master schedule to be developed.

The sales order entry application looks after customer orders, enquiries and delivery quotations and will therefore need to include such activities as availability checking, to see if a customer request can be serviced. This activity will need to be linked to the MPS, since if the customer request cannot be serviced from finished goods inventory, it will need to be provided for there. For future reference it is important that the specific customer order is 'pegged' to a specific batch in the MPS. If the customer order cannot be serviced within the required lead time from the MPS as it now stands, then the viability of changing the schedule should be examined. This ability is greatly enhanced using the simulation features found in a number of MRP (material requirements planning) packages.

The *production planning* activity involves a range of business issues and provides the link between the operation and the other functional areas of the business. As such, it is the joint responsibility of operations, sales and marketing and finance. Issues that need to be resolved at this stage include:

- target sales that are to be achieved;
- target production that is to be achieved;
- inventory target levels;
- major 'make-to-order' or 'buy-in' decisions;
- the link to the annual budgeting process.

The production planning activity links demand forecasting and the MPS and, if carried out correctly, both provides a measure for future performance and can be used to anticipate problems in master production scheduling practice.

The *master production schedule (MPS)* is the statement of planned production for the future. It is normally expressed in finished product terms and, as such, can provide a detailed measure of operational performance. It is the link between the production planning process and factory performance, and drives the entire set of manufacturing planning and control activities.

With such a key role it is important that the MPS is managed successfully. One the major causes of failure of MRP systems is poor master scheduling practice, and this fact needs to be recognized organizationally. It is important that the organization structure reflects the needs of the system, and that the appropriate individuals are made responsible for master scheduling practice. In addition, the appropriate policies and procedures must be in place to support the activity.

Key considerations to be made whilst appraising the MPS are:

1 *Planning horizon:* The horizon should reflect the longest lead time to respond to scheduled production needs, taking into account stock policy. For example, if we have decided to run with no stock of a component with a six-month lead time, if we failed to set the MPS with a planning horizon of greater than six months, then whenever we wanted that particular item to service production requirements we would always be too late! In practice, the trade-off is the realism of extended planning horizons against component or raw material stockholding costs.

2 *Level of detail:* The level of detail within the MPS should be the minimum needed faithfully to reflect production requirements. If we try to build too great a level of detail in the schedule then the supporting demand forecasting activity will become very complicated and expensive (and unrealistic!). Efforts put into simplifying product structures for planning purposes can really help in this regard.

3 *Reliability:* The MPS needs to be reliable and, in this context, schedule stability is a requirement. Too many changes in the schedule cause disruption and affect productivity. Many firms 'freeze' early schedule time periods in order to achieve this stability – that is, schedule changes are not normally allowed in this 'frozen' period in an attempt to achieve stable production. However, again there is a trade-off because too much rigidity in the schedule will be reflected in a lack of responsiveness to customer requirements, the consequent need to hold excessive inventories, and therefore increased costs of running the operation.

4 *Realism:* The MPS needs to be realistic, so there must be a tangible link to the production planning process. In addition, it must be capable of being successfully executed. A major contributor in this area is the complementary 'rough-cut capacity planning' activity, which is covered in the next sub section.

However, the acid test is actual schedule achievement by the factory, and closed loop feedback from the downstream areas is vital to the maintenance of the schedule's realism. By this feedback mechanism the MPS can reflect any actual problems, including capacity and material shortages.

A master production schedule audit checklist is included at the end of the chapter (p. 120).

Rough-cut capacity planning involves analysing the MPS in order to evaluate the associated operations capacity requirements. The 'rough-cut' aspect indicates that it is normally only confined to key or aggregate workcentres, and that it is carried out with less frequency than detailed capacity planning – usually at monthly intervals. However, it is a vital component in ensuring the realism of the MPS and will highlight potential over- or underloads, thus allowing schedule changes to be executed. The advance indication of production bottlenecks can also serve as a vehicle to suggest potential areas of subcontract activity for the future.

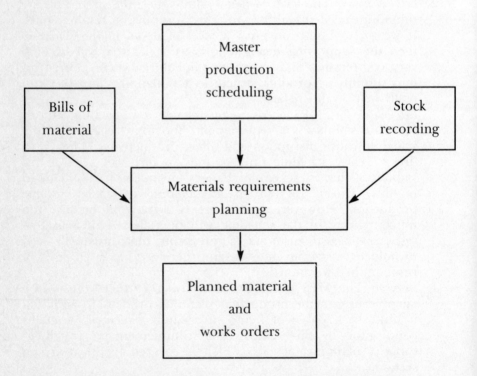

Figure 5.3 From MPS to planned materials and works orders

Master production schedule to planned material and works orders

In order to translate the MPS into material and works order requirements there are further system building blocks needed (see Figure 5.3). These are the bill of materials and inventory recording modules respectively, which are used by the materials Requirements planning module to determine the future material and works orders needed to achieve the MPS.

The *bill of materials or formulation* maintains the basic data for defining products and their structures. As such, it contains a list of components for an end product or assembly, together with the product structure, recent approved changes, and a procedure for handling options and variants and so forth. Some products, typically the 'formulation-type' products would be reflected in a similar fashion, with the intermediate products held as the equivalent of sub-assemblies. In this latter case, the bills of materials are generally simpler and characterized by fewer levels.

Care taken in structuring the bills of materials – say, into families – can pay great dividends in master scheduling practice by eliminating complexity. Since an MRP system is very demanding in terms of data accuracy, the appropriate organization needs to be set up to ensure that changes and amendments to bills are authorized and controlled as well as for the initial creation of the bill itself. Typical required data accuracy in this area is 98 per cent. A bill of materials audit checklist is provided at page 121.

The second module in this section is *inventory recording,* which provides a basic accounting system for all types of inventory, handling all associated transactions for goods receiving, inspection, receipts to stores, issues, transfers and adjustments and so on. At any one time, this module will provide the inventory balance for any item held on the system and will provide the trigger for cycle counting amongst other activities. An accurate reflection of the 'on-hand' balance is vital for success of the MRP module, and the supporting policies and procedures need to be in place to ensure that this is the case. An audit checklist for inventory or stock recording is provided at page 122.

The third module in this section is *material requirements planning,* which contains the logic for the MRP activity. This is illustrated by Figure 5.4. The logic is as follows.

The 'gross' requirements are derived from the MPS and the 'on-hand' inventory together, with orders already placed on suppliers or released to the shopfloor being subtracted to give the 'net' requirements. This is the requirement that will be covered by planned orders.

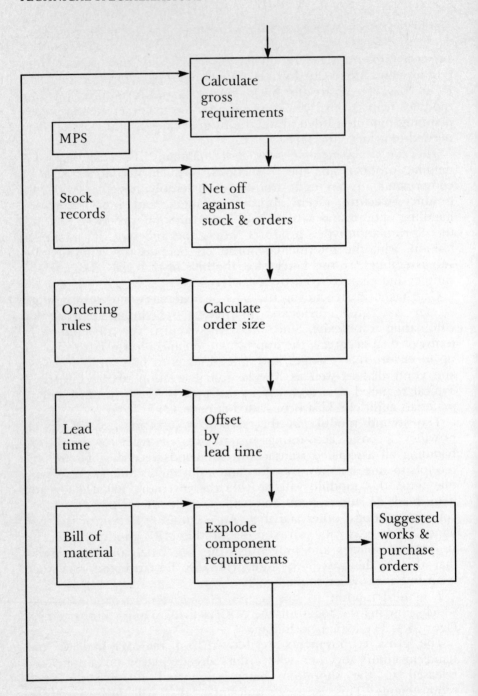

Figure 5.4   MRP logic

In order to calculate the magnitude and the timing of these planned orders, it will be necessary to apply the firm's ordering rules and offset this by the supplier or factory lead time. The firm's ordering rules relate to the selected inventory service level and the degree of safety stock necessary to cover the uncertainty present in both demand and lead time. In addition, there will be the application of a re-order quantity rule. The use of these techniques has been covered in Chapter 4.

The resulting planned orders are scheduled to be released on the basis of the normal purchasing or manufacturing lead time, to ensure that the items will be available when required to service production needs. If the items are assemblies or intermediate products, the system will now explode these planned orders to develop requirements for the corresponding sub-assemblies or raw materials, using the bill of materials module. The process is then repeated at this level, commencing with the gross requirements.

The output is a series of time-phased suggested orders which, if released and executed in accordance with recommendations, would enable the MPS to be achieved. The other point is that this schedule would then have been achieved in line with the firm's inventory policies.

One of the critical tasks with any MRP system is to ensure that the planning process represents reality and, apart from data accuracy, a key decision is how frequently the system should cycle. If it cycles too infrequently then the data within the system will be out-of-date, will fail to reflect the current position, and the system will fall into disuse. If it cycles too frequently then the system response could become too 'nervous', and it is debateable whether the organization could cope with the continual reviews and changes.

With this in mind, MRP systems fall into two categories: regenerative and net change. The regenerative system carries out a full regeneration each time the system is cycled – that is, previous plans are discarded, a new MPS is calculated, the gross to net conversion is carried out for the schedule, and the whole process of applying ordering rules, offsetting by the appropriate lead time and suggesting planned orders is repeated at each level in the bills of materials. Obviously this is a time-consuming process and requires that the supporting organization assimilates a completely new plan every time. An alternative approach is to use the net change approach where only the changes from the last schedule are subjected to this approach, with corresponding savings in time, paperwork and effort. It is akin to 'managing by exception'. With this type of system it is possible to cycle more frequently as there are less downstream implications, and so it is easier to keep the system realistic and hence derive real benefits.

The *benefits* of taking an MRP approach where it fits the business and product feature needs are:

- less inventory holding;
- shorter product lead times, corresponding to less work in progress;
- more delivery promises met with fewer shortages.

Although it is a very demanding application, many firms have witnessed substantial competitive advantage accruing through these types of benefits. However, if the scope of the application is not fully realized and the appropriate organization and policy changes are not made, the adoption of the system can be dysfunctional. An audit checklist for this module is given at page 123.

Detailed production planning and shopfloor control

This part of the system is concerned with the planning, execution and control of the planned orders from the previous stage (see Figure 5.5).

The *detailed capacity planning* module ensures that individual workcentre capacity is available to execute the suggested works orders. In the event of an overload, a range of options are available: these include a temporary increase of capacity through working selective overtime; transferring labour into the overloaded areas; offsetting the load through the use of an alternative routing and hence alternative workcentres; subcontracting; or by the purchase of the item outside. If none of these possibilities is viable, then there is the option to reschedule.

Note that this application illustrates the importance of closing the loop through feedback control to the MPS, since if the rough-cut planning activity is not carried out successfully, then it could well be impossible to implement the schedule at the detailed level once the requirements planning activity has been carried out. The telltale signs of this problem will become apparent at the detailed capacity planning stage.

The *order release* stage applies to both shopfloor orders and to purchase orders, and is a necessary manual stage in the process. (Note that MRP does not take the detailed workcentre capacities into account when it generates the suggested orders – that is, it assumes infinite capacity.) The task is to authorize release of the orders and to set a control on the system to ensure that it corresponds to latest business requirements. An audit checklist for shopfloor control is given at page 124.

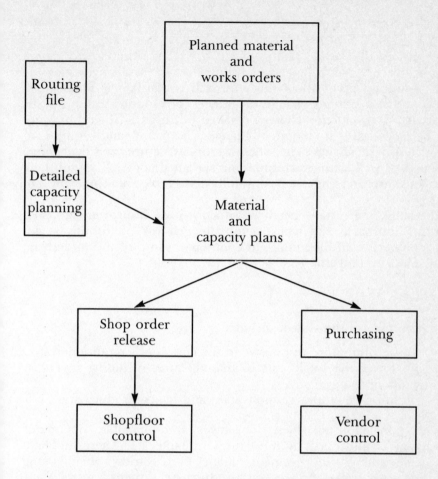

Figure 5.5 Detailed production planning and shopfloor control

This systematic approach to production planning and control has great benefit, but it is necessary to apply appropriate controls on to the system to ensure that the benefits are being achieved. This set of controls does not just apply to the detailed shop order release stage, but rather to each stage in the process. Typical control considerations are given in the planning and controlling the flow audit checklist at page 125.

'Just in time' philosophy

The 'just in time' (JIT) philosophy is a way of running production that is fundamental to Japanese production and productivity gains.

A significant point about this approach is that it is a 'philosophy' and not just a systems change. In fact, it corresponds to the holistic approach to production strategy detailed in earlier chapters. In order to be successful it requires changes in plant and equipment characteristics, changes in organization structure and personnel practices as well as the corresponding system changes. If any of these elements are missing then the full deliverable benefits will not accrue.

Certainly, there have been well-documented improvements cited for this approach, and whilst a fully-fledged JIT philosophy is not appropriate for all operating environments, some of the underlying principles certainly are.

Objectives

The objectives of the system include:

- To become more responsive to the customer's requirements;
- To lower the total costs of manufacture (including inventory holding charges);
- To improve employee motivation and hence productivity.

The translation of these objectives into tangible operations advantage is illustrated by the figures in Table 5.1. These highlight the wide-ranging improvements made in a variety of operating environments and against several 'productivity' dimensions.

Several points arise from these figures. First, JIT is not just an inventory reduction system, although there are incredible reductions in inventory possible as illustrated by the Table. Second, the system allows the facility to become much more closely attuned to its marketplace, with significantly reduced work in progress enabling faster throughput lead times and hence far speedier delivery response. There are also additional derived benefits in the area of performance to specification, potential capacity utilization gains and better use of space.

The JIT approach certainly does appear to hold real competitive edge advantages, provided that it fits the firm's product characteristics and chosen operations strategy.

Table 5.1
JIT benefits

	Automotive components	Flexible packaging	Electrical cons. goods	Mechanical equipment	Fashion goods
	Repetitive	*Process*	*Repetitive*	*Job shop*	*Repetitive*
MFG lead time reduction	89%	86%	85%	83%	92%
Productivity increase					
direct	19%	50%	n/a	5%	⎱ 29%
indirect/salary	60%	50%	38%	21%	⎰
Scrap/rework reduction	50%	63%	26%	33%	61%
Purch. mat'l price reduction	n/a	7%	n/a	6%	11%
Inventory reduction					
raw material	35%	70%	50%	73%	70%
WIP	89%	82%	85%	70%	85%
finished goods	61%	71%	90%	0	70%
Set-up reduction	75%	75%	94%	75%	91%
Space reduction	53%	n/a	80%	n/a	39%
Capacity increase	n/a	36%	n/a	n/a	42%

Prerequisites

There are certain prerequisites for success and, whilst these might limit the applicability of the total approach, it does not mean that elements of the system are appropriate for a wide range of environments. The prerequisites for introducing an effective JIT approach are:

1 *A high degree of planning:* It would be very dangerous to attempt to introduce this approach without significant pre-planning. This is not a 'quick fix', but a different philosophy to running production. A typical lead time schedule is given in Figure 5.6.

   It is noteworthy that the underlying principles of the change are not difficult to understand, but a significant amount of time needs to be allocated to communicate the benefits and pitfalls of approach, both internally to employees and externally to suppliers and customers.

2 *Flexibility in resources:* In order to gain the benefits of this approach it is first necessary to achieve responsiveness in the resources consumed by the firm. This flexibility includes the ability of the plant and equipment to handle small batch sizes easily and without significant changeover-time cost penalty, and also workforce flexibility in terms of job demarcation and retraining. A fluid responsive management structure is therefore needed to handle day-to-day problems. An interesting point arises with bonus schemes, some of which have the effect of encouraging large batch working. Obviously, in such an instance, the reward mechanism would be out of tune with the needs of the business and would have to be modified. A further example of the need for flexibility arises when the purchasing department choose potential suppliers. The price dimension, so often used as the discriminator, is just one part of the picture. The more appropriate choice would be for the chosen supplier to have the ability to deliver frequently in small quantities, with on-specification products at an economic price. This would allow the firm to run with far reduced inventories and would encourage it to build up better, longer-lasting relationships with its suppliers. The benefit to the supplier could be increased volume of business with the customer (reflecting the associated tendency to reduce the absolute number of suppliers), and a more visible and predictable relationship.

3 *Level production rates and a limited range of production variants:* The approach is best serviced by maintaining a level of stability in

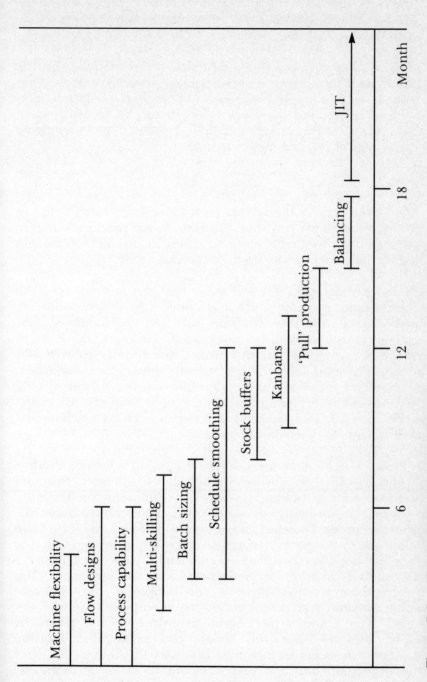

Figure 5.6 JIT implementation schedule

the MPS, thus allowing a smoother production flow within the factory and heightening the opportunity to give the schedule visibility to chosen suppliers. There is an impetus to standardize products and production processes.

Note that it is very important that the operations chain is configured to enhance its predictability – that is, that we have reliability of supply, reliability of factory on-specification output at required rates and so on. It can be seen that there are some very strong parallels between the underlying principles of JIT and quality management.

Principles

The main principles of the system are to eliminate waste – that is, any activity which adds cost, but not value to the product – and, in concert with this, avoids the need to invest in inventory while still meeting the customer's exact needs at the exact time.

Improve activities that add value and reduce those that just add cost The important actions are those which add value to the product, and any operations activity in this direction that can be translated into financial advantage should be encouraged. However, there are a wide range of existing operations activities that do not effectively add value but add cost instead and which should be eliminated. Examples of these include any overproduction that is not directly matched to customer requirements, together with the associated inventory, internal non-value-added activities such as machine set-ups, waiting time and inventory moves.

Reduce inventory The intention is to achieve the benefits of a flowline type process with the corresponding ability to meet customer requirements without holding inventory. A commonly used analogy is to liken the inventory to water in a river which hides the problems, or rocks. Therefore, if we want to reduce inventory, drain the water out of the river in stages so uncovering the rocks, and at the requisite point remove them permanently. If we do not take a staged approach to inventory reduction, or if we attempt to skim over the problems, then there is the danger of the operation becoming unstable, with disastrous effects on output.

At each stage it will be necessary to consider the role played by inventory, and to take the action to render that function unnecessary. For example, it may be necessary to eliminate the need for the decoupling function played by inventory by reducing the impact of a process choice change, combining operations, relocating equipment or eliminating the need for a machine set-up time. In all cases, it is the problem that must be treated not the symptoms! What is required is a permanent solution.

Improve the operations focus on the customer   It is also necessary to match the output of the operation to the needs of the customer and so operate with a minimum of finished goods stock. This is achieved by running the facilities with minimum batch sizes, pulling production through so that earlier sections in the plant are totally synchronized with later sections and, in assembly-type environments, running mixed model final assembly with a sequence of products running down the same assembly line.

If this approach is taken, it is vital that flexibility is engineered into the facilities, organization structure and personnel policies.

Set up the appropriate customer and supplier linkages   It is very important that the production facility is viewed as just one stage in the operations chain; thus, if significant changes are mooted for the production facility, it is vital that their impact is assessed on the other component parts. In particular, the effect on suppliers and customers should be evaluated.

With reference to significant suppliers, it is very important that they are involved in the change process itself. As mentioned earlier, the criteria for an approved supplier status can change, and this needs to be communicated early in the planning stage.

So far as the customers are concerned, they should see tremendous benefits that they themselves can convert into competitive advantage for their own businesses. The progress into JIT manufacture will be expedited if key customers are involved and are prepared to communicate their future schedule requirements and new product introductions.

The implementation of a JIT approach has the effect of integrating the various components of the operations chain, and bringing customers and suppliers into the same 'family' for mutual benefit.

Involve the personnel   As indicated earlier, the JIT implementation will succeed or fail depending on how successfully the benefits, expectations and pitfalls have been communicated. But there must be an attitude change engendered amongst the total workforce. It is not only the shopfloor which needs to be involved in this process, as the JIT approach will quite dramatically affect the jobs of supervisors, middle management and support departments.

A task force or cross-functional team approach has been found to work well in this application.

An audit checklist relating to the JIT philosophy is provided at page 126.

Capacity requirements planning and scheduling production

Certain approaches have been built up around capacity planning and scheduling. There are a number of systems around which are based on finite capacity planning principles – that is, they recognize capacity overloads and underloads and try to optimize a schedule taking into account the constraints associated with bottleneck workcentres. There are some fundamental principles that apply to scheduling when we take workcentre capacities into account.

Principles

Bottlenecks govern throughput and inventories In any operation, for a given mix of products, there will be some bottleneck workcentres with no spare capacity, and it is these that constrain total factory output. For example, if the bottleneck workcentre breaks down it is not just its throughput contribution that has been lost but, in fact, the throughput contribution of the whole factory.

Just as there are bottleneck workcentres so there will be non-bottleneck workcentres and, by definition, these will have spare capacity at the current level and mix of productive activity. They therefore present no constraint to factory output unless they are so badly scheduled or sequenced that they interfere with bottleneck production.

Scheduling bottleneck and non-bottleneck workcentres The concept of bottleneck and non-bottleneck workcentres has interesting scheduling implications.

Because the bottlenecks influence factory output, if the market demand warrants it, a key task must be to keep these workcentres running on effective production at all times. Workcentre availability must therefore be improved through the application of appropriate planned and preventative maintenance techniques and selective overtime working. The process must be held under control using the latest process control technology, as valuable bottleneck capacity cannot be wasted producing non-conforming product. (It may also pay, in this case, to inspect product on the input side of the workcentre to ensure that valuable processing time is not wasted on inferior or non-conforming raw materials.)

With non-bottleneck workcentres' there is spare capacity and so the application of this practice need not be so stringent. In fact, running these workcentres continuously must increase the work in process inventory, because the relative spare capacity will produce an output in excess of the bottleneck workcentres' capacity, causing a build-up in front of the bottlenecks. The appropriate practice is to be prepared to shut down the non-bottlenecks when they are producing excessive output. Therefore scheduling needs to be modified according to the bottleneck or non-bottleneck status of the workcentre.

Directing improvement efforts Not only do the bottleneck workcentres govern throughput and inventories, but they set the characteristics of the operation. In other words, if the bottleneck workcentre is inflexible, then generally the whole facility will prove to be inflexible and will need to be buffered from the marketplace by investing in stock. Therefore if we want to change the facility's characteristics a good place to start would be at the bottleneck workcentres. In the above instance, it would be appropriate to direct set-up reduction activity to start at the bottleneck workcentres.

Optimized production technology (OPT) is a proprietory scheduling system that attempts to schedule finite resources in order to achieve maximum factory effectiveness – that is, to develop the schedule that improves profitability by simultaneously increasing throughput, whilst reducing inventory and operating expenses.

It operates using set scheduling principles including the following:

- Bottlenecks govern throughput and inventories.
- Time lost at a bottleneck is lost for the whole factory.
- Time saved at a non-bottleneck is a mirage.
- Balance flow not capacity.
- Activation does not mean utilization.
- Transfer batch does not necessarily equal process batch.

The outputs from the system are detailed production schedules for each work-station and a complete set of materials requirements for the chosen planning horizon.

Personal development task no. 5.1

1 Apply the following checklists to your operation to highlight relevant strengths and weaknesses:

- MPS checklist (p. 120)
- Bill of materials checklist (p. 121)
- Stock recording checklist (p. 122)
- MRP checklist (p. 123)
- Shopfloor control checklist (p. 125).

2 Develop action plans to eliminate weaknesses and build on strengths.
3 Implement the actions against an agreed timescale.

Personal development task no. 5.2

1 Determine the control criteria used to judge the planning and control function of the business. The production control checklist (p. 124) can be used as a guide.
2 Evaluate how appropriate this is to the needs of the firm, suggest and implement improvements.

Personal development task no. 5.3

1 Examine the JIT production philosophy, and decide which of the underlying principles can be applied to your organization.
2 Set out an implementation plan paying particular attention to the communication needs.

Personal development task no. 5.4

1 Evaluate how effective your firm is at managing the production flow through the management of bottlenecks.
2 Suggest improvements where necessary.

Chapter summary points

- The planning and control process needs to be an integrated process which fits the needs of the firm.
- There are three principal stages in the process:
  - demand management to the MPS
  - MPS to planned orders
  - shopfloor control

- Each stage should link to the others, with a feedback loop at the appropriate point.
- The JIT approach can show startling 'productivity' improvements if it is appropriate for your operating environment.
- Even if the JIT approach is not wholly appropriate for your environment there are still substantial gains to be made by applying certain elements of the philosophy.
- Bottlenecks govern throughput and inventories.

Essential reading

Bolander, S.F., Heard, R.C., Seward, S.M. and Taylor S.G., *Manufacturing Planning and Control* (in Process Industries), Virginia: APICS, 1981.

Goldratt, E.M. and Cox, J., *The Goal – Excellence in Manufacturing,* New York: North River Press Inc., 1984.

Schonberger, R.J., *Japanese Manufacturing Techniques – nine hidden lessons in simplicity.* New York: Free Press, 1982.

Vollmann, T.E., Berry, W.L. and Whybark, D.C., *Manufacturing Planning and Control Systems,* Illinois: Irwin, 1984.

Audit checklist

Application Area: Master Production Schedule

Audit Objective

To establish whether the master production schedule (MPS) is realistic, planned in accordance with available capacity and reflects the sales forecast modified through stock policy.

Points to Consider

1. Is the planning horizon appropriate?
2. Are the appropriate time periods used (weekly then monthly: firm/flexible)?
3. Is the MPS planned using 'rough-cut' capacity planning techniques?
4. Are spare items included?
5. Is the MPS linked to the sales forecast using the stated finished goods inventory policy?
6. Is the plan based on the correct level of detail, i.e. end items or families of products?
7. Does the MPS account for lead time considerations?
8. How often is actual performance compared with forecast?
9. Large arrears destroy the accuracy of the plan.

Detailed Tests

1. Review actual performance against plan and investigate deviations.
2. Establish the procedure for capacity planning the MPS and confirm the method for matching load with capacity.
3. Investigate recent delivery performances together with the level of arrears.

Audit checklist

Application Area: Bills of Materials/Formulations

Audit Objective

To establish whether bills of materials (BOMs) are complete, accurate, technically up-to-date and reflect current product-structures.

Points to Consider

1. Is there a defined management policy for BOM?
2. Is there a BOM for every appropriate product?
3. Is the documentation satisfactory and supported by procedures and authorization checks?
4. What internal controls are in existence?
5. Specific problem areas could be:

initial inaccuracy	scrap allowance
obsolescent items	material specifications
bulk change routines	extraction rates
technical changes	alternatives/substitutes
effectivity dates	options/variance/phantoms

Detailed Tests

1. Redundant bills of materials?
2. Confirm the existence of a control system for raising, amending and deleting BOMs.
3. Check compliance with established procedures and authority levels.
4. Confirm accuracy and completeness of sample BOMs.
5. Note that BOM inaccuracies may be highlighted by monitoring unplanned issues and receipts to stores.

Audit checklist

Application Area: Stock Recording

Audit Objective

To establish whether the stock recording system is an accurate reflection of stock movements and balances for goods held in accordance with stock policy.

Points to Consider

1. Are the appropriate stock transactions recorded?
2. Is the prime documentation adequate and supported by the relevant procedures?
3. Are inventory balances accurate and promptly reported?
4. Is there correct treatment of non-conforming items?
5. Is there adequate security of both physical stock and records?
6. Is there correct segregation of duties?
7. Is there a control system that ensures the completeness and accuracy of documentation?

Detailed Tests

1. Physical verification checks.
2. Confirm the policy re-authorization levels.
3. Is there a statement of formal procedures and objectives?
4. Test for unauthorized access to records and materials.
5. Test for completeness and accuracy of information.

Audit checklist

Application Area: Material Requirements Planning (MRP)

Audit Objective

To establish whether material requirements planning (MRP) system produces accurate planned requirements (production plan) in accordance with the defined master production schedule (MPS).

Points to Consider

1. Are the MPS, bills of materials and stock recording systems accurate?
2. What assumptions are built into the MRP system re-ordering rules, lead times, etc?
3. What parameters underlie the MRP system?
4. How are planned requirements translated into actual works and purchase orders?
5. How frequently does the MRP system cycle?

Detailed Tests

1. Individual tests on MPS, BOM and stock recording systems, as per their own checklists.
2. Review of key control documents and print-outs.

Audit checklist

Application Area: Production Control

Audit Objective

To establish whether the detailed production plan is realistic, planned in accordance with available workcentre capacity and reflects the requirements of the master production schedule (MPS).

Points to Consider

1. Is the planning horizon appropriate and are suitable time periods used?
2. Is the production plan produced using either finite or infinite capacity planning techniques?
3. How is workcentre capacity established?
4. What assumptions underlie the determination of capacity, e.g. efficiency, utilization, shop calendar, etc?
5. What is the limiting capacity factor?
6. How is workcentre load established and what is the accuracy of standard times, routings, etc?
7. What method is used to successfully match load and capacity?
8. Is the production planning and control system sufficiently flexible to cater for changes in the MPS?
9. What key reports are produced by the system and how is job priority established?

Detailed Tests

1. Review actual performance against plan and investigate deviations.
2. Confirm the procedures for loading, establishing capacity and matching within the production planning system.
3. What is the level of unplanned activity, e.g. overtime, subcontracting, arrears, etc? Also, is there significant underutilization?
4. Is there an undue level of progress-chasing activity?
5. How often is the plan rescheduled?
6. Large arrears destroy the accuracy of the plan.

Audit checklist

Area: Planning and Controlling the Flow

Topic: Control Checklist

Subject	Target	Findings
1. Master Schedule		
– Performance to schedule	> 95%	
– MPS vs production plan	95-105%	
– MPS arrears	> 2%	
2. Material Planning & Production Control		
– Material availability	> 98%	
– On-time completions	> 95%	
– Rescheduling activity	< 10%	
3. Capacity Planning		
– Load vs capacity	95-105%	
– Arrears	< 1 week	
4. Data Maintenance		
– Inventory record accuracy	> 98%	
– Bill of material accuracy	> 98%	
– Transaction accuracy	> 98%	

Audit checklist

Area: Planning & Controlling the Flow

Topic: Just in Time (JIT)

Subject	Findings
1. Prerequisites	

1. **Prerequisites**

   - Range of pre-planning activity
   - Degree of flexibility in resources:
     - equipment
     - organization structure
     - people's attitudes
     - scheduling system
   - Market demand characteristics:
     - level of market schedule
     - range of variants
       - simplification?
       - rationalization?
       - process compatibility?

2. **Activities**

   - Plan to reduce activities that add cost but no value
   - Inventory reduction programme
   - Scheduling and synchronization of activities
   - Quality lists – (right first time)
   - Focus on customer
   - Customer and supplier linkages
   - People involvement

6 Managing the facilities: the acquisition process

Introduction

The acquisition of fixed assets is a *structural* decision which helps mould the future characteristics, and hence the operations capability, of the firm. Each acquisition choice should be viewed primarily in the light of its potential to enhance the firm's competitive advantage, as decisions made in this area impact on the ability of the firm to service its marketplace effectively, and should support the firm's competitive strategy.

It is important that each incremental capacity decision should fit within the overall strategy set for operations. For example, if the key operations task is to develop responsiveness to the marketplace then volume and/or variety flexibility should be a major consideration when appraising equipment selection, and could outweigh direct operating cost savings.

For this reason, a formal decision process should exist to appraise the acquisition of new or replacement facilities, the objective being to ensure that each decision made reflects both the need to support the chosen strategy for competitive advantage as well as the need to earn an economic return for the shareholders.

The characteristics of the decision mean that a large number of factors need to be considered at the appraisal time, and it may be dangerous in the long term to be guided by solely short-term financial considerations. A wrong choice made at this stage can effectively lock the company into a poor operations capability for years to come and hinder the achievement of competitive advantage.

This highlights the need for a facilities strategy.

Facilities strategy

A facilities strategy provides a major link between the competitive advantage set for the firm and operations capability. It is a basic framework that underpins selection decisions and helps to ensure consistency of decision-making. Typical issues that need to be resolved at this stage include:

- Location of facilities
- Type of facilities capability
- Timing of additional capacity increments
- Sizing of additional capacity increments
- Role of integrating linkages

Issues that arise when considering the *location* of facilities include the desire to be close to the customer and/or the major suppliers, or to the availability of certain scarce resources – for example, skilled labour. It may be that the importance of any of these factors can be eclipsed by the attractiveness of such factors as grant aid, but it should always be remembered that location decisions are structural changes with effects on competitive capability which can easily outlast shorter-term inducements.

The wish to be close to the customer or supplier may be prompted by the need to minimize the impact of transportation costs on total product costs. This is obviously a key consideration when we are concerned with commodity-type products where it is difficult to differentiate from other competing products. In this case, in the absence of any other basis, competition will be through price, and a key task for the operations manager will be to structure the lowest-cost operation in the industry. If this is achieved, the organization as a whole will derive competitive advantage.

Location plays a large part in achieving this benefit, particularly where plant location is included as part of the total logistics chain. Again, this is an instance where structural decisions of this nature are not just an operations responsibility but rather a business decision with significant operations influence. It will certainly be the responsibility of the operations manager to highlight the linkage between operation location and achievement of the key operations task.

The desire to be close to a key resource (such as skilled labour) is prompted by the needs of the production process. It should always be borne in mind, however, that underpinning this desire is the assumption that the present process is appropriate and will continue. With rapid advances in technology, a large number of previous constraints are being removed; plant location must therefore reflect skill requirements not just for the present but as technology advances in the future. This will clearly have an impact on the plant's degree of capital intensity and also on the type of skill that may be in short supply. An example is given in Table 6.1 which represents the changed profile of a typical manufacturing unit for a large organization.

Table 6.1
'Typical' manufacturing unit after introduction of process technology

Area	% change over 5-year interval
	Change
Production Operatives	Down 12%
Clerks and Office Workers	Down 7%
Craftsmen	Down 11%
Technicians	Up 14%
Engineers and Scientists	Up 62%
Supervisors, Foremen and Chargehands	Down 10%
Salesmen	Same
Welfare and Personnel	Same
Managerial	Up 17%

The Table illustrates the effects of new process technology introduced on the shopfloor. There has been an effective deskilling of the workforce requirement, together with the gain of shopfloor productivity. It is interesting to note that the introduction of the new technology has led to an increased demand for supporting skills – technicians, for example – both to maintain the new equipment and engineers to process plan and to redesign products to realize the competitive advantage inherent in the new equipment. The move to this new type of process technology may have removed the restriction of one type of skilled labour shortage only to replace it with another.

It may be that the location decision is impacted by the desire to develop close customer or supplier linkages in order to gain competitive advantage through plant and scheduling flexibility. For example, with the 'just in time' approach, the philosophy is to reduce waste. A plant location that is close to the customer effectively reduces transit stocks, and allows the customer to gain the full benefit of the supplier–plant flexibility which can be translated into a financial advantage through lower stocks, reduced supplier lead times and so on. In this instance, plant location is an overt sign of customer commitment and can develop competitive advantage unique for the supplier and correspondingly great for the customer.

Another issue that arises at the facilities strategy stage is the *type of facilities capability* that is to be provided. For example, would the operation be better served by a single or many plants? A major consideration here would be the effect of economies of scale. If the operations' key task is to compete on a cost basis, then the single larger plant would normally provide that return due to potential increases in process efficiency, more effective amortization of fixed costs and so on. However, there is a price to be paid for large-scale operation with regard to difficulties of control, the corresponding move towards a strongly functional organization, and the potential for loss of responsiveness to market demands due to the inflexibility of the process of the organization. It is very important that the decision of whether to opt for a single or multiple plant set-up is linked carefully to the operation's key task. However, more and more technology development is directed at engineering flexibility into large-scale plants to derive the competitive advantage of a low cost base, together with volume and variety flexibility.

This highlights another concern which needs to be addressed at this stage – namely, the degree of plant flexibility required. Obviously this is linked to product features and market characteristics with regard to the breadth of the product range and the demand pattern throughout the typical year. If we are configuring a facility to handle a wide product range or a range that is subject to a large number of new product introductions then a key operations task will be to acquire the ability to respond flexibly to these demands. This objective will require flexible plant with rapid changeover times, a flexible planning and scheduling system together with an appropriate organization structure which develops the responsive linkages both internally and externally (for example, with suppliers). The impact of these requirements will need to be recognized at the facilities strategy stage.

If we are considering a facility to service a marketplace with a seasonal or erratic demand pattern, then we will need to trade off the requirement to hold finished goods stock with building volume flexibility into the plant. This can be achieved through sizing the plant generously to service maximum demand (although there is an obvious cost penalty with this approach) or be reducing the capital intensity of the process and using temporary labour to bolster production at peak times. Again, these issues will need to be addressed by a cross-functional team at the decision stage.

A related decision will have to be made with regard to new technology. There is no doubt that technology can radically change the way an operation services its marketplace. It can be a very effective way of promoting change, but there are risks. An unproven technology can consume inordinate amounts of resource in developing deliverable benefits and, for this reason, the firm will have to ensure that the technology suits its product range and that it is capable of applying the technology for competitive advantage. For these reasons, firms may decide to become technology-followers rather than leaders, thereby allowing someone else to undergo the learning experience to apply the new technology effectively. However, there is, of course, the risk that the application of the technology gives the other firm an unassailable competitive advantage not only through better servicing its customers but also by changing the characteristics of the industry itself.

This attitude towards new technology is influenced by how the firm defines its industry and develops new markets. A firm which sees its focus as technology-oriented – possibly based on an unique production process – will have an attitude towards research and development of protecting its superiority in that field and of trying to launch new products through that technology focus. If however, it sees its major emphasis as being product-related, then it will adopt a correspondingly different approach.

The firm's attitude towards risk-taking will also colour its judgement. Technology, as with other things, has a life cycle, and the timing of when to use the technology is a critical decision. However the *timing* issue is not just related to new technology, but is a critical factor in facilities-type decisions. Three basic policies seem to exist, the first being to build capacity in advance and in anticipation of market requirements. This approach has the advantage of signalling intentions to other players in the marketplace, and can be used as a pre-emptive strike to prevent others following the same route. Indeed, some industries are characterized by the leapfrogging of potential suppliers in laying down capacity. Of course, building capacity in advance of the market requirements does carry the risk that the market fails to materialize, through an incorrect estimation of demand or possibly through the appearance of a more favourable close substitute. A remedy may be to adopt a more aggressive pricing policy to try to use the spare capacity, but it is questionable whether this approach is tenable in the long term.

A second approach is to wait until the market exists and is undersupplied and then to build to meet the unsatisfied demand. Inherent in this approach is the acceptance of a short-term loss of possible contribution by not gearing up to immediate market demand as it appeared. This approach carries less direct market risk, but there is a great danger that a competitor will have recognized the same opportunity and be quicker off the mark to meet it. Should the competitor choose to lay down sufficient capacity to permit an aggressive pricing policy to bid for additional business this could result in a loss of market share.

A third approach is to attempt to match plant capacity with market requirements and to build neither early nor late. Obviously, to make this approach achievable in reality will require an intimate knowledge of the marketplace. If the firm is a large player in the market, then it may be able to influence the market to its advantage and so make such an approach tenable.

A complementary concern to the timing of the next capacity increment is its *sizing*. Both issues are inextricably linked. The immediate concern is to optimize the new plant's level of utilization, which can be paramount in commodity-type businesses where it is important to realize the economies of scale involved. However, it could well be that strategic business reasons outweigh the normal sizing considerations and, in order to prevent a competitor entering the market, a plant is built to a size which would not normally be justified but is used to establish a significant barrier to entry to a new player by creating a now oversupplied marketplace.

With plant sizing, care must be taken to account for changes in process technology and automation which, in certain industries, have changed the rules with regard to optimum size. New technology has greatly influenced the degree of integration possible with previously discrete stages in the process, has in certain instances greatly reduced the amount of initial capital investment and, as a derived feature, permitted the use of smaller focused units in locations close to the markets with similar product unit costs to the previous large centralized plant.

A significant point made throughout this section is that any decision to add capacity cannot be taken in isolation because it is a fundamental business choice as to how and where it wants to address its marketplace. The point has already been made that the operation is seen as just one stage in the integrated supplier chain, and no capacity decision should be undertaken unless the complementary *integrating linkages* have been developed. Indeed, facility-type decisions will impact on the type of employees required by the organization, as well as the appropriate organization structure neccessary fully to derive the benefits of any new technology.

A list of issues that arise with facilities-type decisions is given below:

1   Location of facilities:
    -   customer/supplier linkages;
    -   proximity to other factors that could promote competitive advantage;
    -   grant aid;
    -   impact of incoming or outgoing transportation costs;
    -   impact on focused facilities approach;
    -   inpact on scheduling flexibility;
2   Type of facilities capability:
    -   single or multiple plants;
    -   economies of scale;
    -   strategic risk, e.g. single sourcing;
    -   location of many suppliers;
    -   volatility of the marketplace.
    -   focused or general purpose;
    -   life cycle implications;
    -   marketplace volatility;
    -   product prospects.
    -   dedicated or flexible units;
    -   link to life cycle;
    -   volume flexibility;
    -   variety flexibility;
    -   fashion-type product.
    -   orientation – product/process;
    -   concept of core technology;
    -   method of new product development;
    -   emphasis on taking process technology into other applications;
    -   product development is totally compliant with market needs.
3   Degree of capital intensity:
    -   advancement of necessary automation;
    -   labour availability and skill level;
    -   process consistency;

- tightness of product specification;
- flexibility;
- availability of finance;
- learning curve.
4 Attitude towards new technology:
- leader vs follower;
- ability to support new technology;
- available technology infrastructure;
- risk-averse vs risk-taker;
- stage in the technology life cycle.
5 Timing of new capacity increments:
- before:
- risk of market failing to materializing;
- risk of close substitute appearing;
- barrier to entry;
- costs cheaper in inflationary times;
- signalling of intentions.
- after:
- risk of competitor taking initiative;
- lost margins and contribution;
- lesser market-related risk.
- matching:
- accuracy of market forecasts?
6 Sizing of additional capacity increments:
- utilization;
- barrier to entry/pre-emptive;
- optimum plant size, e.g. scale economies;
- link to marketplace demand.
7 Role of integrating linkages:
- customer/supplier;
- organization capability.

The above check list illustrates the strategic nature of this type of investment decision and how it relates to the business and market needs. The next stage in the process is to subject the decision to a financial appraisal.

The acquisition stage

Characteristics of investment decisions

Capital investment decisions characteristically involve the firm in spending large sums of money in the present to enhance operations capability in the future. Such decisions may support the company's need to expand volumes or market share, to diversify its product range or to get closer to its existing market through cost-cutting, enhancement of the product specification and so on.

The characteristics of the decisions, namely that:

a) large sums of money are normally involved
b) the effect of the decision is long-lasting
c) they involve a forecast of the future

differentiate them from revenue-type decisions, and mean that the firm needs some basis to compare and rank competing projects. This has been the traditional role of financial appraisal.

These techniques have developed in order to decide whether the financial benefits derived from a particular type of project justified its original capital outlay, and to establish a set of financial guidelines for project classification, and hence comparison. However, as mentioned earlier, this is only one part of the decision process. It is very important that the decision is seen first as a way of enhancing competitive capability and is then subjected to a financial, technological and behavioural appraisal.

Objective for capital expenditure projects

There is no inherent conflict in this approach – indeed, it is fully consistent with the theoretical objective for capital expenditure projects: *to maximize shareholders' wealth*. However, this definition does not include a time horizon. So are we attempting to maximize shareholders' wealth in the short or long term? There is a danger that short-term pressures will force us to take a view of project selection which may not be in the company's best long-term interests. Screening procedures should be set up to ensure that this type of situation is not allowed to predominate, and that a more balanced or portfolio approach is taken with project selection instead. In other words, at any one time, a firm should have a spectrum of projects with differing risk/return profiles. Obviously, the firm will expect projects involving high risk to offer correspondingly high returns to compensate for the uncertainty involved, and this introduces the concepts of risk premium and project classification. Typical project classifications are:

● new ventures

　　　　　　　　e.g.　diversification
　　　　　　　　　　　expansion or penetration of
　　　　　　　　　　　existing markets

- replacement decisions
  - e.g. using existing technology
    using new technology
- social ventures
  - e.g. non-profit-contributing decisions

The risks associated with the different project classifications are quite different. For example, investment decisions that support diversification strategies would normally involve a much higher degree of risk than a straight plant replacement decision involving proven technology. Both decisions should be subject to scrutiny, but the diversification decision should involve commensurately higher returns.

The intention is to achieve a balanced portfolio of projects, so balancing the risk, and also to achieve a balanced spread of project life cycles, so balancing the funding requirements. This is illustrated in Figure 6.1.

In order to achieve these objectives, we need to consider a variety of techniques for project appraisal.

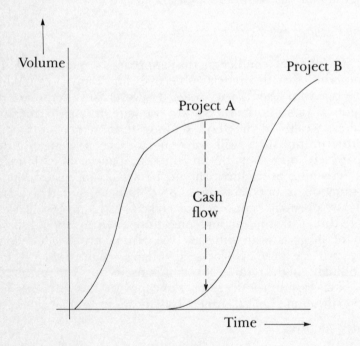

Figure 6.1 Project portfolio planning

Methods of financial appraisal

Techniques of financial appraisal exist to establish the financial attractiveness of a particular investment, and to provide a basis for comparison amongst competing projects, particularly when investment funds are limited.

Each method establishes a concept of the project's financial return for comparison against an acceptance standard. Therefore, in order to evaluate the methods available, it is appropriate to consider how the particular financial return is calculated, together with the derivation of the firm's specific acceptance standard.

The following methods will be considered:

1 payback method
2 return on capital employed method
3 discounting methods:
   – net present value
   – internal rate of return

Payback method

The principle of this method is to establish the cash flows throughout the project's economic life, and then to determine the number of years it will take to recover the cost of the original investment. This is the payback period for the project and may be compared with the firm's 'acceptance standard' for project payback.

A simple example is given below:

PROJECT A

Original Investment	£30,000
Net Cash Flows (In)	
Year 1	£5,000
Year 2	£12,000
Year 3	£13,000
Year 4	£14,000
Payback Period	3 Years

The advantage of this method lies in its simplicity of application. Once the relevant project cash flows have been established it is an easy matter to compute the payback period, which can then be compared to the company's acceptance criteria. For example, if the firm has set two years as the acceptance criterion for projects of this type, then the example shown would not be acceptable and, on this basis, should not be pursued.

However, the payback method has a number of limitations. Since it does not consider any cash flows occurring after the payback date, it will prefer projects that have high initial returns – that is, projects that will rapidly pay back the original investment. But what happens after the payback period? These cash flows are not considered by this method. A situation could arise where a project that generates low initial returns but builds into substantial cash inflows could be rejected in favour of another project showing higher initial returns which tail off quite rapidly, even though the first project is in the firm's best interests when both are compared over their total economic life.

So what is the payback method really telling us? It tells us for how long our original investment is out there, at risk, in the marketplace. As such, it is not necessarily a project profitability indicator, for the reasons mentioned earlier, but it can be likened to a project risk indicator. That is, the longer the payback period, the greater the financial risk associated with the project. Note the emphasis on financial risk, for, in common with other financial appraisal methods, payback period gives no indication of the technological or behavioural exposure associated with the project.

Later on, we will consider how the firm's acceptance payback criteria are set, but it is worth commenting at this stage that too inflexible an approach in applying payback criteria could result in too much emphasis being placed on the short term at the expense of providing operations capabilities for the longer term.

In summary, payback is still used by firms to measure project financial acceptability, but its most powerful application is as a risk indicator when used in conjunction with other more appropriate financial methods.

Return on capital employed method

This method establishes the project's average annual return as a percentage of the original capital investment. This represents the project's return on capital employed, which may then be compared with the firm's acceptance rate.

Returning to our previous example:

PROJECT A

Original Investment	£30,000
Net Cash Flows (In)	
Year 1	£5,000
Year 2	£12,000
Year 3	£13,000

Year 4	£14,000
Average Return per annum	£11,000
Return on Cap. Empl.	c.37%

The return on capital employed method, unlike payback, does consider project cash flows over its economic life. Indeed, it tries to establish a concept of project return or profitability that is comparable with ratios used to measure the performance of the firm as a whole, namely return on capital employed (ROCE) or return on investment (ROI). It is relatively easy to see that if a firm is consistently accepting projects with ROCEs lower than the average for the firm as a whole, it is gradually eroding the wealth of its shareholders, and vice versa. So the firm's average ROI provides a guideline basis for acceptance criteria under this method.

However, the method does have limitations, since it takes no account of the 'time value' of money. In other words, it classes £1 of income received today as equivalent to £1 of income received in, say, three years' time. In fact, they are not equivalent because £1 received today gives an opportunity to invest that money now and earn additional returns before the other £1 is received in three years' time. For example, if an available investment rate of 10 per cent is applied, then, with compound interest, the £1 received today would be equivalent to £1.33 in three years' time. So any project appraisal method that attempts to measure the financial attractiveness of the venture without considering the 'time value' of money will overstate the effects of income flows received in the future at the relative expense of those received now. It is for this reason that the return on capital employed method has limited appeal and has, for all practical purposes, been replaced by methods that do take this into account.

Discounting methods

Discounting methods exist to take into account the 'time value' of money. The concept of discounting can be thought of as the reverse of compounding.

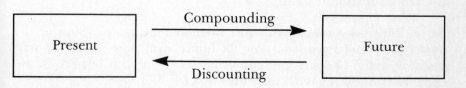

In other words,

Compounding is used to determine the future value of present cash flows

whereas

Discounting is used to determine the present value of future cash flows

The following table compares the future value of £1 after compounding, with the present value of £1 after discounting, using a compound interest and discount rate of 20 per cent respectively:

Year	Future Value of £1	Present Value of £1
0	1.000	1.000
1	1.200	0.833
2	1.440	0.694
3	1.728	0.579
4	2.074	0.482
5	2.488	0.402

(using a rate of 20%)

From the table it can be seen that, if a discount rate of 20 per cent applies, then £1 received in five years' time will only be equivalent to £0.402 received today (because I have foregone the opportunity to invest that money at 20 per cent). Any financial appraisal method that ignored this factor could therefore lead to poor financial investment practice. Two methods have evolved to overcome the shortfall:

● The net present value method
● The internal rate of return method

Both methods apply the concept of discounting to determine the present value of future cash flows.

Net present value method   With this method the present value of the project is found by discounting all future cash flows at the chosen discount rate. The net present value (NPV) of the project is the algebraic sum of the individual cash flows.

If the NPV is positive, then the project is returning better than the discount rate. It is possible to use this method to compare a variety of projects for their performance against the chosen rate. A simple example is given below:

Year	Discount Factor @ 10%	Project X		Project Y	
		Cash Flow	Present Value	Cash Flow	Present Value
0	1.000	(1,000)	(1,000)	(1,200)	(1,200)
1	0.909	600	546	600	546
2	0.827	500	413	700	579
3	0.751	55	41	200	150
Net Present Value			0		+75

In this example it can be seen that, when a discount rate of 10 per cent is applied, the NPV of project Y is greater than that of project X; therefore, all other things being equal, Y would be preferred to X.

Internal rate of return method   This method follows a similar format to NPV, but this time the discount rate is found by iteration, giving a net present value of future cash flows of zero. This represents the project's internal rate of return. Various projects may then be compared on this basis.

In the following example, the internal rate of return (IRR) is 10 per cent, as this is the rate at which the net present value of the project is zero.

Year	Project Cash Flow	Present Value at Chosen Discount Rate		
		9%	11%	10%
0	(1,000)	(1,000)	(1,000)	(1,000)
1	600	550	541	546
2	500	421	406	413
3	55	43	40	41
Net Present Value		+14	−13	0

Summary of financial appraisal methods

In practice, the best approach to financial appraisal of capital projects is to use a combination of payback, the financial risk indicator and a discounting method – probably net present value.

In all cases, the 'mechanics' of each method are simple to understand, but it is far more important to understand the underlying assumptions that generate the forecast cash flows in the first place. It is too easy to be seduced by the apparent exactitude of the method, forgetting that the forecast cash flows are only accurate to, say, ± 10 per cent. This introduces the concept of uncertainty or risk into the analysis. We have already mentioned how the acquisition of fixed assets is a structural decision shaping the future profile and characteristics of the operations area and, as such, it is subject to a range of uncertainties at each stage in the project life cycle. The next section considers the risks associated with project cash flows and looks at ways to evaluate the effect of the risk on the project viability.

Risk and uncertainty in capital projects

In order to evaluate the risk associated with particular capital expenditure decisions, it is important to consider the range and timing of the cash flows associated with the typical project (see Figure 6.2).

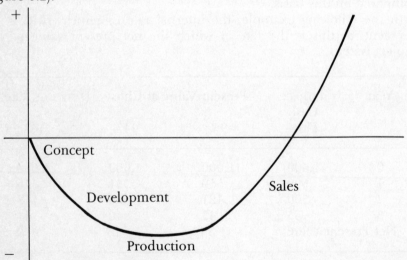

Figure 6.2   Project cash flow

Projects are generally typified by having to spend money now to earn a return in the future. Figure 6.2 illustrates a typical project cash flow profile over its economic life cycle. The initial investment would involve large cash outflows in the project's early years. After the project is commissioned, we see the generation of a stream of net cash inflows representing the excess of sales over operating costs. At the end of the project's life, we may obtain the benefit of any residual or scrap value as a cash inflow.

There are several implications of this profile for risk analysis:

1   The cash flows of the early years are not as affected by the application of discounting techniques as are those of the later years. Therefore, any project overspend or failure to get the project commissioned on time (and therefore delay to the stream of net inflows) will knock holes in the project's discounted rate of return. We need some quantification of the chance of this happening.

2   At project appraisal time, all cash flows are forecasts or best estimates of future performance, and rely on a range of assumptions. They are therefore at risk.

3   We need to question the basis used to establish the project's economic life. If we are operating in a fast-moving technological environment, then the chances are that the plant will be technologically obsolete before it actually 'wears out'. We need to assess the effect of this occurrence on the project's viability.

This is the role of sensitivity analysis.

Sensitivity analysis

For any project there are a large number of variables or underlying assumptions which could affect its financial viability. Typical examples are given below:

1   Forecast Demand
    • How will the marketplace move during the project life cycle?
    • How realistic are our market share estimates?
    • Is this a high-risk diversification strategy or a lower-risk market penetration strategy?
    • What factors could change it drastically?
    • How are the competition likely to react?
    • How price-sensitive is demand?
    • How mature is the market and are there still established barriers to entry?

2   Level and Phasing of Initial Investment
   - How predictable is the technology?
   - How reliable are suppliers and subcontractors?
   - How fully are internal costs researched?
   - How realistic are the commissioning time estimates?
3   Efficiency and Operating Costs
   - Are we breaking any new technology barriers?
   - What new factors might cause problems?
   - What do we know about the reliability of performance of this type of plant?
   - What utilization figures relate to the efficiency claims?
   - How sure are we about material usage claims?
   - Are we susceptible to employee relations disputes?
4   Residual Value
   - What criteria do we use for replacement dates?
   - Will the plant or equipment suffer technological obsolescence?
5   Underlying Assumptions
   - Inflation
   - Economic growth
   - Interest rates etc.

Sensitivity analysis attempts to evaluate the relative importance of changes in each of these factors to the project's potential financial success. One way to test sensitivity is to calculate the effect on the net present value of an incremental change in each of the factors. For example, what would be the effect on the project NPV if the estimate for market share was to change by 1 per cent? By applying this technique to each of the relevant factors, it would be possible to highlight the sensitive areas – that is, those factors that will have the greatest impact on project viability.

For example:

Factor	Change in NPV for 1% difference (£000's)
Market share	70
Selling price	80
Direct labour cost	3
Material utilization	7

When we apply sensitivity testing here to the individual project factors it can be seen that any change in the achieved market share, or selling price, will have a disproportionate effect on the project's financial performance. The effect of changes in the labour or material factors pale by comparision. Therefore, attention should be focused in the market factors to confirm the accuracy of the estimates; this will give some indication of the risk and also suggest which actions can be taken to improve actual performance in these areas, since they are fundamental to generating better-than-forecast returns.

Project rate of return

A critical decision in the application of financial appraisal techniques is the selection of the firm's 'acceptance' rate of return. A variety of factors influence the decision and may best be highlighted by considering two rates – the minimum rate and the target rate.

Minimum Rate

The minimum that the project must return corresponds to the firm's cost of capital. Any project that returns less will, in financial terms, be eroding the wealth of its shareholders and should therefore be rejected if its acceptance is only appraised against financial criteria. (Note that the project may still be accepted for other non-financial considerations.)

What, therefore, constitutes the firm's cost of capital? A good maxim is that projects are not normally considered to be financed from specific sources of funds as this short-term view could be prejudicial to certain projects, depending on the particular financial market structure at the time they were proposed. A better approach is to use the weighted average cost of capital (WACC) for the capital invested in the business. The two costs to be averaged are: the opportunity cost of equity funds (that is, subscribed capital and retentions), and the actual after-tax cost of non-equity funds (that is, preference shares and borrowings).

The cost of equity capital relates to the returns expected by shareholders within the company. This can be expressed by the formula:

Cost of equity capital = $D / P + G$

D is the net dividend paid
P is the current share price
G is the expected percentage growth

Therefore, for a company which has paid a dividend of 10p with a share price of 100p and has expected dividend and profit growth of 5 per cent, its cost of equity capital is 15 per cent.

The cost of non-equity capital is the after-tax costs of the various types of longer-term capital, and can be combined with the cost of equity capital to obtain the company's weighted average cost of capital:

Capital	After-Tax Cost	£
Equity	15%	100,000
Non-equity	10%	50,000
Weighted Average	13.3%	150,000

In this case, any project should return a minimum of 13.3 per cent if there is not to be an erosion of shareholders' wealth. This figure is considered the minimum because, if a large number of projects are accepted with rates below this threshold, then in the longer term there will be a dilution of earnings and hence an inability of the firm to maintain its competitive position. However, this figure is probably not the target rate for capital projects considered by the firm, as there will be a range of modifying criteria. These are considered in the next section.

Target rate

One modification that can be made to the minimum rate involves the concept of the opportunity foregone by deciding to accept the project under consideration. In other words, if I could invest the funds required by the project at minimum risk in a bank account returning 10 per cent, then, by deciding to go with the project, I have effectively decided to forego that option which represents the project's *opportunity cost*. On a more realistic basis, I should be comparing opportunities relating to the same risk criteria – that is comparing the opportunity cost of projects that have the same degree of riskiness.

One of the inescapable facts of new projects is that they are all concerned with the future and that they all therefore include an element of risk. Sensitivity analysis represents one attempt to quantify the risk involved, but it also needs to be taken into account when we decide the financial acceptance rate or target rate. In broad terms, the greater risk associated with the project, the greater returns that will be required to compensate for that risk. This introduces the concept of differential rates for different projects, based on a datum target rate for a risk-free investment plus a *risk premium* element as compensation for the risks associated with that class of project.

Certain classes of project have a greater inherent risk than others. For example, a project to lay down a new facility to diversify a firm's capability involves the risk of taking new products into new markets, together with a possible process technology risk. The implied risk here is far greater risk than with a project which is simply an upgrading of present productive capacity. The firm will require greater returns from the first project as compensation for the additional risks involved. This constitutes the additional risk premium.

To ensure that this principle works in practice, firms will need to develop criteria for classifying projects so that differential risk premiums may be applied as a matter of course. Once this has been done, and the supporting procedures documented, then a key task of management in a capital-rationing situation is to develop a *portfolio approach* to project management selection, with a balanced range of projects in each risk class. This concept could be extended to cover also the 'quality' of the businesses within a particular firm's portfolio, so that a low-quality business could be confined to just sustenance-level capital with fast payback, and a high-quality business would conversely be eligible for development capital with longer payback. The rationale here is that the high-quality, growth-opportunity business is the seedcorn for tomorrow's prosperity.

A further consideration is that, over time, the firm will have developed norms for acceptance rates of returns for different classes of projects within different business environments. In this instance, the norm rates become the project acceptance thresholds, and individuals are encouraged to present projects that match these criteria.

Personal development task no. 6.1

1 Carry out a facilities strategy audit with regard to:
   - location
   - type
   - timing
   - size
   - integrating linkages

   The checklist on pages 133–134 can highlight more detail.
2 Evaluate how successfully the firm's strategy meets the needs of the marketplace and make recommendations for improvement.

Personal development task no. 6.2

1 Determine the methods used within the firm to appraise the financial success of capital projects.
2 What other criteria are taken into account?
3 On what basis are the firm's rates of acceptable return developed and what account is taken of risk?
4 For your next capital project submission, evaluate the sensitivity of the project to the key influencing variables.

Chapter summary points

- The acquisition of fixed assets is a structural decision that greatly influences how the firm interacts with its marketplace.
- In line with this, firms need to develop a facilities strategy.
- Financial criteria are not the only basis for project acceptance or rejection.
- Financial appraisal methods must allow for the riskiness of individual projects, and employ some methods of sensitivity analysis.

7 Managing the facilities: operating and maintaining the assets

Introduction

The maintenance of the operation's capability to service its marketplace is essential if the firm is to achieve or maintain its competitive advantage. However, as a result of age or usage, the performance of fixed assets will usually deteriorate and may break down. The role of the maintenance organization is economically to maintain the operational capability – that is, to ensure that the facilities are available to provide on-specification output whilst minimizing total operations costs. This trade-off is illustrated in Figure 7.1 which illustrates the costs associated with the maintenance of facilities. The first set of costs relate to maintenance activity. These represent all the costs associated with providing a maintenance service, and it can be seen that, as the level of maintenance service rises, so too do the associated costs. Typical costs would include maintenance labour and supervision, holding costs for spare parts, consumables and so on. The second set of costs are related to equipment failure. These split into two categories: corrective and indirect failure costs. Corrective costs relate to the direct costs associated with effecting the repair – for example, the time spent and the replacement parts consumed. Indirect failure costs relate to the unplanned losses of output – which, for 'bottleneck' machines, equates to total plant output – and any associated consequential losses as a result of non-conformance. Generally, indirect failure costs outweigh corrective costs.

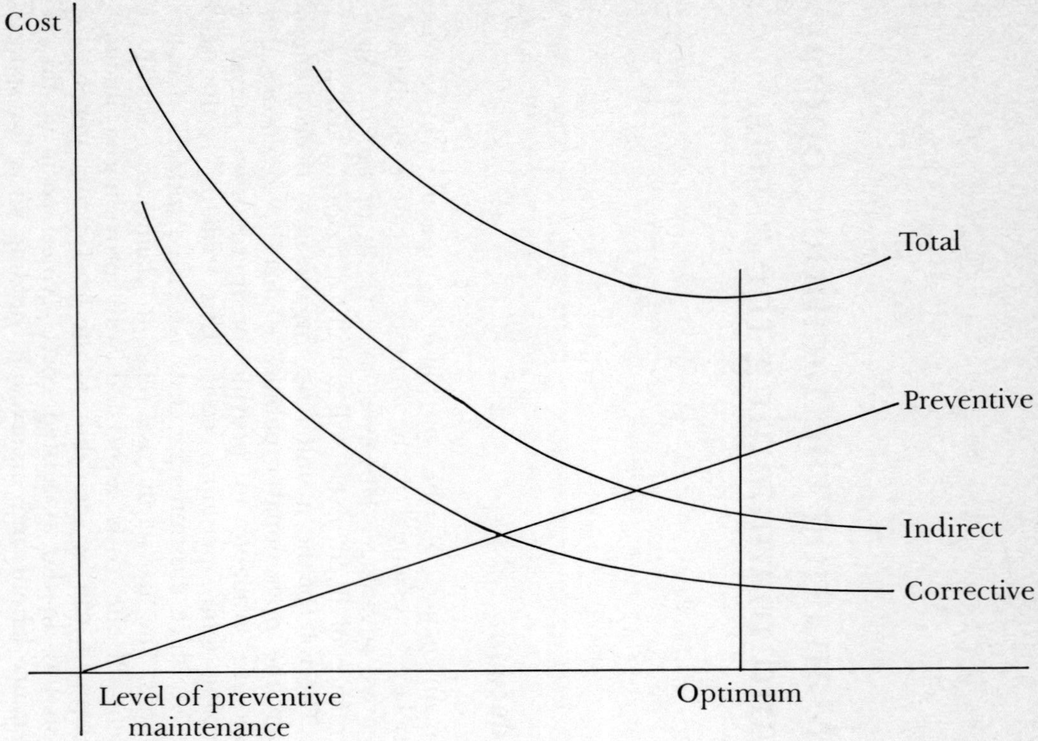

Figure 7.1   Costs and the level of preventive maintenance

The graph illustrates the level of maintenance service that optimizes the maintenance activity versus failure cost relationship, where total costs are lowest. A firm following a cost leadership strategy should certainly aim to operate at this point. A firm operating a differentiation strategy will still need to maintain cost proximity with its competitors to be effective, and will thus need to be aware of the trade-offs involved. The aim is for maintenance activity to support the firm's desired competitive advantage and, within that context:

to provide the level of service that optimizes the total cost–facilities availability relationship.

Note that this relationship assumes that all legal requirements are met, including local rules concerning health, safety and waste/effluent management.

The role of maintenance

The development of a strategy for maintenance involves a range of structural decisions. These are:

- WHAT categories of assets are to be maintained?
- HOW, or on what basis, should they be maintained?
- WHEN, or with what frequency, should they be maintained?
- WHO should do it and what range of skills are required?

These decisions should all be answered with a focus on servicing the competitive advantage set by the firm. We will now take each decision type in turn:

What categories of assets should be maintained?

One of the first decisions that has to be taken is on the scope of maintenance activity. Although the principal activity is directed at ensuring that the main operations processes are available and functioning correctly, a wide range of other facilities will need attention. Typical categories include:

- Production plant and machinery
  - bottleneck plant
  - non-bottleneck plant
- Utilities
- Transport
- Land, buildings and associated support functions

Each of these categories reflects the total failure cost–availability relationship highlighted earlier. For each category we will place a different emphasis on deciding how it will be maintained, its frequency and who will do it.

For example, in the case of bottleneck plant and utilities, the effect of a breakdown would be catastrophic in that total plant output could be lost, so, although the corrective costs may not be significant, the indirect failure costs certainly will be. For this reason, it may be appropriate to have a high level of preventive maintenance activity, rapid in-house service in the case of a breakdown and possibly stand-by plant available in the case of utilities. In this instance, we are prepared to endure high maintenance activity costs in order to raise equipment availability.

Non-bottleneck plant, by definition, has free capacity and so we may decide to apply a differential level of maintenance support here, in order to reduce maintenance activity costs. (Note that the indirect failure costs are lower in this case.) This policy is acceptable provided that the level of plant failures in this area does not start to affect the operating performance of the bottleneck plant.

For the land and buildings, response time may not be so important, and so this is an activity that could be placed with external sub-contractors. In other words, the maintenance activity costs associated with keeping an in-house capability are not warranted by the level of service required. A similar type of argument may be put forward for the transport fleet where it may be more economical to sub-contract the associated maintenance activity.

These policies would be totally consistent with supporting the chosen strategy for operations, and different maintenance decisions would need to be taken for the different categories of asset if the maintenance organization is to support the business needs effectively.

How, or on what basis, are the assets to be maintained?

The basis for maintaining assets can be related to the way in which they fail, and it is on this basis that the decisions can be made regarding the degree and direction of preventive maintenance activity and so on.

Basically, assets fail in one of two ways – either on a random basis or through age-related causes. Typical age-related failures are caused by parts wearing out or corroding, the effects of fatigue or general physical deterioration. Random failures could include accidental damage, overloading or a variety of unknown causes.

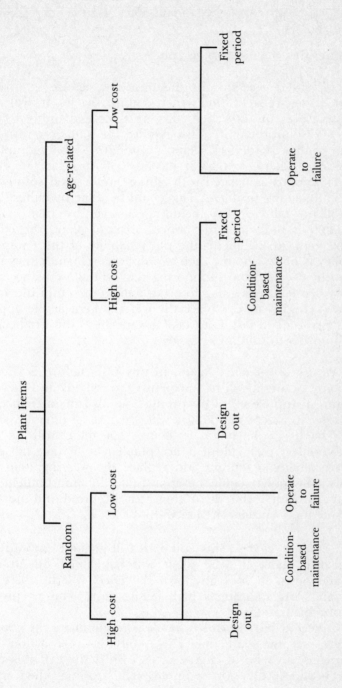

Figure 7.2 Choice of maintenance strategies

153

We could further categorize failures by including the associated failure costs, both corrective and indirect. Figure 7.2 highlights the range of choices.

Consider first the age-related failures:

Age-related, high-cost failure In this instance, failure is predictable, since it is age-related, and when failure occurs it will be very expensive either in corrective costs or associated indirect costs (for example, lost production). This typifies the situation with wearing parts on either bottleneck plant or utilities – for example, plant compressors. There is a great incentive in this case to avoid the costly disruptions associated with failure, and a good solution would be to eliminate the problem. This could be done by either designing the problem out, or by including a stand-by item. Generally, redundancy is built into the critical areas of plant, the effect of a stand-by item greatly increasing the reliability of the equipment. If this policy is not economic then two options remain: either to set up some form of condition monitoring that will allow us accurately to predict when failure is going to occur and so pre-empt the associated disruptive effects; or to replace the wearing item at the appropriate fixed intervals. The task is to take advantage of the predictability of failure in order to minimize its costs.

Age-related, low-cost failure Again, in this case, failure is predictable, but when it occurs it will be inexpensive to remedy and there will be minimum disruptive effect on production. Two maintenance choices exist: either to accept that failure will occur at set intervals and allow that to happen (the rationale being that there will be so little disruptive effect that failure is acceptable); or to take advantage of the predictability of failure and replace the wearing item at fixed intervals. This policy could be appropriate for non-bottleneck items of plant, provided the disruption that occurred did not cascade down and affect bottleneck plants.

Random, high-cost failure This is the area of greatest exposure for the maintenance manager. The plant will fail, albeit on an irregular basis, and when it does go down the effect will be disruption to output and correspondingly high failure costs. These represent the 'war story' plant items.

The critical activity in this instance is to eliminate the problem by designing out the part that fails. Only by this action will the maintainance area be in charge of its own destiny. If this option is neither economically nor technologically feasible, then it will be necessary to experiment with the plant to see if some crude condition monitoring relationship can be established. For example, it may be possible to associate a temperature rise in an associated part with failure of a component. The reason may not be clear, but if the empirical relationship holds good it will be sufficient to try to eliminate some, or all, of the disruptive effects of failure.

Random, low-cost failure Here, the item fails on an irregular basis but causes little disruption either to the production flow or to maintenance corrective costs. In this instance, the correct policy would be to operate the plant until failure occurs.

Therefore, by adopting a policy to maintain plant on the basis of its failure, we are trying to optimize the total cost – availability measure set for the maintenance organization. By implication we have included a range of maintenance activities:

- Planned:
  - Preventive
    - Running
    - Shutdown
  - Corrective
    - Breakdown
    - Shutdown
- Unplanned:
  - Emergency

Planned maintenance activity will include preventive maintenance tasks which could be carried out either whilst the equipment is running – for example, lubricating, condition-monitoring and so on – or at the preventive maintenance shutdown time. Typical preventive tasks that could be carried out at shutdown time include inspection, fixed interval replacement and so on.

Corrective maintenance tasks can also be included under planned maintenance activity and typically include the replacement of failed items either at the next available shutdown (if it is possible to wait) or at the time of failure. The significant point is that, in setting out our plan for maintenance activities, we are planning in plant breakdowns, usually for random, low failure-cost items.

In addition, there is the *unplanned or emergency breakdown*. In general terms, the emphasis should always be on prevention through maintenance policy planning rather than accepting emergency breakdowns as a necessary evil.

A survey into the time spent on the major maintenance categories yielded the following results:

Category	%
Preventive	19
Corrective	34
Emergency	20
Indirect	
Capital work	11
Reconditioning spares	10
Waiting time etc.	6
Total	100

The figures are useful as a basis for reducing avoidable costs, such as emergency work.

When, or with what frequency, should the assets be maintained?

The category of maintenance activity will impact the frequency with which it is carried out. As previously stated, planned preventive maintenance can be carried out either whilst equipment is running or at a shutdown.

Shutdown periods should be planned well in advance. They should be planned so that immediate period replacements are carried out and that any unexpectedly worn-out, dangerous or suspicious items are inspected and changed as necessary. The timing of the shutdown will reflect the state of the machinery, the manufacturer's recommendations, in-plant experience and the implications of failure.

Good maintenance planning requires system, organization and accurate data. For example, service record data are an essential component in determining planned maintenance timing.

Note that communication of intent is very important if there is to be minimum disruption to production. This point illustrates the relationship between authority and responsibility. Very few managers have full operating authority in all areas for which they are accountable. In the case of maintenance there is a joint responsibility for the efficient operation and maintenance of plant, equipment, buildings and facilities. It is usually described in such a way that engineers maintain plant and operations staff run it, but in fact the success of each is dependent on the expertise and goodwill of the other. The next section will consider one aspect of this, and report relationships in more detail.

Who should maintain the assets?

There are a range of basic choices to be made in this area, and the correct answer will relate to the aspect of maintenance service that is appropriate for the particular category of asset considered. The introduction of more sophisticated technology has also brought to light important issues in this area.

Own staff or subcontractors A consideration here is the level of expertise that is required to maintain the equipment. Where very specialized knowledge is required, together with a large knowledge-base back-up, as for example in the case of computer hardware and software installations, then firms could well be predisposed to subcontracting that maintenance activity out to specialists who have the skill and infrastructure to support that application. An exception to this would be where that equipment constitutes the firm's core technology. In this instance, the firm will want to maintain the confidentiality of its process and will also strive to develop the in-house capability to maintain it. Because in-house maintenance availability implies a faster and more responsive service, additional benefits will also probably accrue in that area of speed of response. With external maintenance services, speed of response is covered through a contractual agreement with timings being agreed at the outset. Normally the faster the response rate the more expensive the service charge! In the case of substantial installations serviced by a third party, the contractor may well install someone permanently on the client's premises.

Some organizations choose to maintain an in-house capability and to subcontract peak loads – for example, shutdown activity. The rationale in this case is to optimize the service level–cost trade-off. A further instance of this is where firms employ a differential approach to the maintenance of (for example) land and buildings, where they are prepared to subcontract this activity, realizing that response time is normally not critical and that it is not cost-effective to maintain a complete in-house capability.

Centralized or decentralized The firm's attitude towards a centralized or decentralized maintenance activity will reflect process choice, the degree of process technology involved, and its attitude towards the response time–maintenance cost trade-off. The benefits of decentralized maintenance activity are that the maintenance personnel develop specific local plant knowledge, often associate themselves more with the success or failure of the production plant involved, and normally provide a faster response time due to physical proximity and the enhanced plant knowledge. There is also less possibility of 'passing the buck' to other maintenance personnel, as staff are now dedicated to particular items of plant.

The disadvantage of this approach is that it is normally more costly than a centralized set-up because it may involve a degree of duplication of activity, there is the need for increased personnel including support staff, and the 'productivity' of individual maintenance staff may be lower.

This calls into question how we measure the productivity of maintenance personnel. Are we interested in their actual contact time or in machine availability? Again, we are in the realms of the trade-off situation where what really matters is response time – particularly with respect to bottleneck plant. It then boils down to how we can selectively improve the maintenance response time whilst minimizing the total maintenance costs.

Multiskilling: the role of the technician and the operator　The needs of new equipment and technologies have placed greater demands on the skills of the individuals needed to maintain it. Whilst there have been substantial advances in the reliability engineering field, and also in the equipment self-diagnosis arena, the nature, diversity and interrelationship of the technologies involved have meant that the traditional skill demarcations are not as appropriate now as they once were. Some trade unions have been quick to recognize this and have capitalized on the opportunity to further their members' prospects. Others have been slow to accept this change in emphasis, with the result that some firms are not yet able to support the new equipment with the degree of maintenance workforce flexibility that is required. This is an issue that needs to be resolved to the benefit of all if world competitiveness is to be achieved. It will also involve substantial retraining activity to prepare individuals for the new challenges.

Linked to this is the role of the operator with regard to maintenance activity. Trends in this areas are focused on giving the operator the authority and training to be able to carry out simple routine maintenance activity. The benefits are many if the change is managed correctly, as there is less likelihood of split responsibility for machine performance, and the operator associates closer with the machine and is generally more sensitive to its needs. With technical processes, it may be that the operator does not realistically have the technical skill to take on the maintenance task and, in this instance, consideration should be given to employing qualified maintenance individuals to run and maintain the equipment. Whilst this may incur a cost penalty if we consider the concept of productivity relating to the key operations task, this approach may be more beneficial.

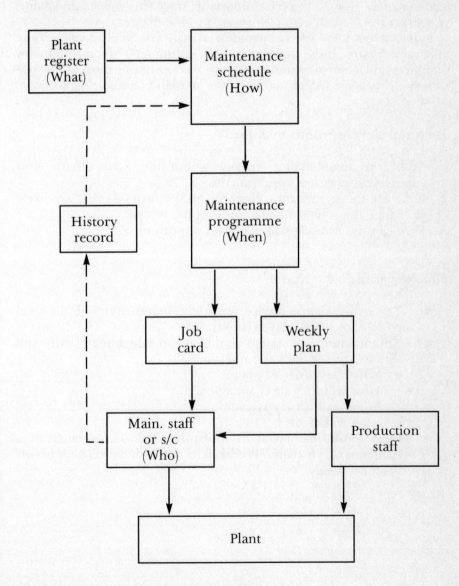

Figure 7.3　Maintenance control system

Maintenance planning and control system

A diagrammatic representation of the maintenance activity is given in Figure 7.3 which illustrates how in practice the basic maintenance decisions are addressed, and also highlights the integrated nature of maintenance work. A very important stage in the maintenance process is the feedback loop illustrated in the diagram.

This systems view of maintenance activity has lately been greatly enhanced with the application of computerized maintenance planning and control systems. A more recent application is the use of 'expert' systems to aid maintenance preplanning and diagnostics.

Personal development task no. 7

1 Audit the maintenance activity within the firm to see how effectively it matches requirements.
2 What are the significant influences on the business that are likely to change the role of maintenance in the future?
3 How can the firm capitalize on this opportunity?

Chapter summary points

- The maintenance service provided should optimize the total cost–plant availability relationship.
- Any maintenance system should be an integrated activity and should answer the basic questions:
    - What categories of plant?
    - How will they be maintained?
    - When will it be serviced?
    - Who will do it?
- Care should be taken in measuring the performance of a maintenance activity. Productivity should be related to the business needs.

8 Managing quality: quality management

Introduction

Quality management is not new. The principles, the techniques and the methods have been available to, and practised by, many generations of operations managers. Rolls Royce and Mercedes were using Total Quality Control in the early part of the twentieth century as the lynchpin of their manufacturing strategy. They achieved this by thinking through and making decisions in three areas of attention:

1 The whole company attitude of superb quality products;
2 Setting a very high level of design quality;
3 Conforming completely to that level of quality.

The secret of their success was, and still is, their unwavering intention to produce exactly what they set out to make – in their cases, superb motor cars. There are many good methods, there is a wealth of statistical and analytical techniques and there are highly sophisticated automatic processes available to operations management. However, they are only of limited use without the thrust and enthusiasm for quality attainment which the chief executive must implant in the minds of every member of the company.

This chapter deals with the management of quality. First, we explore the philosophies of different exponents of quality; second,

161

we look at the four jobs of quality management; third, we use the concept of quality cost to devise strategies for quality management.

A philosophy for quality

In management the old saying 'Cometh the hour, cometh the man' might be extended to read 'cometh the need, cometh the techniques'. When industry was expanding rapidly the principles of specialization led to production lines, high volumes and reduced costs. When world wars created the added urgency for efficiency and product reliability, then the laws of statistics were invoked to provide sampling schemes and statistical quality control. All of these were based on the practice and habit of management control, and worker conformance to regulations and procedures.

Japanese economic development

Later developments in world trade foreshadowed the emergence of Japan and other Eastern nations. With their dependence on imported materials and energy they had only one way to turn in order to compete with Western nations – the route of quality and price. Japan has followed that route relentlessly since its emergence as a real trading force after 1945, to such effect that Western companies – American and European – have been forced to follow their example or perish. Some have not survived the ordeal. Many have studied the implications of competing and discovered that radical changes of management style and attitude were required; that new charters with their unions were essential for any form of competitive edge to emerge.

The difference in style is so marked that, while senior management still dictate on matters of strategy, the successful operating of good companies is a matter for everybody, managers, so-called workers and union officers. It becomes the right and duty of everybody to consider how to improve the quality of performance of the company, in all respects. Now, this marks a radical shift in attitude, which has gained in pace as it has moved from industry to industry, from manufacturing to service companies, from retail to finance houses, from high street banks to the City of London and Wall Street.

These changes, forced on companies by economic necessity, are paralleled by the increasing success of methods and techniques advocated by practitioners and writers in quality control. In the

1960s Juran[1] and Feigenbaum[2] in the USA were advocating Total Quality Control, as a response to the demand for higher quality and the increasing cost of achieving it. Later, in the 1970s, the theme of managerial awareness was being further emphasized with the catchphrase 'Right first time', and in Britain attention was being drawn to the costs of quality and to strategies for defect prevention (for example, Caplan[3] and Seder[4].)

The return of borrowed techniques

As the Japanese achieved economic ascendency in the 1980s their operational management style was studied in detail and attention drawn to various techniques and methods. One of these is Quality Circles, in which groups of employees meet regularly, of their own accord, to discuss and make improvement decisions about aspects of their own work. There are many different versions of Quality Circles and a sizeable literature has grown up. Initial attempts to set up Quality Circles are often unsuccessful, usually because the initiative is halfhearted, the support insufficient and the intention for change of style is not company-wide.

Scenarios for the rising industrial performance of countries like Mexico and Egypt show further pressures being placed on Europe. In order to face this competition and the pincer movement from America and Japan, European companies who intend to survive will have to include quality as a major plank in their strategy. Many have started to do this, and often it has meant a reversal of attitudes. Call it Total Quality Control, Total Quality Management, 'Right first time,' or whatever, the essence of this movement is that:

1 Everybody in the company has a stake in good quality;
2 Everybody thinks about how to improve quality;
3 Everybody knows that when they make proposals, they will be acted upon;
4 Everybody will be kept informed about progress;
5 Managers will spend long periods of time with operators, providing resources, helping developments, making things happen.

To achieve that kind of attitude of mind, chief executives need to invest a large part of their own time; they need to convince all managers that they are serious and that they will not accept any other way. British Airways changed their staff attitudes towards customers with their 'Putting People First' course, a contribution towards their long-term objective to become the best airline in the world. In particular, they spent time with operations managers, where the change of company style would perhaps have the greatest repercussions. In the past, quality improvement efforts had largely been left to operations managers, but when other company activities were also working on quality then the overlap would greatly assist their efforts. If any programme is to succeed in some way or other, the ordinary employees and the more junior managers have to want to be involved. Experience shows that this requires persistence, together with a large investment of time, money and enthusiasm on the part of senior managers.

The four jobs of quality management

There are four jobs which quality management must complete. They cannot be carried out by any one manager, but the operations manager has a strong interest in all four and a direct responsibility for some of the parts. They are;

1 new product specification;
2 product improvement;
3 process improvement
4 inspection.

We now intend to discuss each one, pointing out areas of direct concern to operations managers and those issues where liaison with other functions is essential.

New product specification

High quality is a meaningless phrase. To one person it means a high quality of design, in other words the Rolls Royce or Jaguar motor car, with very high levels of specified performance, reliability and appearance. To another person it means that his Volkswagen 'Beetle' always starts, that it runs well and that very little goes wrong with it: in other words a high quality of conformance. Quality of design must be correctly specified for all new products and services and, while this sounds straightforward enough, it often fails to happen.

New products originate from several sources:

1 The customer specifies what is wanted.
2 Marketing sees a chance to create a new market.
3 Salesmen bring in an idea from their territory.
4 Technologists find a new way to perform a service.
5 Operations develop a new process for manufacturing or creating a service.

Whichever of the above are the originators, sooner or later all the others will need to be involved in specifying the new product or service. Often new products need only minor alterations to existing offerings – for example, many toiletries, some insurance policies. However, when radical changes are made, new product committees or project groups are required, which will need to answer hundreds of detailed questions in producing the new specifications. However, there may be some more fundamental decisions to take, which may even entail changes in corporate strategy.

Table 8.1
New product questionnaire: Part 1. Strategic issues.

Marketing
1   Will the product need new marketing approaches/techniques?
2   Do we have the expertise to do this?
3   How much will it cost and how do we get it?
4   How long before the expertise is installed and running?

Selling
1   Will our current sales force be able to sell this service?
2   If not then do we need specialist sales people?

Operations/Engineering
1   Can we make this product with our existing plant?
    (This question must receive an honest answer or there will soon be quality problems.)
2   If not, is the plant available and how much will it cost?
3   How long will installation and development take?
4   Will we need new operations staff, or could they retrain?

Technology
1   How far has this new product been developed?
2   How long before we can send it to operations?
3   How much more development expenditure is needed?

The questions in Table 8.1 are the fundamental ones. Other more detailed questions will need answers, but often these are discounted when presenting the case for strategic change and/or large capital investment. We will take just one example to make the point. In operations, if a basic change of strategy is needed, say, from high volume to single or small batch special items, then where will the new plant be built? Certainly it should not be allowed to run alongside existing machinery, however tempting the prospect might be for saving money.

Table 8.1 shows us that quality of design can be a strategic issue. New product specification is frequently the trigger point for strategic change and points up a vital issue for operations managers. It is to ensure that they are not left to cobble together a new development whose strategic issues have not been adequately explored.

When the strategic questions have been settled there will be many items of detail to be ironed out in the detailed specification. To discover a major design fault, or a major engineering problem after manufacture has started is too late. To discover that the administration and operations details demanded of a new financial package are beyond the skills of the administrative staff after the package has been launched is a recipe for disaster. All these questions are part of the management of quality, because, if the time is taken to work them out carefully, there will be few failures during the creation and delivery of the product or service.

Product investigation and improvement

Much of the previous discussion is also relevant to product improvement, but here we are concerned with existing products. There are several reasons for investigating existing products:

- to rectify quality faults;
- to reduce operations costs;
- to improve quality as a reply to competition.

The attitude of mind behind this work is a concern for quality. It may be to raise the level of design quality, it may even be to raise the standard for conformance to that quality. When cost reduction schemes were in vogue many years ago there was a frequent scaling-down of both these quality criteria – an attitude of 'Let's try it on and see what we can get away with'. Modern market pressures preclude this option.

The replacement for such schemes was the concept of Value Engineering. This was a forerunner of Quality Circles and has a number of similarities in operation. In each case, a mixed-level group of staff come together periodically with the objective of improving performance in one way or another. In each case there should be a voluntary attendance at meetings, the ideal being for staff to initiate their own membership of the group. The difference is that Value Engineering is concerned with products or services, whereas Quality Circles have a wider brief – the identification, analysis and solution of their own work-related problems.

The dyers, Hicking Pentecost, used a number of action teams to 'chip' away at quality problems, some large, many small, but all contributing to better customer goodwill and higher profits. After the members of each team had been trained in the philosophy and techniques of Total Quality Management, in their own time, then the team would turn its attention to a particular situation where quality could be improved. By looking to basic issues the company achieved great gains in product reputation and customer goodwill.

Process investigation and improvement

The scope of this book does not permit a detailed examination of process investigation, which is usually a highly technical area, whether it be in manufacturing physical products, using machinery as a service function, or in providing highly technical, but intangible, services like finance, banking, insurance and the law. However, there are one or two issues which operations managers must address in order to assure and manage quality.

Process capability This is the ability of the process to meet the specifications demanded of it, and process capability studies are designed to measure the limits and adaptability of that process. The purpose in carrying out the studies is to ensure that quality is being met in existing products, but also to determine in new-product investigation whether the process is capable of consistent quality manufacture of the proposed product. In the manufacture of a piece of engineering equipment, the quality engineer will seek to determine the limits of accuracy of the process involved, so that they will know whether the specified tolerances are consistently possible on that machinery. In exactly the same way it is possible to examine the capability of machinery to 'process' a service which it is producing, because it usually produces a measurable result. In banking, insurance and other services, the operations activity can involve both machinery and people, and the process capability studies often involve the combined efforts of people, high technology communications, and computing equipment. Studies might well be concerned with the limits of accuracy of that process in providing an existing service at different volume levels, perhaps as a prelude to the installation of better computing systems – for example, a new form of building society account, or the effectiveness of the processing of a particular class of insurance work, where the speed of processing is causing trouble.

Other uses of capability studies will be to provide machine operators with a profile of the machine performance under controlled conditions, and this may help operations managers in placing operators on suitable machines. In buying a set of new or second-hand machinery a capability study would be invaluable;

finally it would also be useful as a means of deciding which machines are used for which products or services.

Inspection

When we discuss quality costs later in this chapter we include appraisal costs, failure costs and prevention costs. Appraisal costs will cover the whole of the inspection area, whether it be at the start or finish of the sequence. Inspection is something to be avoided if possible, or at the very least reduced to a minimum safeguard check. Such an objective makes us think about how to do it. Let us start with the oft-quoted observation, still as true as ever: 'The costs of failure grow enormously as you progress, stage by stage, along the production process: they reach a maximum if your product or service fails after it reaches the customer.'

Citycorp see 'considerable evidence' that avoiding errors contributes as much to containing costs as technology does.

When P.A. Management Consultants[5] researched the reasons why successful companies concentrated totally on quality they listed six major factors:

1   The success of international competitors who do take quality seriously.
2   The rising expectations of customers.
3   Quality differentiates companies from the opposition.
4   The narrowing of supplier bases by quality-conscious companies.
5   Growing evidence that sustained growth in market share comes from sustained quality.
6   Sustained cost advantages result from concentration on quality.

All of these factors are important, but the fourth is of particular interest to us in the context of inspection. The reasons for keeping to a small number of suppliers are self-evident – less opportunities for poor quality, the ability to control the quality of their output, and the chance to demand quality guarantees. All buyers strive for the perfect supplier, one who guarantees quality and has such a good quality record that good inwards inspection is rendered unnecessary.

The obvious deduction from this is that we should inspect as early as possible in our own processes and demand guarantees of quality from our suppliers. This leads us to supplier quality assurance schemes, where the company inspects suppliers' production units, then if necessary installs auditors or managers to help their quality management processes. These are well known among top British, continental European and American companies, the best being extremely effective. Suppliers are expected to guarantee their quality and replace all defective products immediately. The reality of this situation is that all goods inwards inspection is cancelled, but that it becomes a statistical sampling process for intermittent verification of quality.

In-process inspection comes in three forms, depending on the process. Continuous processes are suitable for automatic control, as are many batch processes in manufacturing companies and this control is itself a powerful quality assurance factor. Second, the periodic testing of products, using statistical sampling techniques, is applied at predetermined points in the process. However, those points must be chosen with care. They will be most effective where radical alterations, which could go badly wrong, are made to the emerging product. Third, and far more important, is the quality attitude of the operator at every stage. Every operator, every supervisor, every manager can improve product quality, but the operator will have by far the most immediate effect:

- in making good products;
- in stopping defectives;
- in improving processes and quality.

Hence the popularity of task forces, Quality Circles and 'Right First Time' campaigns.

Figure 8.1 shows the sequence of inspection, together with some of the techniques, methods, even philosophies which are associated with the cost-effective management of quality. Not least in effectiveness is the attitude and perception of the customer. One way to obtain reliable information about his attitude is a carefully worded customer perception survey, in addition to the normal feedback from salesmen. It is often devised and carried out by operations staff, who will meet the user of the product in order to get an honest and accurate assessment of performance, reliability and quality level.

In summary, inspection is an area where considerable progress can be made in attaining satisfactory quality, often with a reduction in cost, by using the right tactics and giving the ownership of good quality to everyone involved in creating the product or service.

The costs of quality

There are two ways of looking at the cost of quality. The first is to consider cost for its own sake and use the examination to determine strategies to reduce cost. The second is to recognize that, in reducing

169

cost, the only sensible way of doing so will also lead to better quality, the product will be right first time and people will be drawn towards an attitude of quality improvement. Quality costs are best listed under three categories: appraisal, failure and prevention.

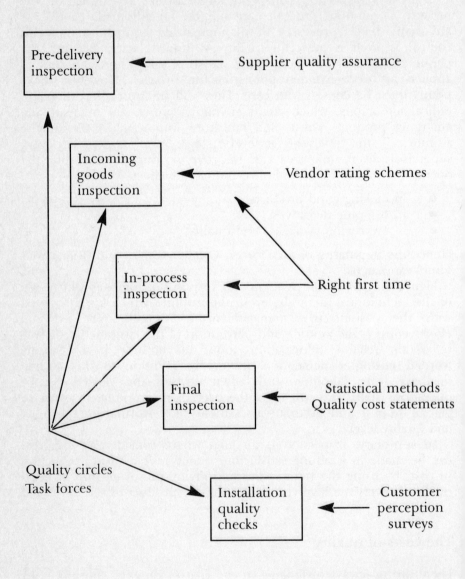

Figure 8.1   The sequence of inspection: some aids to effectiveness

Appraisal costs

These are the costs incurred at every stage in product/service inspection. In manufacturing they include:

1 all goods inwards inspection;
2 every form of inspection on the way through the process, whether it be automatic or human;
4 final inspection and testing;
5 in certain cases, testing or inspection after delivery.

In companies providing services it will be all forms of inspection of the process of giving the service. Examples might be:

● the successive checking of documents in an insurance administration office;
● The quality checking of consumable materials used for dry cleaning and the final inspection of the clothes after pressing in a dry cleaners.

It will also include the periodic quality auditing operation carried out during and after product manufacture, usually by independent personnel; the cost of HM inspectors in schools; the contract-testing of equipment, products or services at the customer's premises after installation. Finally, there is the reconciliation of counter transactions in the high street bank at the end of the day's trading. Any office, providing any service, is subject to appraisal costs.

Failure costs

Any costs incurred when the product or service fails, at whatever stage in the delivery process or after delivery, are classified as failure costs. They are real and can be measured. They include the cost of scrap, at whatever stage the failure is revealed. Obviously, the earlier they are found the less they will cost. In computing the cost of failure there are two things to consider:

1 the cost of waste material, less scrap value;
2 the opportunity cost when the process/production unit is busy.

In the second case, it is irritating to be forced to remake while other orders are waiting to be processed. These comments apply to all internal failures. However, some of these failures may be rechargeable to outside agencies. If suppliers change the specification of their product, or fail to reach agreed specifications, then failures may cause consequential losses in the process. While most companies disclaim responsibility for this, the reality is that intense competition amongst suppliers will encourage a settlement if the business is to be maintained. None the less everyone agrees that avoidance of failure in the first place is a far better policy.

So far we have dealt with internal failures, the ones that we manage to keep in-house, even if our operating costs suffer accordingly. However, the other, often more damaging, failures are those which take place at, or on the way, to the customer. Some examples of this category of failure are inadequate product packaging, unsuitable transport, substandard product appearance and/or performance, reworking or rectifying the product at the customer's premises, replacement product or materials, consequential loss claims for a variety of reasons and the processing of complaints. This last one has even included the cost of a special complaints department set up to minimize customer dissatisfaction. This dissatisfaction is not always easy to cost. Can we really tell why we are only given 5 per cent of a customer's business? It could be our quality in relation to other suppliers. Equally, it could be our price, or perhaps some serious problem we had with rejects a few months ago. Whatever the cause, the arguments are strongly in favour of defect prevention.

Summary of quality activities

In order to gather together this part of the chapter we can expand on Figure 8.1, where we outlined the sequence of inspection. If we now change our scope from inspection to quality we can add several important activities to our list. Figure 8.2 shows the sequence of quality activities in the manufacturing process. Note particularly the work to be carried out in design, with vetting and codes of practice and the need for vendor assessment which is so important in modern business.

Case study: Jaguar cars

The story of the recovery of Jaguar cars is well known. At one time some Americans reckoned that they were very good cars, provided that you owned two, then one could always be off the road for repairs! Two years later Jaguar had to increase capacity to meet the demand for a superb car with extremely high reliability. John Egan, the new chief executive, started the turnaround by demanding an immediate return to high quality by all Jaguar suppliers. That

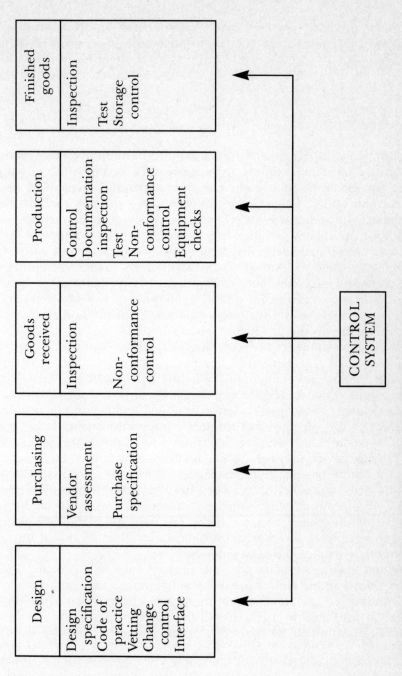

Figure 8.2 Quality activities in the manufacturing process

demand included a guarantee of quality, not simply a promise to improve, and his actions cost some Jaguar suppliers a lot of money. Jaguar executives and staff then turned their attention to many other aspects of the quality of their cars, with spectacular results for their sales.

Prevention costs

'You cannot inspect quality into a product. The best way to produce a quality product is not to produce a poor quality one.' Anything that can be done to prevent failures happening is classified under prevention costs. This category is very wide, and can include items which might otherwise be classed as process or marketing costs. Obvious candidates are all forms of specific quality training, whether for operators, managers, inspectors, functional experts or sales staff. Another is the operation of quality assurance schemes for all manner of materials, supplies and components. The planning of quality, including the strategies for quality achievement, is a prevention cost. Some managers would include those aspects of method study which assure quality in the product or process.

During recent years the widening of quality responsibility and the generation of company-wide quality awareness has attracted much senior management attention. Quality Circles, 'Right First Time' campaigns, Quality task forces, Total Quality Management, quality coordinators, Total Quality Seminars, Quality Suggestions Teams are all part of the strong thrust towards competitive quality being made by those companies who are determined to compete and to succeed.

This great thrust has taken quality away from the exclusive responsibility of operations managers. They now have many helpers in the drive towards quality. The effect has been to raise the cost of prevention considerably, but the consequent savings go far beyond the easily computed cost of rejects. In many cases they mean quite simply the ability to continue trading, rather than go out of business due to low quality and high cost.

When costing systems are well devised they will provide quality cost information, and a breakdown by percentages against a total investment is useful. The argument has always been that, for an extra investment in prevention, the savings in failure and even appraisal costs will be dramatic. Some managers would also argue that the reduction in total cost provides a margin for more competitive bidding.

Table 8.2 shows the comparative figures for all products in a company during a time of difficulty and after strenuous efforts had been made to diagnose causes and prevent recurrence. In fact, the major cause of trouble was defective machinery, the rectification of which produced very useful savings.

Table 8.2
Company quality cost statement 19—

	£	£	%
Faults at customers			
1 Returns (15 different categories)	39,600		
2 Rework at customers	8,630		
3 Claim settlements	29,200	77,430	26.5%
Faults in factory			
1 In-process rejects	26,300		
2 Components	21,400		
3 Materials	7,600		
4 Finished goods	23,800	79,100	27.0%
			(53.5%)
Appraisal/Inspection Costs			
1 Materials inspection	13,200		
2 In-process inspection	21,600		
3 Final checks	29,100		
4 Consumable supplies inspection	14,780		
5 Inspection materials/supplies	8,900	87,580	30%
Prevention Costs			
1 Quality circle admin	15,000		
2 SQA staffing	22,000		
3 Staff training	3,500		
4 Quality planning	7,600	48,100	16.5%
		292,130	100%

A number of points may be made about the figures obtained. First, the failure costs show as much cost incurred for customer faults as for those detected in the factory. This means that they are not being detected in time. Certainly, the figure of £29,100 for final inspection means that the checks are not having the intended result. Also there have been substantial payments, probably for consequential loss, as well as the £39,600 on returned goods. The supplier quality assurance staff have missed out somewhere, with £20,000 spent on component failures. While these were picked up in the factory they should never have arrived and it is to be hoped that the money will be recovered from the relevant suppliers.

A quality cost statement tells the success (or failure) story of the quality strategy of the company during the time period which it covers.

Case study: the human element

The Firestone approach to quality arose from the principle that the thrust should start with the chief executive officer. At a time of reappraisal of its attitude to quality, the corporation moved its emphasis towards people, and this thrust led to the development of a corporate quality policy. Within this policy, it was decided that everyone should have a personal commitment to excellence. Focusing on quality was a way to achieve this excellence, and became a means to change the culture within the organization. A particular aspect was the link to quality cost, a rule of thumb being that every dollar spent on prevention saved ten dollars in failure costs, either internal or external.

A task force was set up to produce a structured quality system, with planned development, part of which was education and training. The significant changes made were:

1 A refocused quality perspective;
2 A concentration on the economics of (cost-driven) quality improvements.
3 Better quality cost systems, focusing on reduction of failure costs.
4 Refocused quality strategy – from techniques to people.
5 A leadership style where people get things done.

The major results achieved were a better market share and better market ratings by their customers.

Case study: emphasis on results

Quality concepts at IBM include:

- Quality improvement comes from management action.
- Everyone must be involved.
- Focus on the job process.
- No level of defect is acceptable.
- Quality improvements reduce total costs.

In translating these concepts into a comprehensive system IBM used Quality Circles, together with many tools and techniques, such as defect identification, cause analysis, corrective action sequences, and the examination of line management accountability. A number of important principles and figures emerged.

1 The defect reduction targets were tightened by 20 per cent whenever that target was hit three times in a row and, in four years, this produced a dramatic reduction in typewriter warranty repairs.
2 When a new product was introduced, the defect rate was required to start lower than that of the old product at that time.
3 Defects must be identified in a device early because, if left until discovered in a system in the field, the total cost of correction will have been multiplied by more than one hundred.
4 In two years the miscoding of information by accounts departments was reduced by a factor of eight.
5 Software quality was improved dramatically by increasing the ratio of in-process prevention/inspection. Over three years the percentages of in-process/final test/field failure changed from 20/31/5 per cent to 64/31/5 per cent with a considerable drop in the total quality cost.

Case study: how to improve the quality of a service

A service business is totally customer-driven. Satisfied customers provide free advertising by word-of mouth. So American Express (Amex) set out to:

1 determine how to measure quality;
2 establish standards of service based on the marketplace, the delivery system, the economics and the impact on customer behaviour;
3 communicate the standards to employees;
4 monitor performance against those standards, (internal and external surveys);
5 integrate the programme into the corporate culture.

As customers are only concerned with the final product, Amex set out to establish customer expectations of quality, then to work out advertising commitments and the position and stance of competitors. They then considered the best way to deliver the service, taking account of both the economics and the constraints. By considering the costs of doing it wrong they arrived at a monthly cost to correct errors. Then they added to this the indirect costs in bad publicity and the people who do not renew. Finally, they examined the level of service required, treating it as an informed business decision. The internal and external monitoring of performance and customer satisfaction showed how far they were succeeding. Amex concluded that quality in a service industry is the same as for a production unit. In their case, it depended on speed, accuracy and a more comfortable service. These factors must be known if success is to be achieved.

Quality audits

Four types of quality assurance system are recognized in the United Kingdom and these are defined in British Standards BS 5750 and BS 4891. Cost-effective quality management systems are specified in BS 4891. In BS 5750, Part 3 covers the simplest products, while Parts 1 and 2 deal with all but the simplest products, with or without the establishment of design. The standards list 23 elements of quality management which are appropriate to one or other of the specifications. Under each element a series of questions are asked about the products under review, and a satisfactory series of answers would suggest a system in accord with the standard. Thus, we have an audit system of considerable use to any company aspiring to a satisfactory quality management system.

An example of a simple audit checklist is given at page 182.
Note how even this very simple audit gives a picture of the quality performance of the company or unit. After this simple assessment more detailed analysis of particular areas of concern may be carried out, thus progressively moving towards excellence without overemployment of resources.

The quality company

One way of summarizing all the issues which we have addressed in this chapter is to consider the difference between the company which is imbued with quality in all its forms and the 'ordinary' company. This difference is well tabulated in a PA/Consulting Services document dealing with Total Quality Management, and shown in Table 8.3.

Table 8.3
The quality company

	'Ordinary' Company	Quality Company
1	Customer satisfaction comes after profits.	Profits come from customer satisfaction.
2	Focus on detecting problems.	Focus on preventing problems.
3	Cost containment through cutting.	Cost containment through disciplined approach to own operations and to the supply chain.
4	Values numbers.	Values people.
5	Low spending on training.	High spending on training.
6	Vague about goals, roles, standards at any level.	Explicit and disciplined about goals, roles, standards at all levels.
7	Treats complaints as a nuisance.	Treats complaints as an opportunity to learn.
8	In awe of technology.	Uses technology selectively under management control
9	Runs by systems.	Runs by people working with other people.
10	Sees quality, productivity, cost reduction as separate endeavours.	Restless search for improvement of the business with quality, productivity, cost reduction as indivisible elements.
11	People do not know where they fit in the quality chain.	Manages the quality chain.

Personal development task no. 8.1

1 Draw a copy of the five boxes in Figure 8.1 (p. 170) for your operations.
2 On the right of each box enter your figures for (or estimates of) the cost of quality pertaining to that area of attention.
3 Enter any of the techniques (e.g. vendor rating) which you employ to assure the quality of your products or services.

4 What is your strategy for inspection?
5 Do the figures which you have just entered in the diagram agree with that strategy?
6 If not, what is your plan for improvement in the inspection activity?

Personal development task no. 8.2

Please answer the following questions about your quality policy in operations at your company and then consider their implication for your own effectiveness as a manager.

1 Do you have any form of quality costing which will produce analyses like Table 8.1 and Figure 8.1?
2 If so, is it possible to produce a quality cost statement by product line or service?
3 If the answer to these is 'No', then how do you know how good your quality record is?
4 Having considered the previous questions, please write down, in one short paragraph, a statement of your quality strategy for the company and your tactics in operations for fulfilling that strategy.
5 Take another look at Table 8.3 on page 179. Are you a quality company or an ordinary company?

Chapter summary points

- Quality management is a strategic issue.
- In effective companies, quality is the principal objective of everybody.
- New product specifications must satisfy all interested parties in the company.
- For inspection, the strategy should be 'the earlier the better'.
- Product improvement schemes are about involving people.
- Quality cost analysis pinpoints areas of questionable quality.
- Quality management is not a management post, but the result of continuous cooperation across departments.

References

1 Juran, J.M., *Quality Control Handbook,* New York: McGraw-Hill, 1974.
2 Feigenbaum, A.V., *Total Quality Control,* New York: McGraw-Hill, 1961.
3 Caplan, R.H., *A Practical Approach to Quality Control,* London: Business Books, 1969.
4 Seder, L.A. *Quality Cost and Defect Prevention,* London: Incomtec, 1955.
5 *Total Quality Management,* London: P.A. Consulting Services, 1986.

Essential Reading

Crosby, P.B., *Quality is Free,* New American Library, 1979.
Total Quality Management, P.A. Consulting Services, 1986. This document gives many examples of companies practising Total Quality Management, and describes the requirements for such a system in a way which will help the operations manager put the principles into practice.

Audit checklist
and Quality Assurance

Application Area

Audit Objective

To establish the existence of an appropriate Quality Assurance system that matches the needs of the company.

Points to Consider

1. Are the quality objectives defined and attainable?
2. What are the qualities within the areas of the company which are matched to the quality objective?
3. What is the level of prevention and appraisal as opposed to the failure costs?
4. Are quality records maintained and accurate?
5. Does the company operate within the guidelines of British Standard BS 5750?

Detailed Tests

1. Measure the achievement of quality costs against plan.
2. Consider sample cost-benefit analysis.
3. Carry out documentation checks.

9 Managing quality: Quality control – techniques and applications

Introduction

Statistical techniques are used in many parts of industry, not least in the operations areas of materials management and quality control. We cannot ignore the mathematics involved, but must choose how comprehensively we treat the subject. It would be inappropriate to attempt a treatise, so our approach will be to explore some of the principles from which particular applications are developed. Our sequence will be to examine:

1 The background of reliability;
2 The principles involved in sampling techniques;
3 A survey of the various types of control chart;
4 Some examples of the application of control charts;
5 A list of sources for more detailed treatment of these subjects.

Variability

When we are asked to manufacture a product, whether by hand or by using machinery, there will be some variability in that work arising from a number of physical and human factors. The science of statistics will help us to study these variations, to assess their effect on the level of quality required by the customer. When a piece of machinery cuts metal to length or diameter, when continuous plant produces sheets of any material to a given width and thickness, when a batch process is measured by the viscosity of the liquid, there will be variations in the results obtained. One way to examine these variations is to count the frequency of the results obtained. So, for a required length of 5cm we might obtain:

30 pieces at 5.00cm
25 " " 4.99cm   25 pieces at 5.01cm
18 " " 4.98cm   17 " " 5.02cm
 8 " " 4.96cm   9 " " 5.04cm
 1 " " 4.94cm   2 " " 5.06cm

This gives us a frequency of the variations, which may be shown as a chart (see Figure 9.1). It also gives a picture of:

(a) Where the middle value lies in relation to the desired (nominal) value. This in turn shows how well the process is centred.
(b) The spread of values. Out of 125 pieces only one is as low as 4.94 and two as high as 5.06.

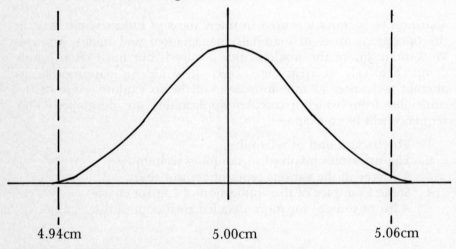

4.94cm   5.00cm   5.06cm

Figure 9.1   Frequency of variations around 5cm

Distribution curves

If we are given acceptance limits of say 4.96 and 5.04 we already have a good idea how many pieces are likely to be rejected. Distribution curves of this type are common for industrial processes,

184

where they have widely differing uses. Process capability studies will often include the preparation of frequency distributions for the work being produced. They give a more accurate description of the ability of that process to meet the production standards required. Very often, the curves obtained are bell-shaped, or normal. They may have a long tail on one side or the other, when they are known as skewed, right or left (see examples given later in this chapter).

The normal distribution has properties which are valuable when measuring the deviation of a set of readings from the nominal value. Obviously the first one of interest is the average of the readings. Remember that two machines may cut 500 pieces each to a nominal length of 5cm, and the average for each machine may be exactly 5cm. However, the spread produced by each might be very different indeed. It may be that only one of the machines is able to reach the specified limits. Figure 9.2 illustrates this point.

In order to get a better picture of the deviation from standard we calculate the standard deviation. This is the root mean square deviation of the readings from their average.

Sample Standard Deviation $\sigma = \sqrt{\dfrac{\Sigma(x-\bar{x})^2}{n}}$

where
$\bar{x}$ = average.
σ = sample standard deviation
n = number of readings.

Strictly speaking, for a population standard deviation we should use $(n-1)$ for n, but if the sample size is high enough we gain sufficient accuracy for our purposes. This question of sample size will arise later, and we must be quite sure that, when testing from a batch or during a run, we take a realistic size of sample, so that n and $(n-1)$ are not significantly different in size.

We are now in a position (given an adequate sample size) to predict how many readings are likely to appear at different deviations from the average value.

1 Take a number of samples of the product from the batch or during the run.
2 Use their values to calculate a figure for standard deviation.

We will then be able to state how wide or how narrow are our process limits. In fact, Figure 9.3 shows that 68.27 per cent of the readings will be inside ± 1σ (standard deviation) from the

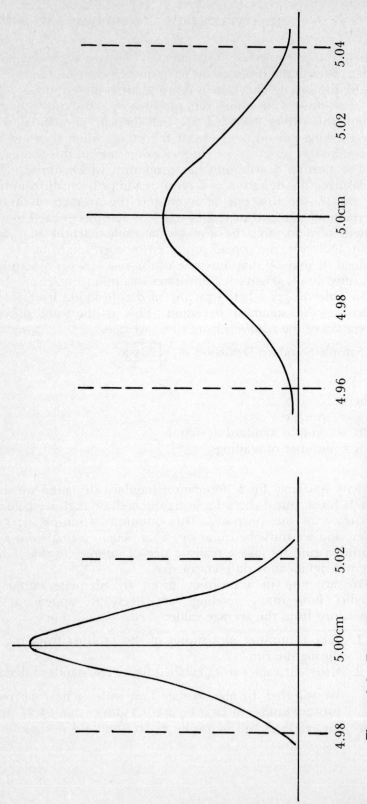

Figure 9.2 Examples of two distribution spreads

average. A further 4.28 per cent will fall between $\pm$ 2σ and 3σ from the average. Finally, 0.27 per cent will lie outside $\pm$ 3σ. The average is a measure of central tendency and enables us to determine variability and deviation in the form of the standard deviation. Another is the median or middle reading in a group. This is used in certain simple and approximate types of testing.

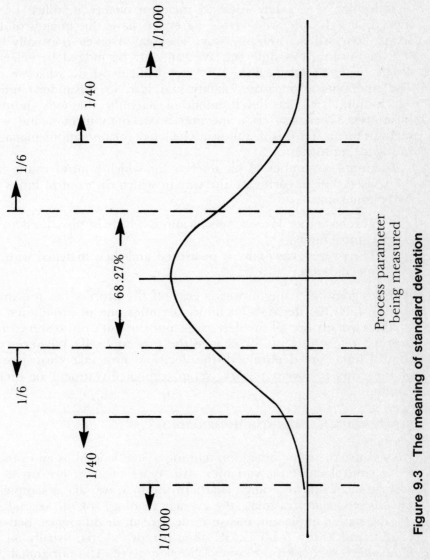

Figure 9.3 The meaning of standard deviation

187

Quality control charts

The use of control charts

The quality control chart has become an expected part of factory operations. It is seen above the work bench, on the wall next to a section of workers, or in the control rooms of automated processes. Significantly, it is rarely used to measure quality in office jobs – indeed, few people who create a service have the quality of that service assessed in the same way. The reason given is usually 'Ah, well in my job it is different. We can only be judged by a feeling about customer satisfaction. It is very difficult to do what we do.' The intention to measure quality can lead to misunderstandings which hold back the development of scientific methods in many businesses. There *can* be a meeting between motivation and work measurement, but this is a topical challenge for operations managers in service industries.

There are a number of parameters for which control charts may be devised, but in each case the way in which the control limits are set is important:

1 The customer gives a specification, which is then used to fix control limits.
2 The process capability is measured and then matched with the specification.

If they agree, then the answer is easy. If the process has too much spread, then the decision on limits becomes one of economics. Do we then inspect out all the defectives, put the work on to some other process, refuse the job, or change the process itself? Whatever way control limits are determined, the decision must take clear account of the costs involved: rework, scrap, capital investment or quality training.

Control charts for variables (Measurements)

We will use the same operation (cutting a 5cm length) as an example for a control chart for variables. Two types of chart are used: the average chart and the range chart. In the first, we take a sample of, say, 20 pieces and calculate the average reading. For the second, we use the same sample and measure the spread, or difference, between highest and lowest readings. We then use two charts, usually on the same sheet, each with the control limits entered. The horizontal axis represents time, the vertical one the property being measured.

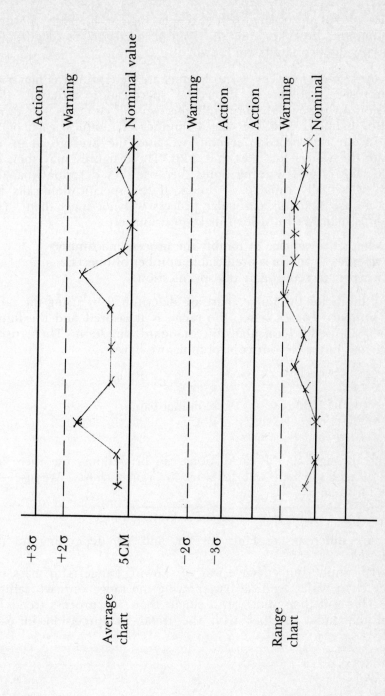

Figure 9.4 Example of average chart and range chart

Samples of 20 pieces are then taken at regular intervals of time, depending on how accurate the control needs to be. Figure 9.4 shows how the two charts are drawn.

Setting the control limits The control limits are determined either from the process capability or from the specification required. (See discussion on page 185). Hopefully the two will coincide, but rarely does this happen. First, we take a number of samples, each of 20 pieces, from the process; second, we find the average, then we calculate the values for $\pm 3\sigma$ and $\pm 2\sigma$. These figures may then be used as control and warning limits, because they describe what the process is actually capable of doing. If the specification calls for tighter limits, then this particular process will not meet them. The operations manager must then make decisions on:

1 whether to replace or modify the process machinery;
2 whether to accept a predictable number of rejects;
3 whether to renegotiate the specification.

Control limits for the range chart are determined by using the same set of samples. For each set, the range is measured and the figure obtained is used to calculate the standard deviation. Then, using average and range for our control limits we have:

	Average	Range
1	$X+3\sigma_x$	$R+3\sigma_r$
2	Nominal Value	Nominal Value
3	$X-3\sigma_x$	$R-3\sigma_r$

Working through all the calculations can be tedious, but there are statistical tables which will help us for range charts. We use the simple formula:

$$\text{Limits} = \text{Constant} \times \text{Average range}$$

There are different constants for $2\sigma_r$ and $3\sigma_r$ depending on the sample size.

A very simple, but effective way of showing range is to mark the average chart with a vertical bar showing the range on each sample taken. This will then show on a single chart the process trend for central tendency, together with the trend for precision in each sample.

Control charts for attributes

A further type of control is when a product is measured either as good enough or rejected, (go/no go). All the calculations detailed above depend on our ability to measure them quantitatively, but this is not always possible. Colour may be measured by spectrometer, but the results need detailed interpretation. Surface gloss and opacity are difficult to measure in practical terms, while some physical shapes would require complicated and lengthy measurement. In these cases, it is common practice to have a go/no go form of inspection, based either on a form of gauge, on an appearance standard, or some other qualitative test. Whatever the attribute used, a convenient control method is to measure the defectives in a given sample. There are three types of chart:

1 Number defective np.
2 Proportion or fraction defective p.
3 Percentage defective.

The standard symbols used are

n = sample size
c = number of defectives
p = proportion defective in sample
$\bar{p}$ = average proportion defective
σ_p = standard deviation for per cent defective

For a given size of sample

$$\sigma_p = \sqrt{\frac{\bar{p}(100-\bar{p})}{n}}$$

Control limits for per cent defective are obtained by using

$$p \pm 3\sqrt{\frac{\bar{p}(100-\bar{p})}{n}}$$

Warning limits may be computed from

$$p \pm \sqrt{\frac{2\bar{p}(100-\bar{p})}{n}}$$

191

Sampling techniques

How do we find out the quality of a production raw material which comes in large quantities, when the testing methods are destructive? How do we find out quickly, and without spending a fortune, the quality level of a product during manufacture? How do we assess the quality of the service given by the nationalized facilities who call on thousands of householders? The answer must be by employing sampling techniques. There are hundreds of applications and innumerable sampling plans available. As with so many services, the result depends on the investment. In other words the more you pay, then the bigger the sample and consequently the more accurate the results.

Modern sampling methods have moved beyond the so-called random samples used in early testing methods. They are based on well-founded principles of probability, developed among others by Dodge and Romig[1] in the USA. Both British and American military authorities publish sampling tables. These cover a wide range of applications, particularly the acceptance sampling of large lots of raw materials and stock in process. Examples include all kinds of chemical solids/powders, wood pulp, small castings, fuels, small metalwork in large lots, nuts and bolts. A further application for sampling techniques is process control. Bearing in mind that the tactics of inspection are to sample as early as possible for continuous processes, the high output will demand some form of sampling rather than 100 per cent inspection. The exception to this will be continuously recording electronic control equipment used to control processes by measuring the product as it is made. In fact, many processes use sampling plans to support the control instrumentation.

Sampling theory

The simple logic behind sampling is that the more pieces we measure, then the more accurate will be the result. However, there are economic and practical reasons for reducing sample size. The laws of probability allow us to build up formulae covering sample size and the risk involved and, for convenience, sampling tables have been worked out for many different situations.

Sampling tables deal with the following parameters:

1   The size of sample required for a given lot size.
2   The amount or number of defective pieces beyond which the batch or lot must be rejected.

Types of sampling table

Two types of sampling table predominate and, between them, they cover most of the important industrial situations. First, there is the table that deals with the acceptance or rejection of a single batch, or lot, on the basis of the sample taken. The most popular form of this is the table for acceptable quality level (AQL). The way it is put together means that we can make such statements about its operating characteristics as:

> For this table, under these conditions, any batch will have an x per cent chance (often 90 per cent) that batches tested at y per cent (often 5 per cent) defectives, will be accepted. We are now talking to the producer of the batch about his chances of success. So the producer's risk here is 10 per cent (in 10 per cent of cases showing 4 per cent defectives the batch will be rejected).

The second type of sampling table deals with the average quality of many batches. In this case, we are concerned with the average outgoing quality level (AOQL). This type of table is much less frequently used than AQL tables. the arrangement here is that there will be a target figure for percentage defectives and that, when any batches are rejected after sampling, they will then be inspected 100 per cent in order to eliminate and return the actual defectives.

Single and double sampling

Sometimes it would help to take second samples, or even multiple samples. The second sample, or double sampling method, will save money if it is used where there are likely to be batches of very high or very low quality. The first sample will pick out the high-quality batches for little expenditure. It works like this:

	Sample 1 Take 60		Sample 2 Take 60
Accept Level	1 defective	Accept Level	5 defectives
Reject Level	5 defectives	Reject Level	6 defectives

So we try the first sample. If 0 or 1 defectives we accept it; if 5 or more we totally reject it. If 2, 3 or 4 we take sample 2 and accept on 0–5 defectives only. From this, it is seen how the first sample takes out the obviously good or bad batches and then only if necessary

193

will the second sample deal with the more doubtful cases.

Having described several simple sampling techniques we should, however, consider the background to the situations where they might be used. If double sampling is necessary, then why accept such variable consignments in the first place? Modern practice leads towards the reduction of raw materials stock through the application of the 'Just in Time' philosophy. Also, there has been an overwhelming insistence on guaranteed quality for all incoming materials. Perhaps the most profitable use for double sampling is for auditing suspect batches as a prelude to negotiating with suppliers a more realistic quality level for their products. However, there are some industries where high output on a continuous basis demands large quantities of raw materials. In these situations, and where destructive testing is impossible, sampling is essential. But it must be employed on the basis that quality levels are guaranteed and the tests are part of a safety monitoring procedure. It should also be remembered that some raw materials are natural products, where variability is not so easily controlled. While valiant efforts may be made to meet specifications and continuous product development is taking place there are some materials which still have a long way to go in the consistency of their quality levels.

Comment

We have given a short description of sampling techniques and so followed our professed intention. Each situation where sampling is appropriate demands individual attention, and the operations manager in that situation will find excellent treatment of all the three major statistical subjects surveyed in this chapter amongst the chapter references.

The application of control charts

Case study: problem diagnosis by control chart

A control chart for attributes was used to diagnose and then cure a damage problem during the manufacture of drive shafts. The chart shown in Figure 9.5 demonstrates how a number of splines were being damaged, while others were measured as being too tight, the proportion defective being unacceptable. Note the 100 per cent sample being taken while the problem was investigated and the return to a zero defect level after the rectification procedure.

Drive shafts					Pre heat treat soft stage (check)			Remarks: insert placed on drill m/c bed – problem solved														
Damaged splines	4		5		3		1	2														
Tight splines	2		—		—		2	1														
DEFECTS	6	0	5	0	3	2	1	2	0	0	0	0	0	0	0	0	0	0	0	0	0	0
SAMPLE SIZE	109	102	101	67	123	98	114	97	96	48	56	96	96	48	96	48	85	72	96	48		
PROPORTION DEF	.055	0	.049	0	.024	.02	.008	.02	0	0	0	0	0	0	0	0	0	0	0	0	0	0

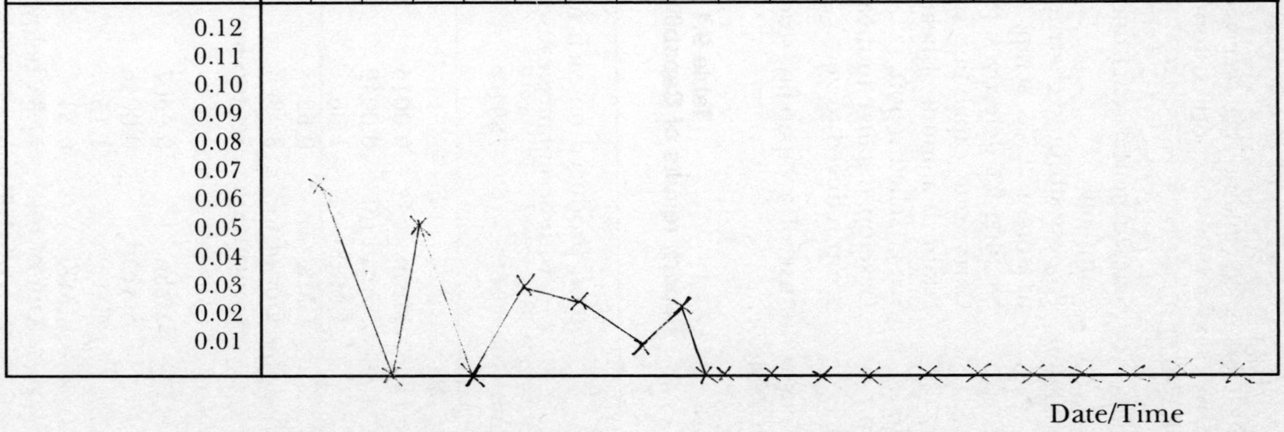

0.12
0.11
0.10
0.09
0.08
0.07
0.06
0.05
0.04
0.03
0.02
0.01

Date/Time

Figure 9.5 A control chart for attributes

195

Case study: – a customer complaint

In this case, a complaint was received by a precision engineering company from a valued export customer. The complaint was set out as follows:

Problem   Shaped helical relief undersize. Telex export customer complaint.

Investigation   Process attribute chart for two machines showed: Heat treatment 2.3% scrap. (Cost/revenue losses shown.) Shaping 0% defectives. (Some rework needed.)

Action   Carry out capability studies on both machines to establish amount of heat treatment distortion.

Results   See attached report.

Action   Developed gauge to measure backlash.

Result   Scrap reduced to zero.

This led to the use of a capability study, for which the report is set out in Table 9.1.

Table 9.1
Report: results of Capability Studies 92116

		(50 off produced on each machine, backlash with acceptance cause measured)	
Machine		7891	6849
Before HT	Mean	0.0015	0.0066
	Spread (6)	0.0049	0.007"
	CM (8)	1.06	0.75
	CMK (8)	0.62	0.10
	Out of tol.	3.1%	37.8% above H.L.
	Conclusion	Set too low	Set too high, too much spread
After HT	Mean	0.0007	0.0058
	Spread	0.0046	0.0068
	CM	1.15	0.77
	CMK	0.31	0.35
	Out of tol.	17.83 below L.L.	14.76% about H.L.
	(Post HT gauge 0.0005" backlash smaller)		
	Conclusion	0.0008" shrinkage	0.0008" shrinkage

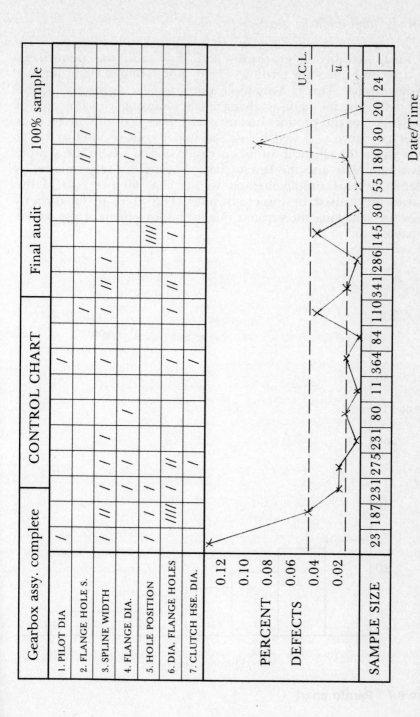

Figure 9.6 Gearbox assembly control chart

Case study: final audit for gearbox assembly

After final assembly of gearboxes a quality audit was performed, using a control chart for attributes, and monitoring a large number of characteristics. This is a multiple purpose chart, giving a picture of the nature of the various characteristics causing concern and of the variability of the product quality over a period of time. Note that the average figure $\bar{u}$ is well below the upper control limit and that there is cause for concern on two occasions, each where the sample size is small. Note also the Pareto chart showing the major causes of problems. By this simple method we see that 60 per cent of the defectives are caused by three attributes. This gives us an obvious strategy for achieving the greatest quality improvement at the lowest reasonable cost.

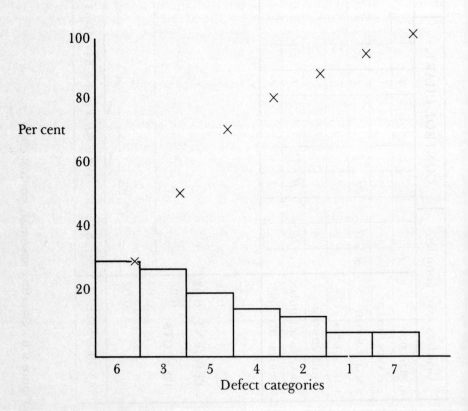

Figure 9.7   Pareto chart

Case study: efficiency improvement targets

Attention to efficiency and quality becomes self-perpetuating when all the individual projects which arise out of a Quality Circle or project group are gathered together in a departmental efficiency programme. The chart in Figure 9.8 shows the gross and net performance for a grinding section cost centre during a period of twelve months. The first point to emerge is the requirement for a continual improvement in the net targets set for each month. Second, the actual performance starts well below the initial target but by month eleven is well ahead of the increasing target.

The means by which efficiency was improved included a number of housekeeping actions, including the replacement of inefficient cabinets, attending to storage racks and relocating oil supplies. A number of specific actions were also taken to reduce set-up times such as rebatching, placing equipment nearer to the machines and changing some setting details. The work being carried out in this section to improve performance was mirrored in all other parts of that particular operations unit. The manufacturing objective for that year included the raising of performance levels throughout all sections and departments to at least a gross figure of 90 per cent. In some cases, that required a very substantial improvement.

Case study: problem diagnosis with attribute chart

It is the aim of any study to come to a clear-cut conclusion, with recommendations that follow automatically from the findings. However, most machinery suffers from multiple influences. In this case, the conclusions point out succinctly what is happening, recommend immediate action, then commission a further study to ensure that correction actually happens. Below is the report of the action meeting covering investigations into oversized gear teeth. Note how outside influences such as shift change were noted and allowed for in the actions reported.

ACTION MEETING
RECORD OF PROCEEDINGS

SUBJECT	Span size XY gear on driveshaft 96449.
PROBLEM	HT attribute chart showing oversize gear teeth on drive shaft 96449. (Span size of up to 0.002″ oversize – will not fit mating parts or pass national service parts inspection).

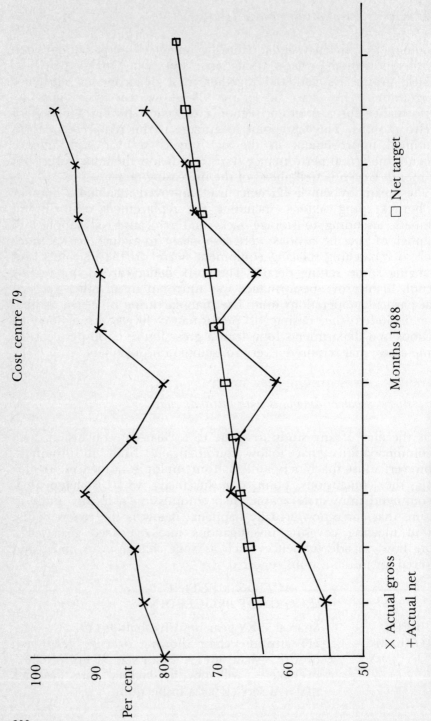

Figure 9.8 Gross and net performance chart

CHARTS   Capability study, hobbed span size for 50 off
                   M/C 7517.
                   Capability study, span size for same 60 off action
                   H.T.
ANALYSIS   Hobbing see analysis 751708.
                   After HT   " 751709
CONCLUSIONS   Analysis of the hobbing showed that bottom
                   limit was already being worked to due to F/L
                   operators being aware that finished gears were
                   oversize. Machine 7517 was not capable. Data
                   badly skewed due to shift change during study. It
                   was decided to lower and open out the hobbed
                   process limits from 1.1975"/1.1965" to 1.1956"/
                   1.1950" with 0.0014" HT growth. This will give
                   finished   size   1.1965"/1.1979"   against   a
                   requirement of 1.1970"/1.1980". This will reduce
                   the percentage of oversize finished gears from
                   38% to zero.
ACTION   Alter layout size to 1.1965"/1.1950" and reissue.
                   Restudy due to skew distribution.
NEXT MEETING. On completion of above study.

Personal development task no. 9

Put a morning aside in your personal planner to review your quality
measurement strategy. Write down, in one sentence, your
understanding of that strategy. Then examine the techniques being
used against the following questions.

1 Do you buy large quantities of raw material? If so how do you
   test it? How much does the testing cost? How many faults escape
   the testing? Has quality improved as a result of testing?
2 Do you use control charts for measuring your process
   performance? If so, are they detecting all process faults, or are
   some being missed, to be picked up later? What can you do
   about it?
3 Are you spending enough money on this type of appraisal?
4 Is your quality measurement strategy effective?

NOTE: This development task is concerned solely with the use of
quality control charts and sampling schemes and their effectiveness.
Wider-ranging work on quality management strategy was suggested
in Chapter 8.

Chapter summary points

- Industrial processes vary in their ability to hold a set reading.
- We can measure the average of the readings and the standard deviation from that average.
- This allows us to measure the ability of many processes to meet specified limits.
- It will also tell us how many rejects we will get for any given set of limits.
- Standard deviation measures process capability.
- Process capability should match product specifications, so control charts should cover both requirements.
- For attributes use per cent defective charts.
- For measurements use average and range charts.
- Control limits for averages $x \pm 3\sigma^x$
- Control limits for ranges $x \pm 3\sigma_r$. $\sqrt{\dfrac{p(100-p)}{n}}$
- Control limits for % defective $p \pm 3$
- Sampling is an answer to destructive testing problems.
- Accuracy costs money.
- Acceptance sampling can be carried out at reasonable costs.
- Double sampling can reduce the cost for very variable batches of products, but is its use a sign of inadequate quality performance?
- Two types of sampling tables cover most industrial applications.

References

1 Dodge, H. and Romig, H. F., *Sampling Inspection Tables,* (2nd edn.), New York: John Wiley, 1959.

Specialist reading

Caplen, R. H., *A Practical Approach to Quality Control,* London: Business Books, 1969. A simple practical treatment of quality control, with good examples of particular applications in engineering.

Crosby, P. B., *Quality is Free,* New York: Mentor Excecutive Library, 1979. Uses many small cases to argue the 'Art of making quality certain'. All about philosophies and attitudes, no technical detail on techniques.

Feigenbaum, A. V., *Total Quality Control.* McGraw Hill, New York, 1961. This is the bible for the designing control charts for all situations, for gathering together the other jobs of quality control, for process studies and for a detailed study of sampling. Highly recommended for technical thoroughness in particular applications.

10 Managing the finances: financial planning and budgeting

Introduction

All management decisions have some financial effect. This is particularly the case in the operations area where managers are making decisions involving significant proportions of the company's assets with corresponding effects on profitability, financial strength and cash. Therefore, an awareness and understanding of the financial implications of operations decisions is vital if the operations manager is to be effective both in achieving objectives and in communicating with other managers.

This understanding should include an appreciation of how the financial performance of a business is planned, reported and controlled, the importance of budgeting in this process, and an awareness of how financial techniques can be used to aid specific decision-making. This chapter will be concerned with the aspects of financial planning and control that are important to the operations manager, whereas the next chapter will consider the impact on decisions that are relevant to the operations area.

Basic financial statements

The effects of management decisions are represented in a firm's financial records. At the end of a convenient period, usually a month, an abstract of the records is prepared to show the total effect of the decisions taken during that period. This abstract is normally summarized into two main documents: the profit and loss account and the balance sheet, which are prepared in line with standard accounting principles and conventions. In this section we will consider both these documents together, plus one other – the cash flow forecast.

The profit and loss account is a statement which illustrates the results of trading in a particular accounting period, whereas the balance sheet represents the firm's end of period financial position. The cash flow forecast represents an estimate of the cash implications of the firm's anticipated future trading.

The profit and loss account

This operating statement provides a comparison of the values created in a given period with values consumed in their creation, according to the accounting conventions used. Some conventions are widely used and accepted. Others, such as the treatment of depreciation of fixed assets or the valuation of stocks – both of interest to the operations manager – are decided by the company.

An example of the presentation of a profit and loss account is given in Figure 10.1, and it can be seen that it attempts to match costs against revenue in order to establish an operating profit which can be used (after taxation) to satisfy shareholders' requirements.

The statement follows a logical pattern and corresponds to a format that would be used for management purposes, there being greater detail than is required for disclosure in the formal external reporting requirements of the Annual Report.

Referring to the statement, the major items are as follows.

Sales This figure represents the value of goods and services despatched and invoiced in the period. The date of payment is not relevant. Note that it does not necessarily correspond to the sales value of goods and services produced in the period, as there could have been either a build-up or run-down of finished goods stock. The test for acceptance is that the goods have been both despatched and invoiced to the customer.

Cost of sales This is the cost of production that is associated with the goods and services actually sold, and it is calculated in two stages. The first stage is to determine the total cost of production; the second stage determines the part of that total cost that is attributable to sales:

PROFIT and LOSS ACCOUNT

Raw Materials			Sales	900
Opening Stock		95		
Plus Purchases		370		
		465		
Less Closing Stock		105		
Raw Material Consumed		360		
Direct Labour		100		
Direct Manufacturing Expenses				
Salaries, etc.		45		
Services & Supplies, e.g.				
Power & Maintenance		120		
Depreciation		30		
Cost of Production		655		
Plus Opening Work-in-Progress				
& Finished Goods Stocks		115		
		770		
Less Closing Work-in-Progress				
& Finished Goods Stocks		95		
Cost of Sales		675		
Operating Expenses				
Manufacturing	20			
Distribution	15			
Selling	40			
Administration	30	105		
Operating Profit/(Loss)		120		
		900		900
Other Expenses		10	Operating Profit/(Loss)	120
Profit/(Loss) before Tax		115	Other Income	5
		125		125
Tax		60	Profit/(Loss) before Tax	115
Dividends		16		
Transfers to Reserve		24		
Undistributed Profit		15		
		115		115

Figure 10.1   Profit and loss account (or operating statement)

1 Determine the total cost of production:
   - raw materials actually issued and consumed;
   - wages earned by the direct labour force;
   - direct manufacturing expenses; including:
   - wages, salaries and associated charges;
   - services, e.g. power and maintenance;
   - supplies, e.g. consumable items;
   - depreciation charges, which represent the reduction of earning capacity of the fixed assets during the period.
2 Determine the part of the total cost of production that is attributable to sales. That is:
   - total cost of production
   - plus the value of work in progress and finished goods at the beginning of the period
   - less the value of work in progress and finished goods at the end of the period

Note that the extent to which manufacturing expenses are included in the cost of production will depend on the costing conventions in use.

Operating expenses These are the operating expenses not included in the cost of sales. They tend to be grouped by the relevant business functional area - for example, manufacturing, distribution, and so on. The major items are:

- salaries and indirect wages earned in the period;
- services consumed in the period, e.g. rates, insurance etc.;
- indirect materials consumed in the period, e.g. stationery;
- depreciation of non-manufacturing assets, such as cars or office machinery.

Note that the relevant value for inclusion in the profit and loss account is the value consumed in the period, which will frequently differ from the amount paid in the period.

Other income and expenses These are items which are unrelated to the firm's trading activities and could include the receipt and payment of interest.

Notes and comments The excess of revenue over total expenses is the profit for the period, and the final stage of the profit and loss account shown is the allocation of this profit. The first claimant is H.M. Inspectors of Taxes, and the amount due is calculated according to the appropriate tax legislation and deducted from pre-tax profit. The second claimant is any class of shareholder that has prior rights to a dividend. The balance is the amount available for ordinary shareholders, and a decision will need to be made by the Board on the proportion to be paid as a dividend, the proportion to be placed to specific reserves, and the amount to be carried forward as undistributed profit.

The balance sheet

The balance sheet is a summary that shows a company's state of affairs at a particular date which corresponds to the end of an accounting period. It is arranged to distinguish the sources of the funds used by an enterprise and the use to which those funds have been put. That is, it distinguishes the amounts owed by the enterprise from assets owned by and amounts owed to the enterprise. An example of a balance sheet is given in Figure 10.2.

It can be seen that the accounts are grouped into significant sections. The first main grouping is between liabilities – that is, sources of funds or amounts owed and assets, namely, uses of funds or things owned plus amounts owed to the company.

Consider first the grouping for *liabilities*. The breakdown within that grouping is given in Figure 10.3. As can be seen, the main division of total liabilities is between the amounts owed by the enterprise to its owners and the amounts owed to outside creditors.

The owners' interest is divided into *share capital* and *reserves*. The share capital is the amounts subscribed by the owners and is divided into different classes of share. Ordinary shares normally have the rights to residual earnings after prior claims, and represent the 'equity' of the enterprise. Preference shares have preferential rights to a fixed annual dividend and normally have prior rights in the event of the company's liquidation.

The organization's reserves are split into revenue reserves, which are earned from operating, and capital reserves, which are mainly derived from capital transactions – for example, reserves gained by the revaluation of assets.

The amounts owed to outside creditors are divided into long-term or short-term liabilities. The convention is that a liability is considered to be long term if payment is due more than a year from the date of the balance sheet.

Long-term liabilities can be represented by long-term loans which are due for repayment at least a year after the date of the balance sheet. Such loans frequently carry a fixed rate of interest and are

OWED BY COMPANY			OWED TO OR OWNED BY COMPANY		
Capital and Reserves			Fixed Assets		
Ordinary	130		Tangible		
Preference	35		Land & Building	30	
			Plant & Machinery	160	
			Furniture & Fittings etc	35	
				225	
Total		165			
			Intangible		
			Goodwill	15	
			Patents, Copyrights etc	5	
				20	245
Reserves		200	Investments Quoted	15	
			Unquoted	5	20
			Current Assets		
Capital & Reserves		365			
Long-term Loans	105		Stocks	200	
Taxation Future	20				
Deferred	15	140			
Current Liabilities					
Creditors	135		Debtors	210	
Short-term Loans	25				
Current Taxation	45		Short-term Investments	45	
Dividends	15	220	Bank & Cash	5	460
		725			725

Figure 10.2   Balance sheet

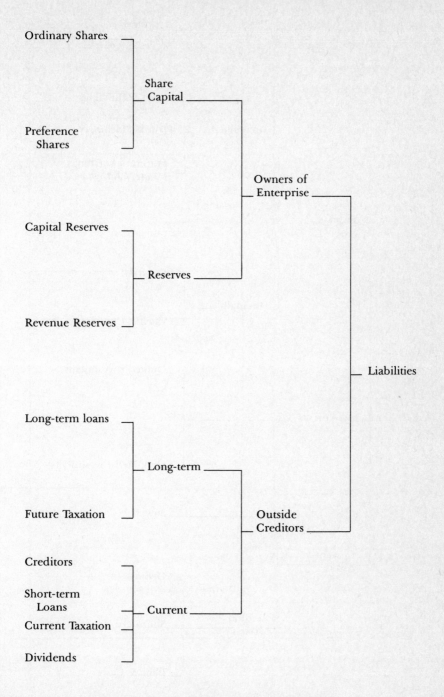

Figure 10.3   Breakdown of liabilities in balance sheet

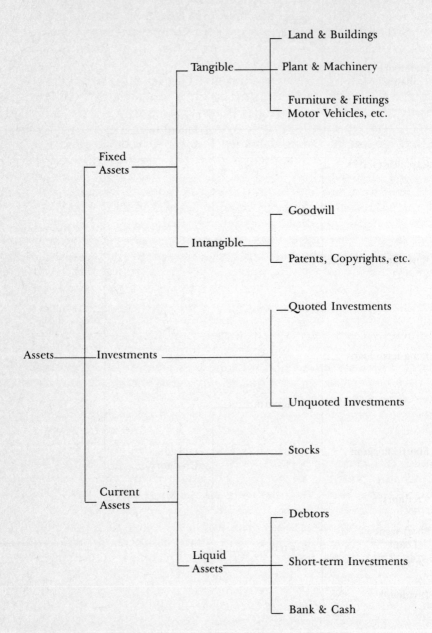

Figure 10.4   Breakdown of assets in balance sheet

secured by a mortgage on specific assets. Future taxation liability is also a long-term liability.

Short-term or current liabilities will include creditors, the majority of whom will normally be trade creditors, together with any other amounts due at balance sheet date – for example, wages and salaries, as well as short-term loans (due within a year of the balance sheet date), current taxation and dividends.

On the *asset* side, a similar chart can be drawn, as illustrated by Figure 10.4. In this case the main subdivisions are the fixed asset, investments and current asset groupings.

Fixed assets represent either physical assets or claims to value acquired for use in trading activities. The physical or tangible assets are the total of the facilities acquired by the enterprise to carry out its trading activities and include land and buildings, plant and equipment, furniture and fittings, motor vehicles and so on. In each case, the value reflected in the balance sheet is the net value – that is, after the deduction of depreciation cost to date.

The *intangible assets* have no physical existence and are divided into two groups: goodwill and patents, copyrights etc. Goodwill represents the excess of the value of the total enterprise as a going concern over the sum of the individual net asset values, and frequently arises when one company is aquired by another.

The *investment* category is normally divided into quoted investments, which refer to investment holdings that have a Stock Exchange quotation, and unquoted investments.

Current assets are subdivided into stocks, which are goods acquired with a view to resale, and liquid assets, which are either money or short-term claims to money.

Stocks are valued at either cost or net realizable value, whichever is lower. One of the issues concerning stock is the basis on which they are charged to production usage. A wide range of methods can be used, including the specific price (that is, the actual price paid for the material bought), an average or weighted average price, or a standard price. Two other methods are the 'first in–first out' (FIFO) approach and the 'last in–first out' (LIFO) approach.

The FIFO method assumes that stocks are used in the order in which they arrived, and so the price charged is that of the earliest consignment actually in the stores. This is very useful for higher-value materials and is likely to give an actual price, or close approximation. The LIFO method charges the price of the most recent purchase, so reflecting current levels of trading. This avoids enhanced profits being reported during times of rising inflation, but is not acceptable as a basis for computing tax liabilities. Both these methods involve significant clerical or computer effort and discipline, and a variety of factors will influence the method chosen – for example, inflation rates, price fluctuations and volume of transaction activity. There is no universally best method.

Liquid assets will include debtors, the majority being represented by trade debtors, as well as short-term investments and cash. The latter figure includes the bank balances as well as actual cash held.

Cash flow forecast

Any business that cannot meet its financial obligations has to stop trading. If a business is making losses, its owners or managers will probably anticipate a shortage of cash, and this expectation will probably be realized. If it is making profits, they will possibly expect the cash to 'look after itself', and this expectation may also not be realized. This is the role of the cash flow forecast – to predict the cash implications of a business trading pattern.

Cash flow can differ significantly from profit, due to the accrual concept on which most accounting systems are based. For example, the profit and loss account is designed to show the amounts of income and expense relating to the accounting period and not the amounts of money received and paid in the period. Because of these differences in timing, cash forecasting techniques are used to:

- identify the timing and amounts of peak requirements;
- ascertain whether liquid funds or borrowing capacity are sufficient to meet them;
- indicate where additional borrowing capacity must be sought, and how much;
- indicate where operating plans may need to be revised due to cash constraints.

However, the ability to forecast cash requirements will depend on the availability of forecasts or budgets of all items affecting the flow of funds in and out of the business. The operations manager will play a key role in providing that data as part of the business and financial planning process.

Basic performance ratios

It has been mentioned that two essential criteria of success in the operation of a company are profitability and liquidity. A third may be growth. In order to aid achievement of these objectives, certain fundamental performance ratios have become accepted as relevant indicators. As such, they now form a significant part of the planning and control activity within the firm. The value derived from such ratios is much increased by comparison against a standard, and by studying the trends in the figures.

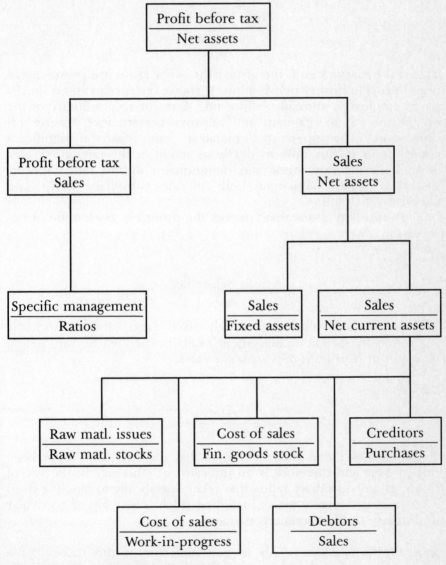

Figure 10.5   Profitability ratios

The classification of ratios broadly follows the criterion measured. The family of ratios that impact on the firm's profitability are indicated in Figure 10.5 and are discussed in detail below.

Profitability ratios

Profit/net assets or return on capital employed

$$\frac{\text{Profit before tax}}{\text{net assets}}$$

This is the main ratio in the group; the other ratios are subsidiary to it and provide further information. It shows the profit earned on the assets employed, normally before tax. A major responsibility of the organization is to maintain and improve performance against this dimension. The operations manager can make a significant contribution to this task, as decisions made in the operations area affect both the numerator and denominator of this ratio. Specific instances become apparent both in the subsidiary ratios and checklist which follow.

The subsidiary ratios that support the profit/net assets ratio are as follows.

Profit/sales

$$\frac{\text{profit before tax}}{\text{sales}}$$

This is probably the most widely used ratio, and is normally supported by specific management ratios in the area of, say, selling expenses or distribution expenses to sales.

Sales/net assets

$$\frac{\text{sales}}{\text{net assets}}$$

This indicates the number of times that the net assets have been turned over and therefore is an indicator of efficiency in the use of funds. It has subsidiary ratios that relate specifically to tangible fixed assets and net current assets including stock. These are of particular importance to the operations manager.

Sales/tangible fixed assets This is one indicator of the success of a company's capital investment policies. For example, a company figure that is low with reference to a realistic industry norm may indicate underutilization of assets. Note that this ratio is of limited use for operating control as there is unlikely to be much change in the level of fixed assets from period to period.

The net current asset ratios include the following.

Stock ratios Here, the basis for control is to relate the level of stock to a relevant figure of turnover. Ideally, an optimum ratio should be established for each principal category of stock, and the actual ratio controlled against this optimum. Appropriate stock control systems should be used to achieve these objectives. Great benefits may be derived from making the correct structural decisions in operations to approach the 'stockless' production ideal.

For raw material stocks, the ratio will normally represent turnover relating to usage:

$$\frac{\text{raw material issues}}{\text{raw material stocks}}$$

In this case, it may be based either on a moving annual total of actual usage or to a budgeted usage for the immediately following period.

For work-in-progress and finished goods stock, turnover will normally be based on cost of sales if a valid comparison is to be made:

$$\frac{\text{cost of sales}}{\text{work in progress}} \qquad \frac{\text{cost of sales}}{\text{finished goods stock}}$$

Operations performance can greatly influence the movement of these ratios.

Liquidity ratios

The principal ratio classifications in this area are the liquid ratio, the current ratio, and the ratios relating to stocks, debtors and creditor performance.

Liquid ratio

$$\frac{\text{liquid assets}}{\text{current liabilities}}$$

Liquid assets represent current assets other than stocks – namely debtors, short-term investments and cash. This ratio therefore relates the company's short-term obligations to the funds likely to be available to meet them. Factors which can affect this ratio are the terms of trading and future funds flow.

Current ratio

$$\frac{\text{current assests}}{\text{current liabilities}}$$

This indicates the 'cushion' that is available to creditors (represented by current liabilities) against the possibility of non-payment if current assets are not realizable at balance sheet values.

Stocks, debtors and creditors/sales

$$\frac{\text{stocks} + \text{debtors} - \text{creditors}}{\text{sales}}$$

This ratio can give an indication of the working capital requirements to match potential sales movements and can therefore be of help when trying to predict future cash requirements.

A further key ratio in this area is the *gearing ratio,* which can be used as an indicator of a company's future borrowing potential:

$$\frac{\text{Fixed dividend capital} + \text{long-term loans}}{\text{equity funds}}$$

If the proportion of equity funds is high, the gearing is low, and vice versa. The level of gearing will affect the company's borrowing capacity, since a high gearing will indicate a high commitment to interest payments and may influence potential lenders into judging that the company's risk is already too high. This could have the effect of restricting the loan capital available to the company.

The financial planning and control process

One of the most important responsibilities of management is that of financial planning and control. Its effect transcends the individual business functions and involves managers of all levels. The process may be subdivided into four main stages which are discussed below.

Strategic planning

The purpose of this stage is to establish a financial objective for the company, to set out the plans by which it will be achieved, and to specify the policies and constraints within which the company will operate. Operations management has an equal contribution to make at this stage through its role of developing a strategy for operations that complements the business strategy, and supporting it with the appropriate facilities and personnel policies.

Profit planning

The purpose of profit planning is to establish a profit objective for the budgeting period, and to establish the major decisions on the course of action to be followed to achieve that objective. The profit objective is normally derived from the overall strategic plan. The output from this stage is a series of planning directives that individual managers can use as a basis for their budgets.

Budgeting

This stage converts the planning directives into departmental operating plans which will achieve the profit and liquidity objectives. These plans comprise a series of individual budgets which are consolidated into a master budget. Each individual budget will contain the planning for targeted cost and profit improvement in each area of operation.

Control

The purpose of this stage is to ensure that the company is managed so that the planned position is attained. It represents a vital part of the process, and its viability is enhanced by the appropriate identification and reporting of deviations from the plan together with the monitoring of corrective action. The stages are illustrated diagramatically in Figure 10.6.

The next section considers the aspects of budgeting in more detail, as this is the area in which most operations managers will be directly involved.

Budgeting

In the budgeting stage, every member of management becomes involved in the financial planning and control process. The success with which budgeting is carried out can determine the profitability and financial strength of the company.

This stage includes

- the establishment, from planning directives, of departmental requirements and of objectives for all accountable managers;

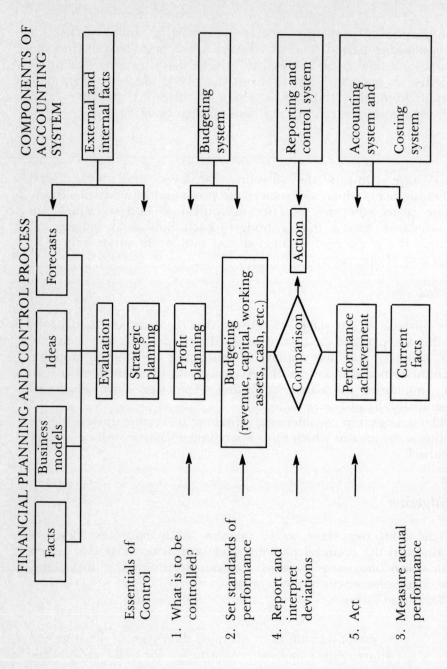

Figure 10.6 The financial planning and control process

- the preparation by each manager of a detailed operating plan for his or her department, which will meet or improve the departmental objective;
- consolidation of all operating plans into a master budget or operating plan, and consolidation with the profit objective;
- the inclusion in the profit plan of a projected profit statement, a balance sheet and a cash flow statement

The principal steps in the setting-up of a budgeting process are detailed below.

Budgeting process

The procedures to set up a budgeting process fall into two categories: the initial steps to set up the system; and the procedures that need to be followed in each budgeting period.

Initial steps

1 *Define the organization structure:* If a formal organization does not exist, then a structure must be set up. It has to be verified that the structure provides for the definition of the limits of financial responsibility and the items for which each manager is responsible.

2 *Establish budget centres:* These are the centres for which separate budgets will be prepared. They will normally be derived from the areas of responsibility as shown in the organization structure, and by the natural divisions of the company.

3 *Establish cost centres:* These are the subdivisions of each budget centre. A separate analysis of cost is required for each cost centre. For example, where the budget centre is the machine shop, the cost centres would be groups of machines or workcentres within that area.

4 *Establish the unit of cost for each cost centre:* In a manufacturing company, parts of the expense budget for production budget centres are derived from budgeted quantities produced at a budgeted price per unit. It is therefore necessary for each cost centre to establish an appropriate unit of cost. This could be man- or machine-hours or actual units of production.

5 *Establish cost conventions:* It will be necessary to establish the cost conventions to be used, so that the most appropriate cost information is collected to service the decisions that have to be made.

6 *Establish resource price and usage standards:* These are necessary in order to establish meaningful raw material and labour budgets. It will require the definition of responsibility for providing these standards and that appropriate authorization procedures are set up.

7 *Establish capital budgeting procedures:* Because capital budgeting is an important part of the budgeting procedure, procedures will need to be set up for the initiation, evaluation and authorization of capital projects.

Period steps

These relate to both the revenue and balance sheet budgets.

1 *Budget–company:* This involves determining the profit objective, as it relates to the profit planning process. From this, the individual departmental objectives can be defined. It is important at this stage to identify the limiting factor and to prepare the volume budget appropriately. For example, a production-limited firm should have this reflected in budgeted volumes.

2 *Departmental budgets – e.g. production division:*
   - *Review and revise performance standards:* The standards need to be reviewed to reflect the changes incorporated into the new operating plan.
   - *Calculate the output from each cost centre:* From the overall production budget a budget of production is calculated for each cost centre. This is converted to output in terms of the cost unit by reference to the standards of usage.
   - *Prepare material budget:* This is derived from the budget volume of production, budgeted usage standards together with standard material prices.
   - *Prepare labour budget:* This is derived from the budget volume of production, operating efficiency standards and the standard wage rates.
   - *Prepare overhead expenses budget:* This is derived from the budget volume of production, standard usage factors and manning schedules.
   - *Calculate standard costs for cost centre units:* These are derived from the budget cost centre output and the budget cost centre expenses to derive the standard 'charge out' rates.
   - *Calculate standard product costs:* The main elements are the standard material costs and the appropriate standard value of cost centre units consumed.

A similar procedure is followed for the appropriate balance sheet items – for example, stock, plant and equipment and so on. The other functional departments will follow the corresponding budgeting procedure for their own functions.

Budgeting climate

In order for organizations to obtain the benefits from the budgeting process, it is vital that top management creates the correct climate or culture.

Corporate culture is sometimes described as 'the way we do things around here', and one pointer to that culture is the attitude taken towards budgeting.

If it is seen as a means of holding down operations and sales managers to targets which are progressively more difficult to attain without reference to the realities of the marketplace, then the whole process loses credibility. It is seen as a chore and leads to long hours of self-justification and excuse-making at the end of the year.

If, however, senior and middle managers take the time to talk through the budget figures, the limiting factors, and the special actions needed to attain the figures, then the process is seen as a realistic basis for managing the business. It becomes the base against which individuals set their own objectives and measure their own performance, and thus the platform which managers can use to devise personal development plans for their staff.

Used correctly, the budgeting process can become a motivational tool. Used incorrectly, the opposite will apply. Because budgeting is as much a behavioural process as a financial control process, the conditions that have to be created in order to achieve success include:

- top management commitment;
- delegation through a management structure;
- accountability for planning and control;
- training.

These are considered individually below.

Top management commitment

The most important single factor in achieving success in the creation and operation of a budgeting process is the commitment of senior management.

One of the main purposes of budgeting is to create, in the whole management team, the attitude of mind that looks for constant improvement in operating performance, by relating management action and decision to their effect on performance. It is a continual process, the benefits of which increase as the attitude of mind develops and as the organization and its managers develop skills in operating the process. If the senior management is seen to be unenthusiastic – particularly in the early stages – there will be little possibility of maintaining the momentum which the continuous process requires.

Delegation

Budgeting is the process by which top management delegates to the management team the responsibility for achieving the company's objectives.

Effective delegation requires that the company define the line of authority from the chief executive to the most junior manager with budget responsibility. It is not possible to institute a budgeting system in the absence of an organization structure defining a line management structure and the items of cost and profit for which each manager is accountable. A meaningful budgeting process cannot be superimposed on an unsound pattern of management responsibilities.

Accountability

Effective delegation requires that managers be accountable for their performance. The bases of this accountability are:

1   the preparation by each manager of an operating plan for their area of responsibility;
2   acceptance by the manager that this operating plan is a standard against which actual performance is to be measured.

The principle of accountability has application both to the preparation of budgets and to subsequent control.

Training

Effective implementation of a budgeting process is facilitated by a training programme designed to suit the needs of the managers involved in the process. It should not just be confined to technical training, but should also include the skills of dealing with people, so reflecting the characteristics of the budgeting process itself.

222

There are obvious links between the budgeting process and management development activity itself. An individual checklist for budgeting activity is set out below:

1 What are the budget areas directly under your control?
2 What are the budget areas outside your control but for which you are held accountable?
3 How do you cope with elements outside your control?
4 Do you understand the objectives and method of the planning and control process?
5 What is your assessment of the control element (accuracy, timing and management climate)?
6 What level of detail do you receive on variance analyses/exception reports, and is it appropriate?
7 What is your involvement in the budget preparation?
8 To what extent do you believe that your performance is assessed and recognized upon achievement of budget objectives?
9 Are you commited to the budgeting process, or is it a chore? If so, what is the reason?
10 What is your budget limiting factor?

Use your answers to compile an improvement plan.

Personal development task no. 10.1

1 Obtain a set of the firm's management accounts and examine how performance is reported.
2 How appropriate are the control measures to the needs of the business?
3 What performance ratios are used in the organization? Are they relevant?

Personal development task no. 10.2

1 Review the budgeting process within the firm.
2 Apply checklist above to see how effective the process is.

Chapter summary points

- All management decisions have a financial effect.
- The basic financial statements are the balance sheet, profit and loss account and cash flow forecast.
- Each statement has a role to play and is compiled according to standard conventions.
- Ratio analysis can be useful to indicate a firm's performance over time.
- The financial planning and control process comprises the following four stages:
    - strategic planning
    - profit planning
    - budgeting
    - control
- Budgeting is as much a behavioural as a financial process.

Essential reading

Buyers, C.I. and Holmes, G.A., *Cost Accountancy,* London: Cassell, 1973.

Sundridge Park Management Centre, *Financial Management Handbook* (not available for general sale).

11 Managing the finances: the impact on operating decisions

Introduction

It has already been stated that a prime motivator of a business is to generate profit. In broad terms,

$$\text{sales revenue} - \text{costs} = \text{profit}$$

Therefore, if we want to know how to generate profits, it is important that we understand how to generate sales revenue and how to control costs. In addition, it is equally important that we comprehend the relationship between sales revenue or volume and costs.

This is where the concept of fixed and variable costs becomes significant, as it allows us to predict the behaviour of costs under varying circumstances. The operations manager is regularly faced with a number of decisions that are impacted by the variability of costs – for example, by changes in product mix through the factory, changes in working practices or by overtime requests, and similar decisions – each of which is affected by the concept of cost variability.

In practice, as volume of activity rises so total costs will rise, but very rarely is it a proportional rise because some costs are fixed and some are variable. An illustration is given by a motor car where the total cost pattern is itself governed by the behaviour of fixed and variable costs. The fixed costs are tax, insurance and depreciation which will be incurred whether the mileage covered is zero or 20,000 miles. The variable costs include fuel, oil and service charges which will generally increase in direct proportion to the mileage. Therefore, when the behaviour of the both cost categories is taken into account, doubling of the mileage will not double the cost; in fact, the total cost per mile falls as the mileage increases.

A similar pattern can be found in many areas of operations. Thus, the first step must be to understand the behaviour of costs that impact on the decision in question, and to do this we need to classify the costs according to their variability relative to output volume.

Fixed and variable costs

These fall into three categories:
1 *Fixed costs* which tend to be unaffected by variations in the volume of output – for example, rent, rates and insurance.
2 *Variable costs* which tend to vary directly with variations in output – for example, direct wages, direct materials.
3 *Semi-variable costs* which are partly fixed and partly variable and, although they will vary with output, do not do so directly – for example, maintenance, cleaning.

Figure 11.1 illustrates the behaviour of the various cost classifications with volume changes. Note that, because every cost is variable in the very long term, the fixed and variable classifications relate to the time horizon for the decision under question. However, the breakdown of costs into these categories underpins several techniques including flexible budgeting, break-even analysis, marginal costing and limiting factor analysis.

Consider the following example, which illustrates the affect of cost variability on profit.

Assume the selling price of an unit is £44, the variable costs per unit are £20 and the fixed costs amount to £21,000 per year. When selling at least 800 units, and not more than 1,200 units, the following would be the profit and loss at three levels of activity:

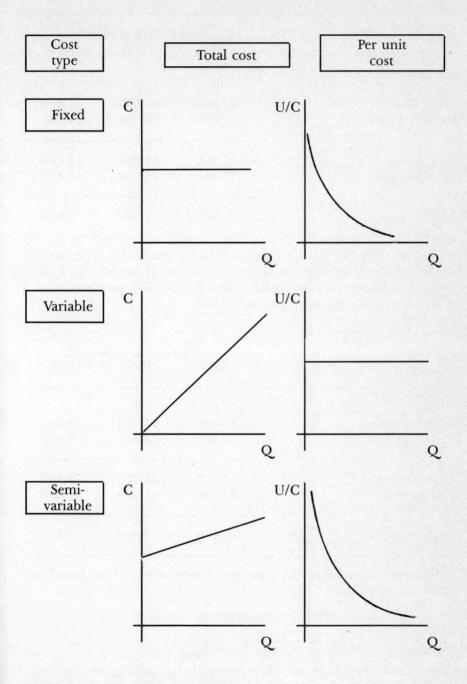

Figure 11.1 Classification of costs

| | Number of units sold | | |
	600	1000	1200
	£	£	£
Fixed Costs	21,000	21,000	21,000
Variable Costs	16,000	20,000	24,000
Total Costs	37,000	41,000	45,000
Sales Revenue	35,200	44,000	52,800
Profit/(Loss)	(1,800)	3,000	7,800

It can be seen that as the volume of sales activity increases so the factory moves from a loss to a profit situation. However, this format is not necessarily the best presentation for analysis purposes, and a more suitable format would be as follows:

| | Number of units sold | | |
	600	1000	1200
	£	£	£
Sales Revenue	35,200	44,000	52,800
Variable Costs	16,000	20,000	24,000
Contribution	19,200	24,000	28,800
Fixed Costs	21,000	21,000	21,000
Profit/(Loss)	(1,800)	3,000	7,800

This format introduces the concept of *contribution,* which is defined by the relationship:

contribution = sales revenue – variable costs

This equation can also be represented by Figure 11.2, where contribution is seen first to be contributing towards fixed costs and then, when they have all been covered, towards profit. In other words, contribution represents the difference between sales and the marginal cost of goods sold.

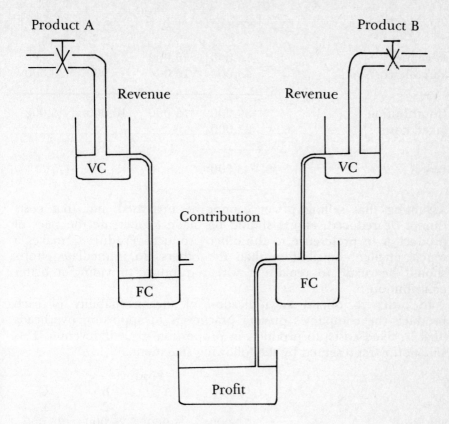

Figure 11.2 The role of contribution

The application of marginal costing depends on the variation of expenses with changes in output. Only variable cost elements are included in product costs (that is variable costs plus the variable element of semi-variable costs). This isolation of variable costs of product from fixed costs provides useful information for decision-making as it allows the effect of changes in volume, price or cost to be readily assessed. The following sections illustrate the concepts applied to a range of business decisions.

Product mix decisions

A factory makes three products each generating the same revenue. The situation is represented by the following financial statement:

		Products		
	Total	A	B	C
	£	£	£	£
Revenue	75,000	25,000	25,000	25,000
Variable costs	45,000	10,000	15,000	20,000
Contribution	30,000	15,000	10,000	5,000
Fixed costs	27,000			
Profit	3,000			

Assuming that selling prices cannot be increased and that costs cannot be reduced, efforts should be made to increase the sales of product A in preference to the other products. Product C makes a much smaller contribution than the others, so immediate efforts should be made to replace it with a product providing a better contribution.

In order to obtain an indication of the profitability of each product, the company's present practice is to apportion overheads (that is, fixed costs) to products in proportion to their revenue. This situation is represented by the following statement:

		Products		
	Total	A	B	C
	£	£	£	£
Revenue	75,000	25,000	25,000	25,000
Variable costs	45,000	10,000	15,000	20,000
Contribution	30,000	15,000	10,000	5,000
Fixed costs	27,000	9,000	9,000	9,000
Profit	3,000	6,000	1,000	(4,000)

This illustrates the comments made earlier where product C is seen to be a lossmaking product. Note that this assumes that the apportionment of fixed costs on the basis of sales revenue is equitable.

Since product C is lossmaking, the company have decided to examine the effects of omitting it from the range:

	Total	Products A	B	C
	£	£	£	£
Revenue	50,000	25,000	25,000	0
Variable costs	25,000	10,000	15,000	0
Contribution	25,000	15,000	10,000	0
Fixed costs	27,000	13,500	13,500	0
Profit	(2,000)	1,500	(3,500)	0

The effect of the decision to remove the lossmaking product has been to translate the factory performance from a profit of £3,000 to a loss of £2,000! This example illustrates how total or absorption costing can lead you to make inappropriate decisions. Although when looking at all costs and apportioning them to product, product C was lossmaking, it nevertheless was making a contribution of £5,000 towards fixed costs (refer to the previous example). Therefore, by eliminating that product from the range, the factory eliminated that contribution towards fixed costs and was effectively £5,000 worse off, so translating a profit of £2,000 into a loss of £3,000.

Note that it is assumed that the fixed costs would be unaltered by the decision to drop a product and also that the turnover of the profitable products could not be increased.

Pricing decisions

In practice, a change in price is likely to lead to a change in volume. In this case, the optimum selling price for a product is that which yields maximum contribution (unit price × volume − variable costs). This could also be defined as the price at which additional revenue per unit is equal to the average variable cost per unit.

It should be emphasized that the practical application of the concept of optimum pricing depends on the availability of reliable assessments of:

- the market demand for the product – that is, the probable volumes of sales at different prices;
- the average variable cost for the range of the probable volumes of sales.

In addition, although this method yields the optimum price in the prevailing or expected market conditions, it does not follow that the optimum price is an acceptable price. For example, it may not be sufficient to cover specific fixed costs and so on.

Limiting factor decisions

There is always a limit to the ability of a business to make or sell its products. Examples include:

- bottleneck processes in the production flow;
- lack of skilled labour;
- funds or cash resources;
- sales potential;
- raw material shortages;
- floor space;
- management time.

At a particular point in time one of these items will limit the volume of the factory's output. It represents the *limiting factor* for production.

It is important that the financial impact of the limiting factor is recognized in decision-making. This is done by expressing the contribution as an amount of money per unit of limiting factor, or as a percentage of the limiting factor. The following example relates to a bottleneck process.

The following information is known about three products relative to £100 of sales in each case.

	X	Y	Z
Hours required on bottleneck process	1.0	1.5	2.0
	£	£	£
Direct Materials	50	70	10
Direct Labour	10	5	20
Variable Overheads	15	10	30
Total Variable Costs	75	85	60
Selling Price	100	100	100
Contribution	25	15	40

When the number of hours available at the bottleneck process is a constraint, it can therefore affect the choice between products, and so it is necessary to calculate the contribution per hour on the bottleneck process:

For product X   £25 contribution per hour
                       on the bottleneck process
For product Y   £10 contribution per hour
                       on the bottleneck process
For product Z   £20 contribution per hour
                       on the bottleneck process

On this basis, where the limiting factor has to be taken into consideration, X becomes the most important product as it makes the greatest contribution per hour of limiting factor.

Where, however, the capacity of the bottleneck process is considerably in excess of production requirements, then Z is the most important product as it makes the greatest contribution per unit of sales.

This approach has great relevance when we use the techniques of bottleneck management to maximize factory contribution.

Break-even point decisions

The techniques of break-even analysis are a useful way of demonstrating the profitability or loss of operating at various levels of output. They underpin the principles used in flexible budgeting, and can indicate the activity level that corresponds to the break-even point – that is, where there is neither profit nor loss. A convenient way to express the relationships is on a break-even chart. Consider the following example.

The company has the following information available:

		£
	Unit selling price	44
	Unit variable cost	20
Therefore,	Unit contribution	24
	Fixed Costs	21,000

The procedure is to construct a graph to illustrate the cost and revenue relationship with volume of activity. The vertical axis shows revenue and costs; the horizontal axis reflects the volume of activity in units. The graph is shown in Figure 11.3.

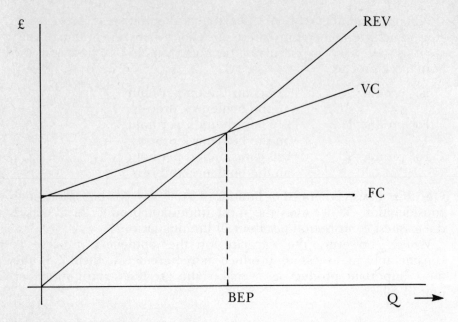

Figure 11.3 Break-even chart

The fixed cost line represents the level of fixed costs, and, as expected, it is horizontal at a value of £21,000. The total cost line represents the sum of the fixed and variable cost elements. This is obtained by plotting convenient points on the graph. The revenue line represents the total revenue from sales at differing volumes.

The break-even point occurs where the total cost line crosses the revenue line – that is, where costs equal revenue – and it is at this level of activity that the business breaks even. If sales are below this level there will be a loss, and if they are above this level there will be a profit.

The break-even point (in this case 875 units) is the point at which total contribution equals the fixed costs, and may be computed from the formula:

$$\text{break-even point} = \frac{\text{fixed costs}}{\text{contribution per unit}}$$

An alternative way of representing this information is through the profit chart illustrated in Figure 11.4. Again, it can be seen that the break-even point is where the graph cuts the volume axis at 875 units.

The relative relationship of fixed and variable costs can be an indicator of the inherent *riskiness of the business.*

If a business is characterized by a high fixed cost element with relatively low variable costs, then quite small volume movements about the break-even point can have quite large effects on profitability and can turn a profitable situation into a lossmaking one. If the business is operating around this point, then its financial performance could be quite volatile. Conversely, a business with a low fixed cost element and relatively high variable costs will experience less marked performance changes around the breakeven point.

With regard to all these areas of decision-making, it should always be remembered that the operations manager's role is to make improvements to operations and hence to business performance.

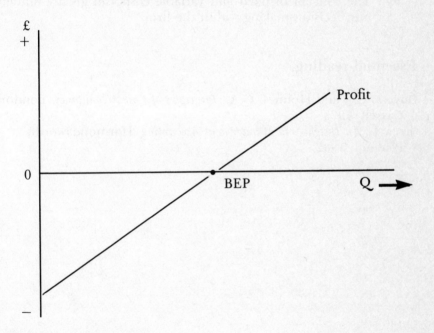

Figure 11.4   Profit chart

Personal development task no. 11

1   Re-examine the decisions that you take in the light of a contribution-based approach.

2   In particular, concentrate on decisions that involve
    -   product mix;
    -   pricing;
    -   limiting factor;
    -   break-even analysis.
3   What improvements can you effect with regard to this type of
    decision-making?

Chapter summary points

-   To understand the profitability of the firm we need to understand the relationship between costs and volume.
-   Contribution equals sales revenue less variable costs.
-   The concept of fixed and variable costs can greatly influence our decision-making within the firm.

Essential reading

Buyers, C.I. and Holmes, G.A., *Principles of Cost Accountancy,* London: Cassell, 1973.
Sizer, J., *An Insight into Management Accounting,* Harmondsworth: Penguin, 1982.

Part IV

MANAGING PEOPLE: IMPLEMENTING THE CHANGES

Introduction

If Part III were to be described as knowing the extent of your job and organizing yourself, then this Part is concerned with understanding your colleagues and organizing them for best performance, both individually and collectively. This bald statement suggests a somewhat cold, practical approach to work organization, but that is far from the truth. This part examines how people behave, both as individuals and in groups. It does this with particular reference to the requirements of operations units, looking for the issues in human behaviour which arise in that environment.

This term of reference dictates the approach taken in each chapter, although the principles expounded are universal to work groups. So we start with personality in Chapter 12. Here we make no attempt to explore the depths of personality, leaving that to specialist works, but list a number of questions about how individuals who work in operations are likely to behave. Then a selection of relevant personality profiles and tests are described, showing where each might be applied.

Chapter 13 deals with motivation, outlining four major factors which lead to motivation in modern working circumstances. These factors provide a context for the whole of management, not simply the manager concerned.

One major managing tool for the operations manager is the meeting. Chapter 14 spends some time exploring various types of meetings common to operations management and asking questions about relevance, organization and membership. This chapter also examines the role of team leader and meetings chairman.

Finally we deal with the relationships that groups, functions or departments have with each other. In operations there are great pressures for conflict, together with a continual need for wise decision-making and foresight to prevent clashes or misunderstandings. This area is well researched and documented, so we refer to the relevant literature, provide case studies from real-life situations and suggest ways to investigate and defuse problems.

In summary, Part IV is concerned with the way in which people behave, both as individuals and in their relationships with other people and other groups.

12 Managing the individual: the impact of personality on motivation

The background to personality

Open any basic text on psychology and look at the chapters on personality. You will find several. You will discover that personality is a wide-ranging subject, linked by some people to intelligence, by others to heredity. You will be told that it is also associated with the physical functions of the brain and body. If you require an all-embracing theory which will predict job-effectiveness then you will be disappointed. This leaves you to consider what use would be a study of personality to the operations manager. To lay out the various theories in detail would provide an absorbing exercise in academic argument and counter-argument. However, our purpose is to provide the operations manager with knowledge and techniques which will lead to a better understanding of how people are likely to behave in the operations situation. One way to focus this requirement is to ask the kind of questions which the operations manager might ask of himself, when seeking advice.

- What is my personality?
- What characteristics should I be aware of?
- How do I differ from my colleagues?
- What aspects of my personality are likely to cause me problems?
- Can I change my personality?

- Can I improve those areas in which I am deficient?
- How do I deal with the differences in attitude and behaviour which I have between my work and my home life?

Before starting to provide answers to such highly focused questions, we need to establish some basic features of personality and then choose the particular approaches which will aid our search for answers.

Problems of definition

Following the arguments of Buchanan and Huczynski,[1] personality concerns attributes of the individual which are both stable and distinctive. Therefore, as they argue, we have to accept that human behaviour does have lasting characteristics and that the distinctive attributes can be measured. This is the beginning of a definition and will allow us to examine those stable attributes. It will also give us a way of measuring them and thus allow us to compare ourselves with other people. However, there are many snares awaiting us, not least the scope of the subject. Do we include intelligence in the definition and is intelligence hereditary? Do we include physical qualities? Psychologists will frame their definition according to how many of these factors they wish to include and, consequently, there are several schools of thought, with many possible definitions.

Reminding ourselves of our aim to examine the way that people are likely to behave in certain circumstances, we should concentrate on those work situations which are directly concerned with operations. Although this has certain definite advantages, it does attract the criticism that we are side-stepping some of the basic issues of personality. But our rationale for this approach lies solely in our objectives, which do not include a wide-ranging survey of the research work on basic personality.

Let us now return to the questions which the operations manager must ponder when looking to his strategy with individuals and groups. While the deep-rooted aspects of personality will always influence behaviour, we all react to the environment in which we find ourselves. Our behaviour is not independent of environmental influence. So if we can devise a series of vehicles which will allow each individual to examine how he or she behaves in their work situations, we might not arrive at a comprehensive theory of personality, but we would achieve a useful result for the operations manager. A good way to move forward would then be to examine some of the many tests and profiles which are now available to the manager and which form the basis of a number of assessment and development programmes for managers.

Psychometrics: personality tests and profiles

Personality testing by questionnaire raises several important questions.

How easy is it to cheat?

In some cases, it is easy and the question raises the way in which the questionnaire is devised and introduced. For recruitment purposes, it would be essential to use a system which signals wrong answers quickly. Reputable recruiters will use such tests or profiles as a means of screening and of providing a starting-point for in-depth interviews. Professional counsellors will use tests which help them to advise managers, rather than assess them. In these circumstances the issue of cheating becomes one of 'self-delusion' rather than the gaining of an unfair advantage. It is not easy to answer a questionnaire really truthfully, however honest one's attentions. It does take a little practice to answer what one would really do, or how one would really behave. Therefore it is advisable to start with one or two simple indicator questionnaires before introducing the major instrument.

Exactly what is the instrument testing?

This is for the tester to consider very carefully. It is quite possible to confuse deep-rooted aspects of personality with our changing attitudes and reactions to the outside world. Questionnaires are quite capable of exploring either issue, but having done so it is essential to make clear the distinction between them. Whether we are introvert or extrovert must be seen to be far more fundamental than how we see a particular work situation at this point in time.

Will the test tell me the personality needed for my job?

No! This question shows a basic misunderstanding of what adds up to effective performance. While some practitioners look for particular traits, and infer that when added together they make up the right personality for one job, that inference is a dangerous oversimplification. What makes a 'good' operations manager is extremely difficult to define in any comprehensive way. Some traits will be very useful on one day, and yet cause all sorts of problems when the situation changes. However, tests and profiles will help to give us a picture of how we are at this point in time and how likely we are to be able to carry out the responsibilities entrusted to us. Heavily qualified this may be, but it still leaves us with some useful initiatives with which to move towards our objective for the operations manager.

How do I get hold of these tests?

Fortunately, the more important profiles and tests are safeguarded against indiscriminate use. While most of them are easy to administer, it is essential that they be interpreted by people trained and qualified to do so. Consequently, most of them are held by those who designed them, or their assignees. Many organizations use such tests, either through the proprietors, or by having members of their own staff properly trained to use them.

Some personality tests and profiles

The PA Perception and Preference Inventory (PAPI)

The Perception and Preference Inventory of PA International Management Consultants focuses on a set of 10 needs and a set of 10 roles, with particular reference to the work setting. In this respect, it covers more areas of preference than most other profiles. It correlates well with several other instruments for some of its needs and roles. A survey of industrial executives and managers suggested that there were seven areas in which a work-style inventory should yield information. They are as follows:

1 work direction,
2 work style,
3 activity,
4 leadership,
5 followership,
6 social nature,
7 temperament.

Various needs and roles are located under each area.

The PAPI is self-administered and self-scored. It consists of a set of 90 forced-choice questions, so that each role or need has nine chances of being preferred. Candidates make their choices for the work situation. Each choice must be made quickly and each question must be dealt with separately and without reference to any others. When the profile has been scored it is transferred to a circular chart in order to make it more visually understandable.

While the reproduceability of the profile is high, there will usually be one or two noticeable changes when the candidate moves to a different kind of job. The PAPI is used in recruitment for interviewing job applicants, in other in-depth interviews, and for counselling. it is important to remember that this instrument is a Perception and Preference Indicator, showing a person's preferences in terms of needs and roles, in the work situation, at that particular point in time. It also demonstrates the perception that the person has of himself or herself. So it gives users the opportunity to analyse the attitudes and values by which people relate to the work situation and to the requirements of their jobs.

The Myers Briggs Type Indicator

The Myers Briggs Type Indicator was designed explicitly to make it possible to test Jung's theory of psychological types and to put it to practical use. It was developed by Katherine Briggs and her daughter Isobel Briggs Myers and painstakingly researched over many years. The questions used were carefully developed, then refined or changed wherever statistical examination left doubts about their credibility. Very large numbers of Americans of all professional and managerial categories have completed the instrument, providing a comprehensive background of information about psychological typing and the different professions. Other nationalities, particularly the Japanese, have used the profile extensively, and a body of knowledge is being built up for British managers. Type theory suggests that every person belongs to one particular psychological type. The factors governing the choice of type are as follows:

First, all people are either perceiving or judging in their attitudes to their surroundings. Then two processes, sensing or intuition describe how they perceive and two more, thinking or feeling, describe how they judge. As well as these attitudes and processes, everybody has an attitude towards the outside world. They are either extroverted, that is outwardly-oriented, or introverted, by which they draw their energy in from the environment. The combination of J or

P with two of the processes and the influence of intraversion or extraversion, a total of four letters, denotes a psychological type, the possible combinations being sixteen. Table 12.1 shows the relationship between the four processes and the attitudes.

Table 12.1
The type indicator

JUDGING by THINKING or FEELING	PERCEIVING by SENSING or INTUITION (processes)
INTROVERSION	EXTROVERSION

Obviously each psychological type has a set of characteristics specific to itself, and people within these types will generally exhibit the relevant ones. Hence, the profile finds its usefulness in interviewing, particularly for recruiting, where the very large body of knowledge will help to suggest the typing exhibited by the majority of successful practitioners in any one profession. There is also the 'know thyself' aspect of the instrument, where a calm, dispassionate reassessment of one's life and career is greatly aided by such information.

The Myers Briggs Type Indicator takes the form of a questionnaire, and requires about 20 minutes to complete. It is marked in a few minutes with the help of a series of templates, giving the psychological type, with a score against each of the four letters. There is then a detailed description of each type, together with an interpretation by the expert who administered the instrument.

The occupational personality questionnaires (OPQ)

Since most personality questionnaires owe their origins, if not to clinical work then certainly to academic research, they have not been particularly suitable for assessing personality in an occupational context. It is not simply that they do not give enough emphasis to those aspects of personality in which personnel practitioners are interested, but also that the actual questions lack any occupational relevance. In view of this, the occupational psychology consultancy Saville & Holdsworth Ltd, developed a new series of work-oriented personality questionnaires, (OPQs), in the early 1980s.

With the sponsorship of over 50 major UK organizations, in manufacturing, banking, retail, finance, transport, service and government, Saville & Holdsworth carried out a research programme to identify those personality characteristics which are relevant to the work environment. Table 12.2 describes this model of personality. Clinical terms or obscure psychological constructs have been avoided in the interests of clarity.

Table 12.2
Personality dimensions measured by the concept model

Relationships with People	Thinking Style	Feelings & Emotions
1. Persuasive	Practical	Relaxed
2. Controlling	Data rational	Worrying
3. Independent	Artistic	Tough-minded
4. Outgoing	Behavioural	Emotional control
5. Affiliative	Traditional	Optimistic
6. Socially confident	Change-oriented	Critical
7. Modest	Conceptual	Active
8. Democratic	Innovative	Competitive
9. Caring	Forward-planning	Achieving
10.	Detail-conscious	Decisive
11.	Conscientious	

Following development work, four levels of questionnaires were constructed:

1 A 30-scale version (concept model);
2 A 15-scale version (factor model);
3 An 8-scale model (octagon model);
4 A 5-scale model (pentagon model).

This means that users of the OPQ have considerable choice in deciding which is the most appropriate questionnaire to use in any particular situation.

Since the introduction of OPQ it has been used with a variety of managerial, technical, sales and clerical populations, and with publicans, air traffic controllers and exchange dealers. The OPQ has also been used in selection, where in combination with the interview, it is used to identify the strengths and weaknesses of job applicants. Other applications include counselling and management development.

The relationship between OPQ and team behaviour, and behaviour in a leader/subordinate situation has shown the ability to predict likely team roles from OPQ. So an important link with the work of R.M. Belbin on team development is established.

(This summary of OPQ is reproduced by permission of Saville and Holdsworth Ltd, 81 High St., Esher, Surrey, KT10 9QA.)

The LIFO method

LIFO stands for 'Life Orientations', a theory developed and applied in a registered training programme and tested by Allan Katcher International, Inc., Van Nuys, California. This theory is based on the assumption that each of us has certain orientations to the world and to our particular environment, and also that we communicate and behave according to what we perceive as our preferred way, using our own combination of orientations.

LIFO theory distinguishes four orientations:

1   supporting/giving
2   controlling/taking
3   conserving/holding
4   adapting/dealing

The combination of orientations for any individual can be ascertained by a standardized and validated questionnaire. The results show which orientations are preferred most and least, when dealing with:

1   routine;
2   conflict
3   stress situations.

Many years of research have shown that a close relationship exists between a person's strengths and weaknesses. Strong points in a character will become weaknesses under excessive use. Someone who is strong on cooperation may at times follow others too easily. Those who excel in analysis may become indecisive during difficult situations requiring immediate action. Self-confidence can become arrogance.

The core of the method is to create increased recognition and insight into our strengths as a basis for using them productively, while avoiding their excessive use (strength management).

Questionnaires and workbooks are available for:

- basic styles
- learning styles
- styles of another person
- selling styles
- organization culture (actual and desired)

One of the most important characteristics of the LIFO method is that it does not suggest that there is only one good style of behaviour. Each preferred orientation is valuable. There is only a question of difference, not of inequality. Through the LIFO method everyone retains his/her own set of values. There is no threat of being criticized or ridiculed for 'what one is'. The LIFO method emphasizes strategies for maximizing the productive use of different styles.

A second essential characteristic is the direct link that can be made between one's function, task, work situation, work problems and cooperation with colleagues and supervisors. This means that the switch to organizational change, distribution of tasks in working and decision-making procedures can be made quickly and effectively.

LIFO applications therefore do not imply a forced way of changing people. On the contrary, the application concentrates on improving the efficiency and effectiveness of the organization. The sole use of the LIFO method for training purposes as an individual learning process is therefore a restricted application.

Applications of LIFO — The theory has found application in North America, Europe, and the Far East, with examples as follows:

1 Development of leadership style.
2 Analysis of organization culture.
3 Management of conflict within organizations.
4 Reducing tensions between departments.
5 Improving communications in teams.
6 Composition of management teams.
7 Improving hierarchical relations.
8 Selection of new employees.
9 Development of selling styles.
10 Solving role conflicts.
11 Matching people to tasks.

(This summary of the LIFO method is reproduced by permission of Personnel Assessment & Communication Training Ltd., 8th Floor, Columbia House, 69 Aldwych, London WC2B 4DX, England.)

Summary

We have summarized four personality profiles or tests, each one with different aims, each one addressing different levels and areas of personality. The PA Perception and Preference Inventory examines the open end of personality and has the advantage that it may be targeted directly at the work situation. It also shows our preferences at that point in time. Reproduceability is good, but nonetheless a change in job will be reflected in changing values in one or two of the needs and roles.

The OPQ questionnaires are also based on occupationally-oriented questions and are useful in predicting team roles. They give a useful set of headings under the dimension of Feelings and Emotions. Again, LIFO addresses the usefulness of our orientations to life, how we approach the world. This helps us to understand how people are likely to react to situations in their jobs, so creating a link between people, task, work situation and colleagues. The Myers Briggs Type Indicator is a method for determining psychological type and in that sense is not solely work-oriented. It does give a more basic picture of personality and is able to show the predominant psychological types found in any career category.

For any given area of work, the operations manager should be able to find, with the help of the experts, a suitable vehicle for examining individual behaviour in that area. An undertanding of why people behave in certain ways is a big step towards managing and developing them wisely and of achieving the very best commercial results from their efforts.

Personal development task no. 12

A personal questionnaire

1 Do you thoroughly enjoy your job, to the extent that you look forward to each new day for the interests that the job will bring? If so, then what attributes do you show that help you to enjoy success in your job?

2 Are there any areas where you feel that you have difficulty dealing with other people as individuals? Can you define them? What can you do about them?

3 Do you have any subordinates who cannot work with each other? Can you pinpoint the reasons? How would you counsel each of them?

4   Are you a risk-taker? What influence does it have on your decision-making?

All these questions point towards attitudes and practices which stem from personality and from personal development. Are you quite clear about all your own attitudes, your needs, your relationships and the way of working which results from them?

Chapter summary points

- Human behaviour does have lasting characteristics.
- Behaviour also depends on working environment.
- Instruments are available to type people.
- Other instruments show preferences at a given time and for a given job.
- A knowledge of the reasons for particular behaviour help the operations manager to lead wisely.

Reference

1   Buchanan, D.A. and Huczynski, A.A., *Organizational Behaviour,* Englewood Cliffs, NJ: Prentice Hall Int., 1985

Essential reading

Briggs Myers, Isobel, *Gifts Differing,* Consulting Psychologists Press, Inc, 1980. This book is about human personality, and might help to find a rationale for some of the personality differences which we all encounter. For the operations manager this may perhaps lead to a more rational reaction to the unexpected ways in which people sometimes behave.

13 Managing the individual: motivation and the impact of leadership style

Introduction

One of the more encouraging features of recent management writing is the realization that motivation is not a simple subject. This is reflected in the sophistication of some of the theories on offer. No longer do we rely on Herzberg[1] and Maslow[2] for solutions which, although simple and appealing, are unable to point out strategies for managers which really work. Academics are exploring many different, but complementary, factors in the attainment of motivated staff. Most of the theories are complex, but it is possible to extract the essence of them in such a way that managers are given pointers for more effective action.

What is motivation?

One way to put together a set of strategies for the operations manager is to concentrate on four factors which are important, to varying degrees, in providing or producing motivation. First, however, we must examine the meaning of motivation. It is when people are eager to, or want to, do their job. How this state of mind arises is of continuing concern to operations managers. Whilst all staff contribute to company success, it is the operations staff who ensure product quality and output standards, often against a background of difficulty or danger. A well-motivated staff will look for improvements, where others would at best maintain the status quo.

The four factors

When a person goes to work, his or her behaviour will stem from either internal capacities, from which attitudes and feelings towards the work will arise, or from external influences such as the culture, the leadership, and the reward/punishment system. The first two of our factors concern internal capacities, while each of the remainder take their origin from external influences brought to bear on the person.

First factor. Motivation occurs when the employee recognizes a link between effort, performance and rewards. (Expectancy Theory)

Second factor. The wants and expectations which the employee brings to the workplace.

Third factor. The ability to obtain and agree work objectives. (Goal Theory)

Fourth factor. How the boss leads. (Leadership Style)

There is perhaps a fifth factor which is often associated with motivation theories, though not strictly part of motivation. This is what the organization, the culture and the management suggest should be the right way (behaviour modification). We will deal with this one later.

If we now look at the four factors again, we find that their lessons for, and requirements of, operations managers are much wider-based than classical theories suggest. We have gone beyond 'How does the operations manager get his staff to work well?' (that is, motivate them); we are now looking at a set of conditions which take in:

1   the whole reward system of the company, in its widest sense;
2   the background and culture which lead to accountability and objectives for all staff;
3   the frame of mind of the person when he or she takes the job;
4   the ability of the operations manager to recognize these factors and to lead individuals and groups according to their quite different requirements.

Now we will examine each of these factors in turn.

First factor

This deals with the link between effort, performance and reward. The basis of Expectancy Theory is that when the employee sees a link between effort, performance and reward, he or she will then be motivated to make that effort. The evidence is that it does work that way. The trick is to be able to define jobs (roles) which allow the job-holder to influence results by his or her efforts – but herein lies the problem. So many employees operate as contributing parts of a whole process and the result is a combination of all their efforts. If employees can be shown that individual performance will get them the results they value then they will make the effort.

The implications for the operations manager are:

1 Find a way to split work into parcels, or specialisms, so that the actions of individuals (or very small groups) can be seen to affect the results. Team or blanket pay awards or bonuses do not motivate.

2 Ensure that each person has the ability to carry out the job properly, the skills required, and the decision-making expertise and knowledge. All workers need the assistance of their managers in helping them to learn the job. The manager will need to explore the way that the subordinate sees the job situation, to ensure that he or she goes about planning and executing the tasks required. Unfortunately, it becomes a very time-consuming occupation for the operations manager. The Japanese are very good at it. There is nothing new in ensuring that each person has the expertise, the training, the skills to do the job. What is *not* so often done is to spare the time to explore how job-holders see their freedom of choice, the decisions they can take and whether these perceptions in fact agree with what the manager intends. This is carried out instinctively by the good operations manager, but it needs to be a systematic process of finding out exactly what are the job-holders' goals and values, whether they be managers themselves, supervisors, technologists, line workers or unskilled labourers.

3 Staff must able to see exactly what rewards will result from what performance, that when someone receives rewards everybody else knows why and for what scale of performance it was given. People want to be able to affect results by their own decisions, but they will not be motivated if they have no control over what is happening.

Second factor

This concerns the wants and expectations of work which people bring with them. They will look for certain rewards in particular ways, quite apart from the nature of the work. It may be that people look upon the job as a means of earning money in order to achieve other goals, but there are many others who prefer working in the open air. There are many different orientations, including working conditions and pay.

Some of these orientations are, naturally enough, similar to those identified by Herzberg[3], but in quite different circumstances. They do, however, point the way towards managerial actions which are not usually associated with motivation. If people have different orientations when should we find out what they are? Surely the place and time to do this is at recruitment. So, for operations managers, the key must be to insist that all staff are given adequate tests and profiles before being employed. Japanese plants in the UK screen all applicants for operating jobs.

Now consider the following case studies, each of which is factual, although the jobs described are in different parts of the world.

Case 1: Bola Bola is African. Bola is fortunate, he has a job at a sugar refinery. Sugar cane is brought in, crushed and the resultant liquors treated in various ways before ending up as the sugar we use as a sweetener and in cooking. Very large tanks are involved in the processes, they may be as deep as 30 to 40 ft. With extensive use they become coated in slime, with a residue of sludge in the base, so they need to be emptied and cleaned. Bola and other workers are lowered into the tanks with cleaning implements. The job is very wet, very smelly and dangerous and the inside temperature is well over $30°C$. Bola and his colleagues are seen having the lowest status in the whole workforce.

Case 2: John John works for one of the high street banks in a provincial city in England. His job is to sort cheques – thousands and thousands of cheques. He works in a saferoom in the basement of his branch of the bank. There are no windows in that saferoom. John works alone, he works to time deadlines in order to keep up with the work. There is no end to the work, it is a continuous process, but it is vital to the continuing efficiency of the bank. John is a young man and has been doing this job for nine months.

Case 3: Hans Hans works as a sandblaster in an engineering factory. He wears very heavy protective clothing, a full face mask, heavy boots and thick protective gloves. His place of work is a fully enclosed booth, where he sandblasts components. The noise level is very high, so he must wear ear protectors, and the temperature is also high. The work is vital to product quality, while at the same time he is a critical element in the output of a group of workers, because his work governs the pace of that group. Hans is well paid, he and his colleagues enjoy a high standing among the workforce.

Case 4: Angus Angus is one of the hundreds of people who fit out ships after the hull has been completed. One particular job is the smoothing of jagged metal with a power tool after sections of the ship have been fitted together. Among the requirements of the job is the need to clean out and smooth a channel well over one hundred feet long. This channel must be accessible, so it is important to clean it out properly. It is of triangular section with 2ft sides, so the only way out is straight on or backwards. Angus is not a young man and the job is physically very demanding. It is claustrophobic and, if not carried out with considerable care, can be dangerous. He has now held the job for eight years.

Most operations managers would be unhappy about having such jobs under their responsibility. Yet most operations units do have unpleasant jobs, boring jobs, or dangerous jobs, and some people do stay in them. The questions which then require consideration are:

1 Why do people do them and stay in them?
2 What can be done about such jobs from a humanitarian viewpoint?
3 What can be done to improve the motivation of the job-holders?

First, there will be many reasons why people stay in them, from the need for money to job shortages or a preference for isolation. It would be a mistake to assume that, because the manager would hate it, then the worker must hate it also. Second, when recruiting for such jobs, it would be better to use psychological profiling to narrow down the field of applicants, rather than endure high labour turnover in the hope that someone will stick. What can be done about the jobs themselves is taken up when dealing with the later factors, which follow below.

Third factor

This is the ability to obtain and agree work objectives (Goal Theory). As we do not intend to repeat the detailed treatment of objective-setting given later in Chapter 17, perhaps the best way to view this factor is to ask the question, 'If a person doesn't know what he or she is supposed to be doing, then how on earth do you motivate them?' People at all levels need goals, something to aim at, a sense of purpose in their work. If they do not have such a sense of purpose they will seek it elsewhere, in outside interests or workplace pressure groups. The ability to obtain objectives is part of the factor, but it also includes an element of agreement, the striking of a bargain with the boss. The evidence (Latham and Locke[6]) strongly supports the idea that people who have attainable but stretching work objectives are well-motivated. However, there are a number of important requirements and conditions which the operations manager must watch carefully:

1 The objectives must be discussed, clarified and agreed, even if the worker does not set them in the first place.
2 The objectives must be capable of quantification, even if a secondary measure of performance is required.
3 After the event there must be open discussion of performance.
4 During the performance of the work, managers must concentrate on providing resources, easing the way, helping technically, giving support to ensure that the objectives are actually attained. Management by Objectives failed principally because, in practice, there was a twelve-month communication gap between objective-setting and accounting for results.

Fourth factor

This external factor addresses leadership style, or how the boss leads. The basic tenet is that motivation is not entirely internal to the individual, or an abstract concept, but that individuals react to external stimuli. It may well be that their reactions are affected by internal or personal needs and desires, but nevertheless it is possible for managers, as leaders, to increase or improve the motivation of their subordinates. This improvement may be the result of management policies, which set the standards by which the company judges performance. It could alternatively be the result of leadership skills shown by individual managers. Either of these initiatives could have a profound effect on motivation, for good or bad. Insensitive discipline procedures, badly thought-out pay systems, inconsistent treatment of different groups, indifference to operations staff by senior management can have disastrous effects on motivation, however hard an individual operations manager works for his team. But what does the operations manager need to do?

Leadership skills for the operations manager

Leadership and the operations manager

All leaders have pressures to face, but the scale and intensity of those pressures vary enormously, as do the variety. In operations they are concerned with:

1 protecting the cohesiveness of the group;
2 acting as a shield against outside disruptive forces;
3 producing on time, with high quality at low cost;
4 changing quickly the style and pattern of production;
5 the need to choose between conflicting demands;
6 the need to keep morale at a high level;
7 the need to coordinate the work of each operations activity with other vital functions in the company.

But how do good leaders achieve all this? How do they resist the pressures, be seen to deal with them for the good of the unit or team, yet at the same time hold the confidence of senior managers as well as their own staff?

The classical approach to leadership was to look for qualities which would define and identify that person, qualities like integrity, wisdom, patience and self-confidence. The suggestion was that leaders are born and that only those already possessing the right qualities would succeed. What proved to be very difficult was to define which were the required qualities and how to identify them in particular people.

Leadership tasks

The operations manager does not always have the time or the ability to do all this, so there is the need for a different approach. This is to look at the tasks which the leader must complete in order to succeed, then to examine the skills required to carry out these tasks. Consider, for example, the shopfloor worker, promoted from amongst his or her mates, or the secretary/typist placed in charge of the friends he or she previously worked with. This person is unlikely to be impressed with a list of qualities, but will probably be saying

'Look, guvnor, I don't know what half these words mean. Just tell me what I've got to do now I'm section leader for the packing bay.'

This is really a cry for help and the manager needs to have some good advice available and be ready to carry out extensive coaching with the new section leader. Between them, they require a structure with which to work, so that the emerging leader can plan his or her own development, practising the skills required for the completion of each leadership task.

One comprehensive structure of this kind was developed at Sundridge Park Management Centre. It gathers together leadership tasks under the four headings of Direction, Motivation, Representation and Development. Each heading lists the essential tasks required, together with the relevant skills, so that the whole structure forms the basis of a comprehensive coaching programme. The first step would be to use the document, shown in Table 13.1, as a diagnostic instrument, assessing the deficiencies in skills. When this is completed, the manager and subordinate work out a programme of skills training sessions. Finally the coaching meetings which all good managers would be running anyway, serve to gather together the skills and give them relevance in the work situation. This results in better motivation, and a noticeable gain in self-confidence by the new leader. It is time-consuming, it is tedious. There will be heavy pressure to postpone meetings for other, apparently more urgent, tasks. A measure of the good operations manager is the ability to resist those pressures and to imbue the coaching sessions with a sense of importance.

Issues for the operations manager

The operations manager has many issues to think about here. It is essential to be able to define the required behaviour accurately and this means having exact knowledge of the circumstances. It is not so easy when the job varies unpredictably and the behaviour required demands judgemental decisions. In these situations we come back to the need for all staff to be fully aware of the background situation in which they have to make decisions. They need to know in detail the limits of their decision-making freedom, so that they are more likely to make the same decision as the boss would in any given set of circumstances.

So the operations manager must be a talker, a communicator, at all levels. Long hours will be spent discussing problems with staff and they will get to know the personality, the temperament and the self-confidence of the boss. Only in this way will they really begin to work as a team.

Table 13.1
Summary of leadership activities

Task	Skills
Direction	
Setting objectives	Summing up the position Making sound and prompt decisions
Eliminating uncertainty	Ensuring that the objective is understood Answering questions Clarifying misunderstandings
Initiating action	Planning and organizing the task Issuing clear instructions Ensuring that individuals know their task Using specialist skills and knowledge in the group
Controlling the group	Coordinating activities Evaluating results Taking corrective action as required
Motivation	
Motivating towards task achievement	Getting commitment to overall objectives and plans Ensuring that all group members feel involved Agreeing individual members' targets Building confidence in the organization and in successful task achievement
Resolving individual and group needs	Understanding each individual's roles and needs Matching the individual to the task Resolving conflict Dealing effectively with grievances Recognizing individual contributions
Using personal style	Winning the loyalty and support of followers Speaking and acting with enthusiasm and conviction Maintaining informal contacts Using a style to meet the situation

Task	Skills
Building group teamwork	Developing mutual understanding and cooperation
	Welcoming consultation and suggestions
	Encouraging group pride and loyalty
Representation	
Representing the group	Combining team membership with objectivity
	Ensuring group achievement receives outside recognition and support
Channelling information	Informing the group of external activities and reactions
	Ensuring that group members know of group progress and results
Maintaining a perspective	Relating group objectives to outside plans
	Matching group achievements to the overall organizational results
Development	
Developing leaders/ managers	Developing own skills and knowledge
	Developing subordinates' skills and knowledge
	Encouraging initiative and self-reliance
	Delegating authority with appropriate control
	Involving individuals in decision-making
	Coaching and counselling individuals
Creating the group's ability to change	Improving teamwork
	Involving the group in the analysis and planning of tasks
	Encouraging the development of new ideas
Integrating the group with the environment	Creating interdependent links with other groups

Context of motivation

There are other theories of motivation, notably the classic contributions of Herzberg and Maslow. They are still attractive in their apparent simplicity and most managers have been exposed to them at some time during their careers. While the academic world is unhappy with the application of Herzberg's theory to some settings, neither theory covers more than a small part of the total requirement for managers. Operations managers need to muster every possible means to achieve high levels of performance. They must have staff who work well together, who are always looking for improvement, who come to work with attitudes and expectations which are in tune with the aims of the company, who strive to achieve more because they know that it will be recognized and directly rewarded. This is the scope and breadth of motivation and each part of this whole must be considered on its own merits.

Personal development task no. 13.1

Complete the following questionnaire on your preferences as a manager. Do you think that you would get the same answers when you are 55 years old, or as a 22 year old and if not how would you expect them to change?

A.   Instructions

The grid shown below may be used to compare each of the factors A to P with every other one. Begin with 'Prestige' and compare it with the next factor, 'Benefits', entering the first letter of your preferred choice in the first space on the top line. Next compare 'Prestige' with 'Changes' and, again, enter the code of your preference in the second square on the top line. Continue to contrast 'Prestige' with all the other factors, entering the code letters all the way across the top line of the grid. Then move on to 'Benefits' and compare it to 'Changes', entering the chosen letter in the first square of the second line. Continue comparing benefits to all the other factors, entering the results all the way across the second line. Compare the rest of the grid in the same way. Add up the number of 'A's from the completed grid and enter the number in the appropriate box marked 'Score'. Add up the 'B's and other letters, entering the results in the correct boxes. If all entries have been counted and correctly added, the score column will total ninety-one. The scores can then be ranked and the priorities will be revealed.

Your ranking	Score		Factor	
-	-	A.	Prestige.	- - - - - - - - - - - - - - -
-	-	B.	Benefits.	- - - - - - - - - - - - - -
-	-	C.	Changes.	- - - - - - - - - - - - -
-	-	D.	Recognition.	- - - - - - - - - - - -
-	-	E.	Salary.	- - - - - - - - - -
-	-	F.	Promotion.	- - - - - - - - -
-	-	G.	Objectives.	- - - - - - - -
-	-	H.	Conditions.	- - - - - - -
-	-	J.	Job Progress.	- - - - -
-	-	K.	Sick Pay/ Holidays.	- - - -
-	-	L.	Security.	- - -
-	-	M.	Facilities.	- -
-	-	N.	Consultation.	-
-	-	P.	Training/ Education.	

Definitions

A. Prestige. Greater prestige and status within the firm.
B. Benefits. Better pension scheme and other benefits.
C. Change. More access to information about changes which will affect you.
D. Recognition. More recognition from your boss when you feel you have done a good job.
E. Salary. Better salary.
F. Promotion. Greater opportunity for advancement and promotion.
G. Objectives. More opportunity to become involved in setting your own and the departmental objectives.
H. Conditions. Better working conditions.
J. Job progress. More information about how you are getting on in your job and more interest shown by your boss in your progress.
K. Sick pay/holidays. Better sick pay and holidays.
L. Security. Greater job security.
M. Facilities. Better social facilities, canteens, club rooms, sports facilities, etc.

N. Consultation. Being consulted more by your superiors in areas where you have specialist knowledge.
P. Training/Education.

This questionnaire, the definitions and the instructions are reproduced with permission from *Moving into Management* by R.C.I. Miller, published by Basil Blackwell, Oxford, 1986.

Personal development task no. 13.2

Who was the best manager you have ever worked for? It might have been the first one you ever had, or the one you work for now. Using just one side of a sheet of A4 paper explain why that person was the best. What did that person do which warranted this sort of praise? Try to concentrate on behaviours (things which he or she actually did) rather than undefinable qualities. List these behaviours, separating them, giving each a one-word heading. Do that before reading the rest of this passage! Have you finished? Now read on. How many of these behaviours are directly concerned with motivation?

Personal development task no.13.3

Table 13.1 on page 260 is a full list of leadership tasks, so there would be some logic in using the whole table for a personal development task. However, it might be more appropriate to take it section by section. Certainly the section on Direction is vital as a first step in leading, so we suggest this for the first task. As this chapter is initially concerned with motivation we then add a second task for this subject. When both have been completed and the implications digested and implemented, then consideration should be given to Representation and Development.

Consider your own leadership performance during the last year. For each major objective agreed with each subordinate, assess how well you have carried out the tasks listed under Direction. For each failure or low mark, consider what can be done to improve your performance. Make a list of intentions and talk with your boss about how to carry them out.

Personal development task no. 13.4

For each of the three people who give you most cause for concern, rate your own performance in motivating them, using the tasks under the Motivation heading in Table 13.1, and employing a scale of 1–5. You may find some of the skills to be more appropriate than others, but an honest assessment will identify areas for you to work on during the next few months.

Chapter summary points

- Motivation is when people want to do their job well.
- There is no single easy technique for motivating people.
- Staff will try hard when they know that their efforts will succeed and when they know that success will be rewarded.
- People bring to their work wants and expectations of that work.
- The ability to obtain and agree work objectives enhances motivation.
- Leadership is only one factor in the achievement of motivation.

References

1 Herzberg, F., *Work and the Nature of Man*, New York: World Publishing Company, 1966.
2 Maslow, A., *Motivation and Personality*, New York: Harper and Row, 1966.
3 Latham, G.P. and Locke, E.A., 'Goal Setting', *Organisation Dynamics*, 8, 1979.

Essential reading

Guest, D., 'What's new in motivation?' *Personnel Management,* May 1984. This article provides a short, well-written basis for examination of the realities of motivation and, as such, is useful for the operations manager. It provides a context within which to work out how motivation happens and how it originates.

14 Managing the team: Generating an effective team – how groups behave

The use and development of groups

What is a group? Charles Handy,[1] quite rightly, sees the need to define a group. He uses as a definition: 'Any collection of people who perceive themselves to be a group'. They will see a collective identity and it is this self-perception which distinguishes a group from a collection of individuals. The distinction is important. Many a manager imagines that he or she is running a group and wonders why some of the members are difficult to manage, or act in a counter-productive way. Some, or all, of the members may not see themselves as a group, despite the fact that there are common objectives, that they need to communicate with each other to do their jobs properly and that, on the organization chart, they all report directly to the same person. One of the immediate results of good leadership is the increased perception that the group has its own cohesiveness.

Why do we work in groups?

Although there are obvious work groups in production units, often with joint responsibility for output and quality, the reality for managers is that they usually work as individuals, only occasionally coming together in groups. The so-called management team is mostly a collection of individuals, managing functions which have little similarity to each other, operating to objectives which at best conflict with each other and at worst are incompatible. At the same time they are managed by a system of one-to-one discussions with their general manager, supported by a weekly or monthly performance meeting for the 'team'. This cynical view of management teams, although biased, serves to spotlight the difficulty of building a group or team who really do work together.

So why the need for groups? There are various reasons, all aimed at increasing total effectiveness.

1 Cooperation. Many tasks are better performed by a group and in some cases, only a group can do the task.
2 Personal safety and support. Most people appreciate support and encouragement. They feel less vulnerable and have a sense of belonging.
3 Mixed discipline. A group containing different specialists can call any one of them into use when necessary.
4 Mutual arousal. When working in a group people will be spurred on to greater efforts than they might perform as individuals.

The purpose of groups

So, if people enjoy groups and work better in groups, what uses should be made of them? Many purposes are listed and the most appropriate ones for the operations manager are probably:

(a) Problem-solving. For management system faults, procedural problems with staff, design faults, quality problems and any problems where more than one department is affected by the results.
(b) Performance review. Regular production, engineering, inspection and other meetings for control and feedback.
(c) Planning. Regular operations planning groups and meetings.
(d) Project groups. To introduce new or one-off projects.

Groups and the operations manager

The operations manager as team member

The management team will operate through a series of meetings on a regular basis – weekly or less frequently. That team will often consist of heads of other specialist departments, depending on the way that the organization is structured. It may include marketing, finance, technical or design or engineering, research and development. Unfortunately there are almost as many different styles of running such meetings as there are management teams, but, if we return to our principles of group behaviour, we can find a way of checking how the management team meetings should be conducted.

Management meetings for performance review

This is probably the most common form of management meeting. The various heads of functions meet at regular intervals, often weekly, to review performance, usually chaired by a general manager. Items reviewed will include production output and efficiency, the need for new plant, performance of new machinery or systems, sales figures and prospects, or changes in the marketplace. This meeting is a halfway house between daily meetings and long-range planning groups. It concentrates on the short-term future and immediate past performance. It looks to the short-term improvement of unit or company performance.

The atmosphere of this type of meeting is set firstly by the objectives and purpose, secondly by the style of the leader, the general manager. First-class chairmanship will prevent an atmosphere where some managers are defending their performance and others are intent on scoring points. The ground rules for such meetings are very important – rules such as:

1   All performance figures should be circulated in advance, with notes and explanations where necessary. It is fatal to mount a meeting and then to present the members with the figures when they arrive. Unfortunately it often happens that way.
2   Discussion on performance will centre on rectification measures for underachievement, and their implications for all other members of the team.
3   Decisions taken will be recorded clearly and concisely, then circulated on the same day with initials against action points.
4   'Any other business' will not be allowed. Very few items of interest *to this meeting* should fail to arise within the normal agenda.

Management meetings for policy review

A more general meeting of the management team deals with wider issues and concentrates on the longer term. Often it is less frequent, say, monthly. It will take reports from other committees such as safety, capital investment, costing, public relations, and determine the attitudes to be taken at these committees, sending them terms of reference and issues to be explored. It is the top group meeting, and as such is vital to the future success of operations and the operations manager.

Policy review meetings: issues for the operations manager

The issues here for the operations manager are varied:

1 It forces a wider view of business than the objectives of each function.
2 It demands a highly detailed knowledge of what is happening in operations and of the intentions of the general manager for the operations unit.
3 It requires a good command of the English language and a confident manner when addressing the team.
4 For personal survival, a knowledge of the aspirations and political aims of all other members is essential, together with the ability to propose clear solutions when others are pursuing those ambitions.
5 The operations manager should have a clearly thought-out strategy for the improvement of the operations activity over the next one to three years, so that all his or her contributions to the meetings have a particular purpose.
6 The operations manager will rapidly develop a working knowledge of personality and of the management style of the general manager.
7 It is not a meeting for managers who do not think long and deeply about their job and the advancement of their unit.

The problem-solving meeting

This type of meeting covers a wide range of subjects: design, raw material quality, market performance, new product performance, provided that the problems cannot be solved by the departments concerned. There is little point in discussing the finer points of purchasing detail in the presence of all the functional heads. The atmosphere here will be different, more relaxed. Problem-solving requires creative thinking and, when a recalcitrant problem is under the spotlight, it is helpful to take a little time going through the techniques of brainstorming. This will create the right atmosphere for thinking creatively. The group will then come together, working effectively, breaking down barriers of attitude, throwing up new ideas for evaluation. The ground rules for this kind of meeting should resemble the following:

1 Only one item on the agenda, with no time limit on the meeting.
2 A set procedure for breaking barriers.
3 No justifying of positions or opinions.
4 Decisions to be taken before adjournment, with action points and initials.

The problem-solving meeting may go further than dealing with individual problems. A growing practice is to take the whole management team away from the workplace to consider future plans and strategies, to work out new organization structures, to plan basic changes in management style and practices. A long weekend, well away from the telephone, where a series of progressive discussions, in the form of a workshop, will lead to well developed plans for change if the meeting is well set up and the facilities are suitable. Such workshops often have a hidden purpose, to bring the management team together and give them time and space to settle down as a group. A wise general manager can achieve considerable gains in team performance by carefully preparing the ground for such events.

Project groups

An important form of group is the project team, which may vary from a semi-permanent full-time team with a leader of seniority in the company, to a small, transient, occasionally-meeting group of three or four people developing a minor system. The project team is a very old concept, brought to more recent prominence by the insistence of NASA on having identifiable project leaders or managers in their contractors. In that way they could always communicate effectively, even on the most complex issues and place accountability for results with individuals. The operations manager will run project teams, be a member of project teams, even deal with them as helper, or as recipient of their services. Subjects specific to operations include:

- new product launch teams,
- plant and machinery replacement project groups,
- new process development groups,

- process control installation and commissioning groups,
- information systems project groups,
- computer-aided production control system teams,
- effluent reduction teams,
- installation teams for plant and services at customer premises.

Matrix management

The special characteristics of project groups are:

1 they have a finite life, a measurable time-scale;
2 they have an easily identifiable objective, common for all to see;
3 they are usually cross-functional in composition.

Project groups set up for such purposes as those above are an integral part of many companies, some having them as major features of their organization. It is then known as the matrix form of structure and is used by engineering companies, civil and construction companies, software houses, computer manufacturers and management consultants. The company is organized in a series of functions such as mechanical engineers, accountants, architects, chemists, and so on. Then, as each project is created, a project manager is appointed, time-scales and budgets are agreed, and then the mixed function team is chosen. Each member of that team has a responsibility:

(a) to the project manager as a member of the team;
(b) to the head of their function for their technical performance.

The heads of each function in turn have a responsibility to provide competent technicians, who are capable of working effectively as part of a team.

Project groups: Issues for the operations manager

There are issues for the operations manager in the number and type of project groups which work in the operations unit. The large project to develop and install a new process will probably have its own full-time team, maybe three or four technical experts. It will call on the operations manager frequently. Careful thought will be needed:

1   to define the project objectives and time-scale;
2   to describe the responsibility areas for the project manager which impinge on operations – for example, can the project manager or any team members instruct operations to perform tasks for them or alter processes?;
3   to describe in detail the help which operations will be expected to give to the project;
4   to determine whether the operations manager should be part of the project team.

These four issues assume a large project, but there are usually many small ones running concurrently. This means that the operations manager could be leading one of them and be a part-time member of two or three others. Perhaps the fifth issue might then be:

5   Are they all really worth doing, or are we overdoing the group culture?

The operations manager as team leader

Here again, regular meetings will take place, with similar requirements of the leader. Performance review meetings may take place daily and the same rules will apply. Despite the time-scales it is equally important that everyone who attends the meeting has seen the figures beforehand. To be made to justify poor performance 'on the hoof' is both destructive to group morale and unprofessional. The composition of such meetings obviously depends on the purpose, but why drag into them other people who do not have a direct interest, or who are not part of an operating department? Service departments can waste long hours attending operations meetings simply to be kept informed of what is happening, when a daily or weekly summary of events would suffice.

Of prime importance for the operations manager is whether to hold such meetings at all. Just because it is 'the daily meeting' or 'we've always had it' is no reason not to review its purpose. The operations manager might send a memo to his team asking questions like:

1   Would you be less informed if this meeting was not held?
2   Why would you want to hold it daily, why not weekly?
3   If it is needed, should you be present?
4   Would some other type of meeting be of more use to us as a team?

He might continue: 'Give me a rationale for a minimum programme of meetings, describing the purpose of each, which will keep us at peak managerial efficiency.' A periodic review of all meetings run by the operations manager will sometimes reach surprising conclusions and is recommended in the personal development task no. 14.2 presented later in this chapter.

Behaviour in groups

In order to be more effective in groups, both as members and as managers, we need to become better observers of what is happening. We can watch how communication is handled, who talks, for how long and to whom. We can observe how decisions are made – decisions about how the group organizes itself and how it carries out the tasks it must perform. It is useful to look at behaviour in groups in two ways – task behaviour and relationships behaviour.

Task behaviour

This is behaviour related to the objectives which the group is trying to achieve. The more expert groups spend an increasing amount of time in task-related behaviour. They will be proposing particular courses of action, giving ideas and suggestions, asking for opinions and facts, clearing up and explaining misunderstandings, summarizing progress.

Relationships behaviour

The relationships between members of the group will be the cause of particular patterns of behaviour. Some members will be keen to diffuse argument or reduce discord. Others will wish to involve everybody in the discussions, to be friendly and responsive, to find ways of meeting every point of view. Every group needs both task and relationship behaviour in order to achieve a reasonable point of view, but new groups in particular find that they spend a large proportion of their time in this way. Neil Rackham and others[2] devised a technique for the examination of this form of behaviour, which is called behaviour analysis and is now used extensively. A list of possible behaviours, together with the names of the group participants, is given to an observer, who then records each intervention by each person during a meeting of the group. In this way a picture is built up of the way that the group is maintaining its own performance. This information is then fed back to the members, as a check on their own impressions of how they behave.

The composition of teams

In 1981 R. M. Belbin conducted a series of experiments with practising British managers, observing the way in which they settled into teams with which they were working. Some took the lead, others became the team thinkers, yet others kept the team well-informed of what other groups were doing. In all, Belbin identified eight different team 'roles', of which each manager would use one or two when working in a team. Obviously each role taken up reflected the attitudes and mental abilities of the participant and was therefore capable of prediction. The work is both valuable and interesting for the operations manager, and a study of the eight team roles should be of assistance in understanding the different ways in which people approach team work.

Personal development task no. 14.1

Examine your performance as a group member by answering the following questions for each group to which you belong. Take yet another sheet of A4 paper, enter these questions, with a column on the right-hand side for action points.

Do I work as part of a group?
What are the problems in this group?
Do I manage a group and also work in it?
Can I resolve the conflict of this situation?
Does my group work as a unit? (If not, then why not?)
Do all members participate fully? If not, then what is the reason?
    Leadership?
    Individual personality?
    Divergent objectives of individuals?
Can I help to generate cooperation and hence cohesiveness?
Is the work flow a challenge? (Or is it too much?)
Do we balance the needs of the group with those of individuals?
Does the group have all the resources it requires?
Do we know the context into which our group fits?
Now give some thought to what you can do to help. Can you talk to the leader about agendas and purpose? Can you influence the meetings from within, planting thoughts in other people's minds, or making carefully designed suggestions? Now fill in the relevant action points.

Personal development task no. 14.2

List each meeting which you run personally and, for each one, record the names of the participants. Then send each one of them a memo asking them what they see to be the purpose of the meeting. Ask them also to give you a good reason for continuing with the meeting. Collate the results. Cancel the useless ones. Refine and constitute the others, giving each member a single sheet with the purpose and procedures for that meeting. Observe how much more cohesive they become!

Chapter summary points

- Good leaders create and develop cohesive groups.
- Groups can perform better than the sum of the individuals.
- Meetings need continual servicing, developing and reviewing.
- The purpose of meetings defines how they are organized and conducted.
- Task and relationship behaviour both contribute to team maintenance.

References

1 Handy, C.B., *Understanding Organizations,* Harmondsworth: Penguin Education, 1981.
2 Honey, P., Colbert and Rackham, N., *Developing Interactive Skills,* Wellens, 1973.
3 Belbin, R.M., *Management Teams: why they succeed or fail,* London: Heinemann, 1981.

Essential reading

Belbin, R. M., *Management Teams: why they succeed or fail,* London: Heinemann, London, 1981. This work enables the thoughtful operations manager to consider the composition of the teams which he or she creates in order to manage operations. It could be used in conjuction with the behaviour analysis techniques of Neil Rackham to develop and blend together an effective operations team.

15 Managing the team: relations between work groups

The symptoms of conflict

Introduction

Operations managers run production, or whatever constitutes the operations activity. However, they can only do that effectively if they receive help from a number of supporting departments. The greater the technology, or the greater the competition, then the more sophisticated the support will need to be. For example, for many years oil companies used global planning systems for production in order to streamline operations and save millions of pounds in logistics and production costs. These planning systems were run by highly specialized managers using sophisticated techniques.

Departments which support operations might include quality control, inventory control, personnel, cost control, purchasing and engineering. They are usually organized functionally, which means:

1 They are groups of specialists.
2 They have specific and specialist objectives.
3 They will be advisers to, or controllers of, what operations do.

These three characteristics may well cause friction – indeed, it is quite common for functional managers to stand on principle and for objectives to become blurred. When this happens, competition will certainly follow and departments will see themselves as being superior to, or more important than, others. Unless that competition is controlled, it may well turn to conflict. It is that subject which we wish to examine in this chapter.

A true story

James Mainwaring trained as a chemist at a provincial university after serving three years in the army. On graduating he joined a large manufacturing company in southern England, where he spent his first year in the works chemists department.

From there he was promoted to production superintendent and, over the next four years, progressed through the plant to become a production manager. During that time relationships between the production units and the sales company were fairly distant and deteriorating. Each one saw the other as a separate company, the sales company preoccupied with revenue, the production units with cost.

One day James was called to see his general manager, who suggested that he should move from production and take a position in the sales company in order to gain a wider experience in the company. It was also suggested that James might act as a technical adviser to the sales managers, in order to improve the relationships.

Next came an invitation to lunch with the two product sales directors at their usual restaurant near Guildhall. James saw this as a good omen and, in fact, lunch progressed quite well. However, while taking cheese he was asked about his background.

'Oh, I read chemistry at —', said James.

One director, looking puzzled, said, 'You went to University then?'

'Yes,' replied James, 'I took an honours degree in Industrial Chemistry.'

The director paused, then pushing forward his plate and leaning back in his seat, he turned to his colleague and said, 'Leslie, do you really think that we ought to have someone with a degree selling for us?'

This true story typified the hostility that can arise between functions when they are allowed or encouraged to compete with each other. James spent the next three years in the sales company, a less than happy experience, although he did achieve some success in reducing the tension which that excessive competition had produced.

A short experiment

It is disturbingly easy to create conflict between groups, and the results can be quite unexpected. There are a number of well known exercises which demonstrate how important it is to create trust between groups if there is to be any hope of real cooperation between them. The exercise 'Win as much as you can' is available[1] as are others and, if there is a problem of hostility between groups in the operations activity, then trying one of them will be both valuable and amusing.

The effects of conflict

The classic work of Sherif,[2] and later Schein,[3] led to an oft-quoted set of observations about how groups behave internally during conflict and how their attitudes towards opposing groups develop.

Schein observed that, while conflict is being experienced, the group will come closer together, as individuals begin to regard the other group as enemies. They feel threatened, so want strong direction from their leader. Hence the leader is given considerable authority. Individuals become very loyal to their group and are at pains to justify everything that the group does and everything that it represents. Their attitude to the other group becomes belligerent, they mistrust the motives of that group and they withdraw from contact with them. They do not listen to what the other group says; they tell them as little as possible.

A further consequence of these developments is that the group will look for ways of winning at the expense of the other group. They will also try to enlist the help of outsiders in their fight. 'So, if we stick together on this one we can't lose.'

The intensity of the conflict will depend on how important each group sees the issue to be and whether they see that winning really matters. Once they have decided that the goal is worth having, they will go for it almost regardless of the cost so allowing themselves to slide into the trap of conflict. All this takes place because they perceive that only one group can win. It is the win/lose situation that leads to the escalation of conflict. If each side can win there may still be competition, but there is no reason for it to degenerate into conflict.

Causes of conflict

The causes of conflict

Handy[4] identifies two fundamental issues underlying the causes of conflict. He points out that symptoms are easily recognized (see Schein), but that causes spring either from objectives and ideologies, or from the maintenance of territory. Among the causes he lists are:

> overlapping formal objectives,
> overlapping role definitions,
> unclear contract.

It is our experience that all three of these causes can create serious problems for the operations manager.

Cause (1) leads us to a study of structure and relationships, covered later, in some detail in Chapter 17. Perhaps the one fundamental piece of the manager's thinking is to work out his or her own areas of accountability, then to agree objectives with the boss. Once this is done, it is important to consider how the objectives fit in with those of other managers, particularly the heads of functions. If purchasing is given the objective of maximizing cost-effectiveness, while engineering is concentrating on superb process reliability, there will be problems. If the sales department are judged on revenue while operations are concerned with cost reduction, then the classic conflict will follow. If the policy administration activity in insurance has strict rules and objectives for accuracy, checking and fault reduction, how well does this fit with the speed and competitive edge demanded of the salesmen?

Causes (2) and (3), as listed by Handy, lead us towards a number of common interdepartmental problems. When the production control department sees itself as the authority which controls or dictates what production does and when it does it, while production sees production control as a service to itself, then trouble will follow. Some of these causes are more basic than others. Role definition, like beauty, is often in the eye of the beholder. Each group will see its own job as more important than will the other group. Some will use that perception as a bid for greater power. They will then interpret the relationship in such a way that they come out with greater authority. This also extends to the interpretation of objectives, which can be expanded to suit one's own aspirations.

Most advisory activities bear a relationship to operations which is capable of misinterpretation. It is essential that the ground rules are laid out carefully, so that each group knows exactly the scope and extent of the other one's responsibilities.

A simple basis for analysis of these relationships is given in Table 15.1

Table 15.1
Sources of conflict in operations groups

	Conflicting Objectives	Role Definition	Contract	Solution	Action Deadlines
Purchasing					
Engineering	X	X			
Costing					
Inspection			X		
Development					
Production Control			X		
Marketing	X				

When there are many departments, the relationships can lead to a pecking order where one group, usually a line department, comes out on top. The other groups are increasingly seen as servicing groups to that department and usually agree to be so. When we can identify as many groups as: operation, engineering, distribution, stock control, product design, purchasing, quality control, development, personnel, production control, research, sales, inspection, raw materials, marketing, cost control, process control and market research, then there is considerable scope for reinterpreting the relationships and the respective objectives. However, there would probably only be three or four major sources of conflict among the departments of each unit or division. Hence it should not be too difficult a task to assess the collective state of that unit or division.

The effects of unclear relationships

When groups are in conflict through relationship problems:

1 Morale in the unit will be low.
2 Loyalty to the unit or company will fall away.
3 Too much time will be spent in argument and conflict.
4 The effectiveness of the conflicting groups will fall away.
5 The groups will actually change their basic objectives.

Once the offending groups are identified, the reasons for conflict established and the basic causes worked out, then some sensible steps may be taken to reduce and finally dispel the conflict.

Leadership style

The severity of problems of conflict depends to a large extent on the personality and style of the chief executive/general manager and on the attitudes of the functional heads concerned. If the functional head has a strong professional background the role definition may become blurred. The managers will then concentrate on their professional expertise, perhaps to the detriment of operations – for example, engineers may insist on shutting machines for repair or maintenance at unreasonable times and without proper concern for operations targets. Personnel may concentrate on procedures for recruitment which slow the process down to unacceptable lead times. If the chief executive/general manager comes from operations then he is likely to favour operations or sales objectives. If his background is accounting then financial control will assume great importance and the advisory or controlling departments may be in the ascendancy during that reign. This in turn will create win/lose situations and conflict will follow.

Solving conflict

Methods of reducing conflict

Schein,[5] having outlined the various symptoms and effects of conflict, moves on to methods of reducing and resolving it. He sees the basic aim as getting each side to talk to the other again. There are several ways to do this, of which he lists three. We have added a fourth, which is to find some way in which the conflict can be made open, so that each side can win. So:

1   Find a common goal.
2   Find a common enemy.
3   Create a sub-group from each party.
4   Make the competition open.

In this way the competition will return to more normal levels of intensity.

Case study 1: Find a common goal

A company making base materials had enjoyed a long relationship with one major customer who converted their product and sold the finished article to stationers nationally. A particular grade of product, worth large sums of money, had been causing trouble intermittently for more than a year. Large quantities had been returned for scrap, the orders then being remade at high cost to the supplier. The manufacturing manager blamed the customer who, he said, was changing the specification every time he ordered. The salesman responsible for the order was under fire from the buyer, who in turn was being pressed by his managers to cancel the order. They had been unhappy about this order from the start. After much agonizing, the salesman called the buyer, suggesting that between them they had better get this one sorted out or 'We'll both be in trouble with our own people.'

The next morning the salesman, together with a well disguised technician from his production unit, met the buyer at the customer's factory. Fifteen minutes later the problem was solved, in two days a new specification was agreed, while after a further week a delivery of material was found to be of excellent quality in every respect. All this was achieved when two members of conflicting groups discovered and accepted a common objective.

In this particular case the common goal was to avoid the wrath of their respective bosses, because they were the two people who would have been seen to have failed and to cost their companies a lot of money.

Case study 2: Find a common enemy

Frequent complaints by sales that the product was always inferior to that of competitors led to open warfare between operations and sales in a company making packaging materials. Sales called the operations staff inefficient, even incompetent, while operations just would not believe what they were being told. Investigations carried out by a sub-group made up from members of sales and operations established that:

1 The product was inferior.
2 The competition was producing better products on similar plant.

The operations unit had repeatedly applied for replacement machinery for one part of the process, but the engineers were adamant that the existing plant was adequate. In that company, the chief engineer enjoyed a position of power in the hierarchy.

When the facts were made known, sales and operations combined forces within a week, formed a sub-group and planned together their campaign against the engineers, who had become the common enemy. Sadly, the final result was the loss of the order, capital investment in new machinery, and a change of engineering management.

When looking for a common enemy it is always good tactics to try to find one outside the immediate workplace groups, or the conflict may simply be transferred to two other groups.

Case study 3: Form a sub-group

Sales wanted to compete with the Japanese in a market for a piece of electronic household equipment. They presented one of the Japanese units as an example of the sort of product to be made. Operations were incensed at this, feeling that they had been 'railroaded' into copying what they saw to be an inferior product. Production were following a tradition of high-quality, conservative, well established products and saw no need to change.

In fact, unknown to operations, the general manager had been holding discussions with market research and sales in order to modernize the product line and was looking for ideas. When market research and sales suggested the electronics product they were only following the lead given to them by the general manager.

The solution in this case was for the general manager to call together the sales manager, a technical salesman who had worked on the project with market research, the production manager and his chief development engineer. The meeting opened in an atmosphere of tension, but when the background was fully explained the tension slowly began to dissipate. However, it was a long time before operations were willing to accept what they saw to be a change of manufacturing strategy.

Case study 4: Make the competition open

The capital investment procedures in one service company laid stress on two factors:

1   whether money was actually available;
2   the justification figures and arguments.

Operations had been trying for the replacement of a complete information and control system, which would greatly improve their efficiency, speed of reaction and quality of service. Purchasing were housed in a very old house away from the remainder of the offices. They were cramped, the roof leaked, and there were many other reasons quoted for investment in new buildings. Each group had failed to gain approval in previous years and the competition in which they were taking part was causing conflict. Each side took the view that the other had a poor case and should not get the money. The competition was now closed and enmity was growing.

Resolution of the problem was achieved by an astute general manager, who called the departmental heads together. He explained that by rearranging the sourcing of funds he would be able to resource both proposals, but only if they met the strict financial and other criteria required by the capital investment appraisal procedure. The conflict was reduced, and each department made their bids for money. In the event, the purchasing department moved into the main offices, but operations failed to justify their new system on technical grounds and it was referred for further search for a better system.

Competition can only be made open when each group is able to gain without forcing the other one to lose.

Commentary

These four case studies are based on real situations, which took place in British companies. Each situation emerged gradually as a sequence of events unfolded. Each one resulted in conflict, caused by influences outside the conflicting groups. Each one shows groups who started off doing their own jobs conscientiously, as they saw them. However, circumstances led those groups into conflict with each other. Often we see the first signs of trouble long before crisis, rarely do we take heed of the warnings early enough. It is only too easy to allow, even encourage, conflict to happen through our normal managerial actions. Experienced operations managers always work hard to ensure:

1   that the structure reflects the important jobs to be carried out;
2   that objectives are very carefully worked out for every operations group in such a way that they do not overlap and cause confusion;

3 that the relationships between groups are clearly and concisely spelt out and that they are fully understood and accepted.

Personal development task no. 15

1 List all the departments that have working relationships with operations.
2 For each one, list the relationship problems, grading them 1-3.
3 Categorize the high-conflict problems under the headings mentioned earlier for cause of conflict – that is, overlapping objectives, overlapping role definitions, concealed objectives, unclear contract.

It is unlikely that there will be more than two or three really serious problems, but those present are worthy of thorough investigation. So take an A3 sheet, list the departments down the left hand side and the headings across the top, leaving large boxes for each. Then analyse the problem for each department and work out solutions for each in the last column.

Finally, make an action plan to put into effect the solutions proposed.

Chapter summary points

- Competition leads to cohesive groups.
- Conflict increases that cohesion and blurs group objectivity.
- Conflict occurs when competition produces only one winner.
- Operations groups are organizationally vulnerable to conflict.
- Defuse conflict by arranging that groups talk to each other again.
- Redefine group objectives and explain them clearly.

References

1 Pfeiffer, J. and Jones, J., *Structured Experiences for Human Relations Training*, vol. 2, University Associates, 1978.
2 Sherif, M., Harvey, O., White, B., Wood, W. and Sherif, C., *Intergroup Conflict and Cooperation*, Norman, Oklahoma: Book Exchange, 1961.

3   Schein, E. *Organizational Psychology,* Englewood Cliffs: Prentice Hall, 1965, p. 81.
4   Handy, C., *Understanding Organizations,* Harmondsworth: Penguin Books, 1981, pp. 224–32.
5   Schein, op. cit.

Essential reading

Child, J., *Organization: a guide to problems and practice,* Harper and Row, New York, 1977. This book deals with the underlying causes of many operations problems – that is, structure and relationships. The chapter dealing with integration is of particular relevance to the discussions developed above.

16 Managing the team: formal negotiations and industrial relations

Context and terminology

Introduction

In the United Kingdom the current state of industrial relations is difficult to establish. As operations managers know, there is a national, possibly a local industrial relations scene, together with the immediate work situation. During the late 1970s and early 1980s significant changes took place at national level and this has affected attitudes throughout the country. The impact of this change has differed from place to place – indeed in some cases it may be more apparent than real. The most comprehensive and up–to–date picture of British workplace industrial relations is contained in a survey of the same name by the Department of Employment, the Economic and Social Research Council, the Policy Studies Institute and the Arbitration and Conciliation Service. This survey was published in 1986[1] and reported on the industrial relations situation during the first half of the 1980s. The survey made a number of observations.

First, despite changes largely fostered by the first and second periods of Conservative administration, many elements of industrial relations had not changed, particularly for the operations manager. In fact, the workplace remains of primary importance as the centre for employment relations, where despite all other issues and external pressures, work must continue.

The second observation was that, in the great majority of workplaces, the senior person dealing with personnel and industrial relations issues was somebody with general management responsibilities. This was particularly true in the private sector, and that person was often the operations manager.

Third, despite the fact that there are fewer strikes, less industrial action overall, and fewer employment law cases brought to tribunals, managers at workplace level are becoming increasingly involved with some types of industrial relations activity. More operational managers reported involvement in determining or negotiating pay and conditions of employment, payment systems and job evaluation. However, the extent of this involvement will vary widely.

Fourth, operations managers will often have most influence over decisions affecting people in the key areas of recruitment, appointment and discipline. Personnel staff were often involved in the introduction of organizational change, but line managers were always involved in technical change.

A fifth point uncovered by the survey is that union membership is decreasing. This gives managers an opportunity to demonstrate better leadership and effective management. The opportunity must not be lost.

There is still a trend towards more formality in procedures which govern relationships at the workplace, particularly in unionized environments. Similarly, trade unions take a greater role in the discussion of pay systems. Greater use is made of job evaluation in determining pay differentials while industrial action still exists in the form of overtime bans or working to rule. In summary, the overall change has been marginal, many of the individual changes being more apparent than real. The industrial relations climate has changed in the United Kingdom, but it does not mean that conflict is no longer prevalent in the workplace, despite the impression sometimes given by the popular press. The survey indicates that the management of people at work is still as complex for operations managers as it has always been.

Terminology

The term 'human relations' usually covers the whole area of personnel management whereas 'employee relations' is a narrower term sometimes used instead of 'industrial relations'. Many people use it to reflect the change in the industrial relations environment. It emphasizes that management is not entirely about dealing with trade unions; that in many cases employees' conditions are harmonized and that they are not represented by unions for collective issues. Nevertheless, managers still negotiate and this chapter is concerned with that skill.

Employment and collective labour law

The traditional view of employment law was that the state should only try to provide a framework within which employers and employees can sort out their differences according to the local situation. There has been a decrease in the influence of individual employment law, largely influenced by increases in the qualifying period of service. However, there has also been an increase in the volume of collective labour law. This form of law can be technical, complex and potentially confusing to the manager. It is also subject to periodic changes which demand frequent updating sessions. Experienced readers will agree that the law does not materially help with the positive management of relations with employees. These facts may create a problem for the operations manager in that he must be fully conversant with current legislation, precedents and practices. Operations managers are unlikely to attempt to manage by using the law but will have a working knowledge of the most important issues. The legal phrase 'A shield rather than a sword' might be appropriate. In these circumstances, our treatment will be to concentrate on the positive management of relationships, on negotiation skills and on the issues facing the operations manager. Current guidance on the law, in clear English, is available in the handbooks prepared by the Department of Employment and held at their local offices.

Informing, consulting and negotiating

Before becoming involved in bargaining it is important to make certain distinctions. Dealing with employees, either directly or through trade unions, may take the form of consulting, negotiating or informing. Informing is direct communication, usually one-way. Consulting is normally a two-way process, defined in law as 'listening with an open mind'. It might refer to an obligation to consider seriously proposals put forward by trade union representatives, while accepting no obligation to be bound by them. That would entail no obligation to come to any form of agreement with them. Negotiation, however, implies some form of agreement. It is therefore important to be quite clear about the issues:

- on which there is an obligation to negotiate;
- where employees will be informed;
- which require that employees be consulted.

Generally the policy should be to negotiate on the narrowest possible range of matters feasible in the workplace. Leading companies such as Marks and Spencer have shown that good management reduces the need for workers to be represented by trade unions. Therefore, in narrowing the range of negotiable matters, good operations managers are positive in managing the situations which might otherwise lead employees to turn to trade unions for help or representation. In this way, they seek to avoid the problems of formal and full negotiations.

Rights and issues

A further matter for definition is the difference between 'rights' and 'issues'. 'Rights' tend to relate to individuals – for example the right not to be unfairly dismissed. 'Issues' relate to the majority, or groups, of employees, and are collective in nature. Trade union involvement in rights is usually about such matters as representation at discipline or grievance hearings. Collective bargaining on behalf of a group of workers will usually concern issues such as rates of pay. There are some examples of full and formal agreement about trade union involvement in disciplinary procedures. However, discipline is more commonly in the hands of management. Employees should have a right or opportunity to be represented, but the final decisions on rights are taken by management. At the same time, such procedures will be subject to examination by outside bodies such as industrial tribunals.

It is therefore important to remember the difference between rights and issues when drafting or revising disciplinary procedures. Codes on discipline are gathered together by ACAS and published frequently to keep in line with any changes in legislation. In summary, rights are not the subject of collective bargaining, although the procedures used when rights are in question may be the subject of consultation. A further principle is to consult to a deadline, but not necessarily to negotiate to a deadline. When consulting without a deadline for a return of views, it is easy to be manoeuvred into a 'no win' situation where one cannot force the pace on the one hand and be accused of failing to consult on the other. However, on occasion, one would wish to negotiate without the restriction of a deadline. There are examples where machinery has been purchased and installed without consultation and without information being given, and that machinery has then stood idle while negotiations proceeded.

The process of negotiation

Perception in negotiation

The differing backgrounds, needs, wants and perceptions which people bring to negotiating, whatever the context, will sometimes cause misunderstanding. It is not uncommon for a negotiating situation to degenerate into disagreement, even acrimony, through the inability of one or both parties to explain or understand adequately the stance that is being presented. Perception is a very important aspect of negotiation and is well covered by Peter Warr in his book *Psychology and Collective Bargaining*[2]. Receivers of information organize material to which they have been exposed so that they can cope with it and fit it into their established frame of reference or grid of experience. As their span of attention is limited, they select only part of the information which is available. These decisions are subconscious and they occur very quickly. People rely on a set of habits and expectations which have built up over the years. As an example, motorists do not expect pedestrians to leap off the pavement in front of their cars, so they pay less attention to them than to the cars in front, which they expect to stop more suddenly.

The processes of observing and drawing conclusions are usually carried out without having to exert conscious control and they operate differently for different people. So habits, expectations, attitudes and prejudices which vary from person to person affect what is seen and the conclusions drawn. As negotiators sit around the bargaining table they observe different aspects of what is happening and draw different conclusions. Individual expectations influence this process considerably; a union representative with no trust in a management spokesman will probably hear that person say things which are obviously unacceptable to the workforce. Other persons present may hear inoffensive, if not very sensible, suggestions. Most people have met this situation and wrestled with the problem of which is the correct interpretation. It is an unfortunate fact that some of the widest differences in perception occur between representatives of management and of workforces.

Negotiating style

A key to successful leadership is self-awareness and, in the context of this chapter, the style one uses in different negotiating situations. In this respect, a useful instrument is the *Negotiating Style Profile* of Rollin Glaster and Christine Glaser.[3] It consists of 30 statements which help to label the negotiating style of the participant. There are five characteristic styles, ranging from what is probably the most effective to the least successful. It also contains an instrument with which colleagues can assess one's style. This allows an examination of the different perceptions of that style, with the opportunity to work on those differences. Statements in the instrument include:

'When I negotiate my interests must prevail for negotiators are adversaries.'
'I enjoy the reputation of tough battler.'
'Half a loaf is better than none.'

These factors are ranked on a 7 factor scale ranging from 'Strongly agree' to 'Strongly disagree'. The resultant plot will illustrate one of five characteristic negotiating styles and will also point out secondary or supporting styles. There is a description of each style and suggestions about what action the participant might need to take in order to improve performance.

Skills of negotiation

One way to learn about effective negotiating is to observe the behaviours exhibited by successful practitioners. This was done in a valuable research project carried out by Rackham, Carlisle and others and published in an article called 'The effective negotiator–the behaviour of successful negotiators'.[4] This article is quoted here by kind permission of MCB University Press.

The researchers observed the behaviour of a group of persons known as successful negotiators in that they were rated as such by both sides at their work places. They also had a track record of significant success in industrial relations and a low incidence of implementation failures. Their method was to examine behaviours used and behaviours avoided.

BEHAVIOURS AVOIDED.

1. IRRITATORS. These were described as certain words and phrases which are commonly used during negotiations and which have negligible value in persuading the other party, while at the same time causing irritation. They are emotive words or phrases such as 'generous offer'.

2. COUNTERPROPOSALS. Skilled negotiators use this tactic much less frequently than average negotiators. The immediate counterproposal introduces additional options which can cloud the issue under discussion. When they are put forward the other party are occupied with their own proposal and are at their least receptive to new ideas. They see them not as proposals but as blocking tactics or a way of expressing disagreement.

3. DEFEND/ATTACK. Because negotiation involves conflict negotiators may become heated, using emotional behaviour. This soon becomes an attack upon the other party, creating a spiral of attack and counter attack. Obviously this leads nowhere positive and usually leaves a wider gulf between the parties than originally existed.

4. ARGUMENT DILUTION. Skilled negotiators use as few arguments as possible, persisting with the one or two most powerful ones. They take the view that the more arguments they use then the more their case is weakened, not reinforced. It is known as argument dilution and creates a snare for many beginners.

BEHAVIOURS USED.

1. BEHAVIOUR LABELLING. Skilled negotiators usually indicate or signal their next action in some way. 'Can I ask you a question?' or 'How many ... are there?' It has the effect of focusing the attention of the listener. It also has the advantage of slowing down the pace of the negotiation, introducing formality, reducing ambiguity and helping to achieve clearer communication. Expert negotiators will try to avoid labelling disagreement. They will give reasons why they cannot accept something rather than state first the inability and then the reasons.

2. TESTING UNDERSTANDING/SUMMARISING. This is done partly by reflecting back comments previously made by both parties. This indicates that they had not been missed and ensures that there is no ambiguity. It also helps to raise issues of implementation; 'If we picked your proposal how would we

deal with . . .'. It is considered important to clear up as many problems as possible so that implementation takes place smoothly.

3. SEEKING INFORMATION. The skilled negotiator seeks significantly more information than does the average one and it is about obtaining information with which to bargain, together with questioning as a tactic to gain control. They have several advantages which the article lists, including their use to gain breathing space, to avoid direct disagreement and to keep the other party active.

4. FEELINGS COMMENTARY. It is perhaps surprising that skilled negotiators are willing to reveal their feelings. They are not emotional, but merely indicate how they feel about particular comments. There is considerable evidence from other psychological work that expression of feelings can be linked to establishing trust.

The conduct of negotiations

Preparation

The first part of preparation is to define the objective of the negotiation. Here it is important to consider what is realistic, to balance the prize desired against the possible costs of obtaining it. It is always possible to fight another day, whereas an unrealistic objective attempted now might ruin any future chances of reaching it. Second, the gathering of facts, the use of painstaking research to fill in all the background to the situation, the checking of all claims or statements for accuracy, are essential to success.

Next define the issues. At this stage a clear picture of the problem is required, not just the symptoms. Behind a surface problem there may be a hidden agenda which must eventually be addressed if relationships are to be maintained or reestablished. The better the existing climate, the more warning will there be of the problem, and obviously informal discussions will help to establish the facts of the situation.

When all this preparatory work is complete, the strategy will be prepared. Strategy is the broad plan, always keeping in mind the ultimate objective. During the performance of the plan, the need will arise for tactics, without which the performance will be inflexible and unresponsive to changing situations.

The negotiation

A useful mnemonic which describes the sequence of operation is BEMA, which stands for Beginning, Exchange information, Movement, Agreement. This sequence may be expanded to the preparation and use of a rough agenda of opening tactics, control, summing up, minutes, action and analysis/implementation.

The opening

During this period there will (hopefully) be an exchange of pleasantries. As people settle to their task there will follow the tabling of issues. For a formal, regular, planned meeting there will normally be an agenda. If, however, the meeting is in reaction to a particular situation then it is important to identify the purpose at this time. This may well be a time for listening rather than making rapid judgements and immediate replies. Restraint may indeed be difficult if remarks made at this opening stage are offensive, or derogatory of management, or particular managers.

Abusive behaviour need not be tolerated and may be handled in a number of ways. One tactic is to ask the leader of the other party if he or she associate themselves with the remarks, to ask if there is any reason for making them, or whether it helps in any way to resolve the issues. An extreme form of reaction to personal attacks is to adjourn the meeting. This is more productive than walking out, which may be dramatic, but can only waste time and means that the meeting must be reconvened at a later date.

Control and tactics

When the issues have clearly emerged there is a need for some form of control and it is at this point that tactics should be considered. In other words, what will be the best approach to solving the problem and how will it fit in with the general strategy? At this stage, it may be useful to call for a recess, or what is sometimes known as a side-meeting. If such a meeting is used then separate accommodation must be made available to each side. It is clearly helpful for management to be able to retire to some private place to discuss progress. Trade union colleagues must be offered the same standard of accommodation and must not be expected to adjourn to a corridor. One advantage of introducing side-meetings is that it helps to keep control and allows a considered, thoughtful and tactical response to the arguments being raised. It also allows consideration of the manner and style in which issues should be developed. It is important to stress the need to keep control. One form of negotiation training is called the Controlled Pace Exercise. It is designed to emphasize the value of keeping a calm atmosphere and a well-paced and slow progression, rather than allowing control to slip.

Summing up

Whenever a natural break occurs, the opportunity should be taken to summarize progress. This summary may be given by one side of their understanding of the issue, of how long an adjournment should last, of their own particular case, or of the common ground. One important reason for summing up is to achieve clarity of understanding for the purpose of minute-taking. Minutes will have been part of the opening agreement on procedure. If they are to be taken, they might be in detail or in a simple outline detailing agreements reached. Local practices vary, but a written record of some kind must be agreed and circulated after the meeting.

Making proposals

At some point in the proceedings there will be some movement, with proposals emerging in the form of 'what if...' or 'could consider...' or 'maybe...'. Proposals or suggestions are an essential part of negotiation in that they move the respective parties closer together. When one side is making proposals the other should never interrupt, but afterwards they will ask questions, clarify, summarize and then respond. A proposal usually has more impact than an argument and is less emotive. The best response to a proposal is a considered counter-proposal, but it must be carefully thought-out and not simply be a way of sweeping aside the contribution of the original one. Counter-proposals should not be introduced until the original proposal has been considered.

Looking and listening

Earlier in this chapter we referred to problems of perception and the importance of looking and listening without prejudice. The expert negotiator, and indeed the expert manager, are always alert to the possibility of non-verbal signals and make use of them themselves. When signals are received they should be confirmed, enlarged and rewarded. If the negotiations are beginning to move ahead then trading will start. The signals of this will be expressions based around the wording 'if . . . then'. There will be an exchanging on the basis that an offer is made after a condition is laid down. Conditions are placed before offers are made so that nothing is firm. If progress continues then moves can be made towards a close and messages such as 'If you do that, then we have a deal' will indicate that agreement is close.

Summary

Once agreement has been reached, then both sides must agree on the exact form and content of that agreement and it should be summarized in writing. There should then be agreement on an action plan showing how the agreement is to be implemented. Good deals are those where both parties have a degree of satisfaction and commitment.

Recapitulation

1 During negotiations keep calm, cool and in control.
2 Test understanding, summarize points covered, seek information and express feelings without emotion.
3 Avoid irritating or emotive words, avoid defence/attack spirals, do not dilute the arguments.

Operations managers are among the most experienced industrial negotiators, and the job presents considerable opportunities for the development of negotiating skills. Even if formal agreements mean that major negotiating is done on a company-wide or even national scale, there are always requirements for workplace bargaining on a factory or departmental basis. So a personal examination of abilities, followed by a development programme may be appropriate.

An audit checklist for auditing the effectiveness and proficiency of the negotiations activity as carried out in your company is given at the end of the chapter (page 301). It may serve to develop organizational action plans as well as personal ones.

Personal development task no. 16

Answer the following questions about your negotiating style and competence. Then, in a second column, prepare an action plan for the development of your skills, not forgetting time-scales for achievement. This plan might include reading, special skills courses, or greater involvement in the practice of negotiating.

1 Do I know my negotiating style?
2 Should I adapt, vary, or change it?
3 Do I prepare thoroughly for negotiations?
4 Do I pick my negotiation team carefully and rehearse adequately?
5 Do I plan the agenda carefully or determine the agenda suddenly after a meeting is called?
6 Do I consider and work out tactics?
7 Do I clarify the common ground?
8 Do I listen and look attentively?
9 Do I take care in how I present information and in how I respond?

Chapter summary points

- Industrial relations law changes frequently and requires a detailed knowledge for complete expertise.
- The operations manager should know enough to use the law as 'a shield rather than a sword'.
- Different perceptions lead to different goals.
- BEMA: Beginning, Exchange information, Movement, Agreement.
- Effective negotiators are cool, calm and collected.
- All negotiations must have a purpose and strategy.
- Know your own negotiating style.
- The end result should be a written agreement in which both sides win.

References

1 Milward, N. and Stevens, M., *British Workplace Industrial Relations 1980–1984. The DE/ESRC/PSI/ACASS Surveys,* Aldershot: Gower Publishing Company Ltd, 1986.
2 Warr, P., *Psychology and Collective Bargaining,* London: Hutchinson, 1976.
3 Glaster, R. and Glaser, C., *The Negotiating Style Profile,* available from Management Planning Resources, P.O. Box 28, Carmarthen, Dyfed, Wales.

4 Rackham, Carlisle *et al.,* 'The effective negotiator', *Journal of European Industrial Relations,* Management Centre of Buckingham, 1978.

Audit checklist

Area: Negotiations

Topic: Effectiveness and Proficiency of Negotiations Activity

Subject	Findings
1. Does the company inform, consult or both?	
2. Are rights and issues distinguished?	
3. Do negotiations commonly reach agreement?	
4. What is the style most commonly used?	
5. Do negotiators avoid: – irritators? – counter-proposals – argument dilution?	
6. Do negotiators use: – behaviour labelling – summarizing – information-seeking? – feelings commentaries	
7. How good is the preparation?	
8. Do negotiators control meetings?	
9. How well do proposals emerge?	
10. Is there ever confusion about agreements?	

Part V
MANAGING YOURSELF: RAISING PERSONAL EFFECTIVENESS

Introduction

Premise

Historically the operations management job has been an unpopular choice for young, qualified people entering their careers. Many more attractive options have been offered by careers advisers in the UK and it is not difficult to find the reasons. Apart from the greater glamour of the City and the professions, the status of operations is seen as being low in the managerial order of preference. Added to this, it is easy to gather together a list of pressures which are always present; they go with the job. Consider some of the factors which govern the way in which operations reacts to the reality of intense competition in worldwide markets:

1　There is a continual drive for staff reductions, however humanely achieved. So the operations manager is usually short of staff, particularly junior managers.
2　Pressure for lowest possible product cost leads to process improvement, faster running and higher utilization of plant and the use of the cheapest effective materials.
3　Reduction of working capital is achieved by 'Just in Time' manufacturing, together with rapid removal of finished goods from stock.
4　Despite these 'invitations' to downgrade the product there is a great drive for better product quality through better design and Total Quality Management systems.

So the life of the operations manager begins to resemble the job description for an archangel!

Theme

In this situation we need to examine how the operations manager deals with all these pressures, how he or she organizes their hectic life. Clear thinking is needed to separate the job demands from the demands of other people and the needs of the incumbent. In other words, getting oneself organized is a prerequisite for organizing other people.

Sequence of the treatment

The failure of 'management by objectives' left a gap in management practice and professionalism. While the principle was right, the emphasis was placed too heavily on procedural matters. The cornerstone of managerial performance is still:

1 knowing exactly the scope of the job;
2 working to a set of regular medium – and long-term objectives.

This Part comprises three chapters, starting with the longer-term. Accountability determination leads to objectives – that is, things which must be achieved in the time period. We use a time-scale of one year for this purpose. In this way, task objectives for managers can be tied to an appraisal system and link with the annual financial planning cycle. Chapter 17 deals with these vital issues.

The breakdown of annual objectives encourages thoughts about personal work style – the way in which we prefer to go about our jobs. This style, made up of our personal preferences for particular ways of working, is important to other people who work with us – peers, subordinates and managers. It is explored in Chapter 18, 'Personal Planning and Agenda-Setting'. This chapter also deals with the detail of medium-term and period planning, helping to distinguish between improvement plans and performance plans.

Finally, in Chapter 19, short-term planning is considered, in particular the setting of priorities and the solving of short-term problems. If this short-term planning problem is approached after dealing with longer-term issues then it will fall into place quite happily. If, however, the major objectives, the personal agendas and the whole purpose of operations are not thought-out and agreed, then no amount of daily or weekly planning will keep the job going for very long. Competition is too fierce for the amateur or haphazard approach to managing operations. Figure 17.0 shows diagrammatically this sequence of planning and may serve as a model, or map, with which to negotiate this section of the book.

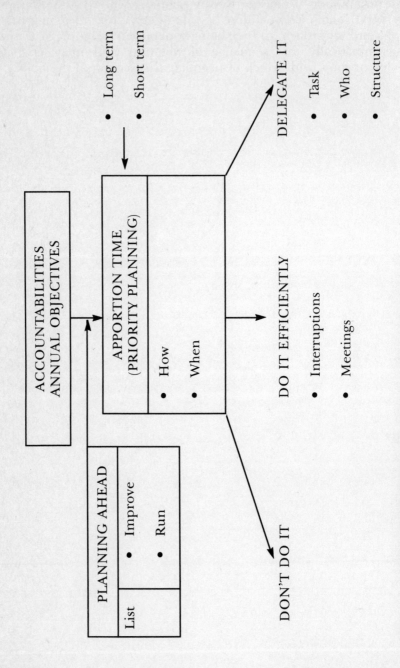

Figure 17.0 Planning the job of the operations manager

17 Accountability and objective–setting

The concept of accountability

The basis of accountability

Accountability is a familiar concept, but its simplicity can be deceptive. It is easy to understand the logic of a superior sharing responsibility with subordinates, but the implications of the arrangement can be complex and far-reaching. The basic concept is that one should be held accountable for the results of one's actions. This is a dearly-held concept in government and politics, where public accountability is formalized. It sometimes leads to the avoidance of decision-making in order to avoid the consequences, and there is already an important question here for managers and objective-setting. If objectives are set so that they can only be achieved by positive action, then no one can sit back and avoid decision-making successfully.

If the concept is that one should be expected to account for one's actions, or stewardship, then an accountability may be defined as 'an area of attention for which one is required to give account'.

Accountability for what?

Case 1: the engineer Joe is a professional engineer, who has been given the job of designing a bridge. His boss charges him with the responsibility for producing drawings and specifications for a structure to meet function, cost and completion date, but what has Joe accepted in his heart as his responsibility? What does he feel accountable for? Possibly only to practise his professional skills conscientiously for as long as the job may take to do, and he may be vague about this. The job runs late because his drawings are late, the boss jumps up and down with frustration, but Joe remains unmoved. He regards his boss's behaviour as an eccentricity of a man who does not realize that 'you cannot be creative to a timetable'. Joe feels deeply upset if any of his calculations are proved wrong, but he never really accepted being accountable for time.

If this company wants their engineer to meet deadlines of his own accord, they must first get him to accept that it is possible to design to a timetable and that it is his responsibility to do so. Just putting in a system for programming design office work will not get to the root of the problem, and will therefore be of limited and transistory value.

Case 2: the supervisor Bill is twenty-eight. Three months ago he was promoted to first line supervisor in charge of four gangs of loaders. Each gang is responsible for keeping a large mixing vessel loaded with raw material on a semi-continuous basis. The work is heavy, but intermittent, with frequent short bursts of activity separated by longer periods of waiting. Boredom is a problem. Most of the loaders are older than Bill, some in their fifties with many years' experience. Bill has already overcome all the technical and resourcing problems of his job – after all, that's why he was promoted. However, he finds great difficulty with discipline and is not yet convinced that he should take on that accountability.

Willingness to be accountable

For a person to be accountable:

- they must know what is expected;
- know what is being achieved;
- have the knowledge, authority and means to influence sufficiently the operations for which they are being held accountable.

A further condition is the ability to control events. Many managers are not in a position to control their work, or at least do not see themselves as being in control. If we wish someone to feel accountable then authority must go some way towards matching responsibility and the person must know exactly what they are expected to do. Often clarification of these things is all that is required to transform their attitude towards being held accountable. More often, however, the problem is more complex.

Self-esteem is part of this problem. True acceptance of accountability means that the person is privately and personally committed to achieving the relevant objectives, and the realization of those objectives becomes a matter of personal pride. Hence the frequent reluctance to accept accountability for objectives which the person feels are unrealistic.

So there is a need to make the person feel confident in their own ability to perform adequately; the opportunity to demonstrate to themselves that they can be successful; the need for guidance and coaching in the job until it is being carried out satisfactorily, with a high proportion of successes. The tough self-starters present few problems in their attitude to accountability, but large numbers of other managers require support, development and confidence boosting.

Multiple accountability

Should the QA manager of the services division of a company report to the group finance director or the managing director? Should a maintenance engineer report to the production manager or to the chief engineer? In the latter case, it is not usually very satisfactory for him to report wholly to one or the other. The production manager is interested in how quickly jobs get done, which job is done next and how the engineer gets on with production staff. The chief engineer is more concerned with the professional competence of the engineer and the level of maintenance costs. One effective arrangement is for the maintenance engineer to report to the production manager for his day-to-day work and to the chief engineer for professional matters. 'One man, one master' becomes less appropriate as management becomes more complex and specialized.

In the first example the position is more senior, the accountabilities will be more numerous, but the job-holder will probably have much more choice over how the job is carried out. If the services division is purely an internal services division to other parts of the company, then the direct reporting line may be to the group finance director. If, however, the division also trades in the marketplace and is run as a profit centre, then the 'bottom line' objectives may well be accounted for to the managing director, just like other profit centre divisions in the company.

Provided that a manager is not expected to be accountable to more than one person for the same things, provided that both he and everyone else are quite clear to whom he is accountable and for what, then multiple accountability is quite practical, and often the only possible arrangement.

Principal accountabilities

We have already defined an accountability as 'an area of attention for which one is required to give account'. Well-written job descriptions will gather together such areas of attention, describing them clearly and concisely, in such a way that sensible objectives may be set for those areas. Unfortunately writing good job descriptions is a deceptively difficult task and many managers suffer through inadequate provision in this respect. So their objectives are too many and too vague, and they do not accept accountability for parts of their job.

A very useful approach is to list one's accountabilities and then to choose a few which are vital to good performance in one's job. These become our principal accountabilities and are defined as 'those few vital areas of attention, where excellence of effort will have the greatest effect on results'. Normally five or six should be enough to cover at least 80 per cent of our job. This follows the universal Pareto principle, or 80/20 rule as it is often known. A similar approach identifies a few key results areas, which have the same effect on results (see Figure 17.1).

An important test of one's understanding of principal accountabilities is to check whether any of them are time-related. If so, then there is an error somewhere. As long as the job remains the same, then the principal accountabilities will remain the same. In order to test all these features of accountability a plant superintendent in a papermill, responsible for the effective management and utilization of a large department and very extensive plant, prepared a set of accountabilities covering the major parts of his job. The result is shown in Table 17.1

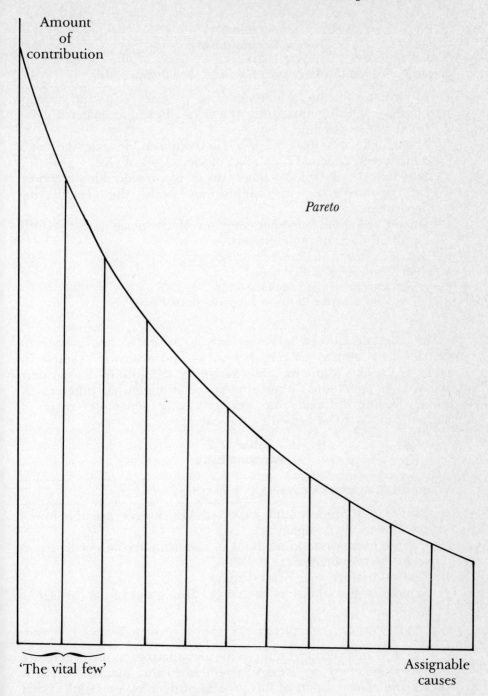

Figure 17.1   The Pareto principle

Table 17.1
Accountability

Preparation Plant Superintendent/Large Mixed Paper Mill

1. Contribute to the achievement of product cost and quality objectives by the efficient treatment of all product material prior to the paper machine.
2. Ensure the adequate supply (in conjunction with the yard department) or wood pulp at an efficient level of cost.
3. Schedule the use of machinery so as to provide adequate time for maintenance, in conjunction with the engineering department.
4. Obtain and hold adequate supplies of chemicals and dyestuffs for all production requirements.

Notes   1. These are not objectives.
2. They do not include time-scales.
3 They describe 'areas of attention' in that job.

The example quoted above is easy to relate to and simple to describe. It is also a real one. Below, we add a second example in Table 17.2. This time we are examining the job of a transport manager in operations, where the scope is somewhat different. A reader finding difficulty in writing clearly separable areas of accountability may be helped by this example.

Table 17.2
Accountability

Transport Manager Electronics/Engineering

1. Ensure that import and export duties/charges are the lowest possible to the company.
2. Choose transportation methods in national inter-factory transport and customer deliveries.
3. Control performance of all carriers.
4. Handle swiftly all claims or changes arising out of the carriage of goods.

Note that in this second example the same factors apply. There are no time-scales, they are areas of attention in that manager's job. A further and essential part of this process of defining one's job is that it has a dramatic effect on morale and motivation.

Case 3: improving confidence John Mitchell is a department manager in a large, multi-product manufacturing unit. Technically competent, good with staff and easy to deal with, John was in many ways an excellent manager, but he never succeeded in running his department efficiently, and poor results did not seem to worry him. It was not all John's fault. His boss was not demanding and furthermore the organization structure made his job difficult. For example, John was required to deal with central services for materials handling, the hiring and firing of staff and for plant maintenance.

After about three years as manager in such an environment, John got a new boss. The new man, more demanding than his predecessor, was immediately concerned about poor departmental performance. Recognizing both John's strengths and weaknesses he did three things:

1   He first demonstrated to John that the department was in fact capable of doing far more than was required. This was done by carrying out a simple work study investigation to measure machine output and to locate the main causes of lost production.
2   He discussed the work study findings with John and together they developed a control statement to record the reasons for lost output.
3   During the next six months he regularly discussed the control results with John and gradually taught him how to decide what had to be done and built up his confidence in getting it done until finally John required very little help.

The new boss has improved John's attitude towards accountability for results by helping him to get a new insight into the working of his department, by smoothing his path and building up his confidence through achieving success.

Objective-setting

Objectives

Many a technique has suffered from being presented as the best thing since . . .' and then being rejected when it fails to solve all problems instantly. One such technique was 'management by objectives' and in this case the rejection was very definite. However, the logic, the good sense, the essential need to set proper objectives at all levels remains undiminished by time, so that we find ourselves repeating many of the arguments of John Humble.[1] and others who wrote so much on the subject.

The origin of objectives

Objectives start right back at the corporate strategy of the organization. They are shaped by the business strategies which follow, and they take on form and substance, numbers and detail as they cascade through the specialist departments and functions of the enterprise. However, it is our experience that most managers do *not* have properly-set objectives. Few middle and junior managers are able to produce on demand a statement of areas of accountability which has any real meaning. There are many reasons for this, the calibre of senior management, changes in marketplace demands, failure to formalize systems and relationships, corporate culture and practices and many more.

Objectives in operations management

In operations management, objectives start to take on form and substance at the level of operations strategy, which ·defines the primary area in which those objectives are set. They have been discussed in detail in Chapter 2, and they immediately define the scope and areas of work for individual managers. The prime requirement for any objective is a position which is to be reached – an 'end state'. The second requirement is a statement of time allowed, the 'by when' element of objective-setting. All other aspects of objective-setting follow from there.

Clarity of objectives

Most operations management jobs are complex, overlap the responsibilities of other jobs and depend on them for their own success. So, in this area, it is important to take account of complexity in stating objectives, to make great efforts to avoid confusion, to state clearly and concisely the end state and to clarify the interfaces and overlap areas. Writers on objectives use the terms:

- clear and concise
- quantified where possible
- challenging to the person
- not overlapping with other jobs
- a means of development

all of which are easily understood in principle, even by the student who has never had to meet managerial objectives. It is more difficult to deal with these requirements in real situations, where the fog of compromise and the confusion of conflicting purpose are evident.

We will start with the example of the preparation plant superintendent studied previously in Table 17.1 (see Table 17.3). Below we have added objectives for each of the four principal accountabilities. Note:

- There is a time-scale.
- All are quantified in some way, either a figure or a yes/no target.
- All are concerned with improving the effectiveness of the preparation plant.

Table 17.3
Accountabilities and objectives

| Preparation Plant Superintendent / Large Mixed Paper Mill | |
Accountabilities	Objectives 19??
1. Contribute to the achievement of product cost and quality objectives by the efficient treatment of all product material prior to the paper machine.	1. To have established every product where departmental process treatment is inadequate, assigned causes, and instituted rectification methods.
2. Ensure the adequate supply (in conjunction with the yard department), of wood pulp, at an efficient level of cost.	2. To have reviewed, with the yard, all pulps in use, and reduced the financial stockholding investment by 25%.
3. Schedule the use of machinery so as to provide adequate time for maintenance, in conjunction with engineering department.	3. Have worked out a regular downtime schedule with engineers for all plant in the department, and have put all plant units through Class B (major overhaul) where required.
4. Obtain and hold adequate stocks of chemicals and dyestuffs for all production requirements.	4. Have established and implemented minimum stock levels for chemicals and dyestuffs.

Have reviewed the whole range of chemicals and dyestuffs used and reduced the number used by at least 50%.

Have reduced the financial stockholding investment by 40%.

We now follow with annual objectives (see Table 17.4) for the transport manager whose accountabilities were shown in Table 17.2.

Table 17.4
Accountabilities and objectives

Transport Manager	
Accountabilities	Annual Objectives 19—

1. Ensuring that import and export duties/charges are the lowest possible to the company.	1. No figure available from senior managers. Must keep figures 'As low as possible'.
2. Choice of transportation methods in UK inter-factory transport and customer deliveries.	2. Keep own transport utilization above 80%. Keep costs/tonne/mile of own transport 10% below carriers' quotes.
3. Control of carriers' performance.	3. Not quantified. Fits in with above.
4. Swift handling of all claims or charges arising out of carriage of goods.	4. Handle all claims up to £x,000, without further complaint, and reduce total claims on company by 10% annually.

This example is taken from the objectives of a real manager and it is clear that he will have difficulty in carrying out either no. 1. or no. 2. satisfactorily. At the end of the year there will either be a disagreement about his level of performance, or the appraisal will be carried out superficially. In either case he will become disillusioned with the appraisal process.

Quantifying objectives

Few managers enjoy writing or agreeing job descriptions. Fewer still like the process of setting objectives, either with bosses or subordinates. Often they feel that they are dealing with immeasurable factors. Yet there are very few worthwhile objectives which cannot be quantified to some extent. When the engineer cannot measure a variable directly he looks for a secondary measure which will act as a proxy. In the same way, the manager can frequently find an alternative way of approaching a difficult objective. Here are some examples:

1   Improve efficiency of major process streams to a satisfactory level. (Raise the efficiency of plants A, B and X to 80 per cent efficiency and 93 per cent utilization by end of this year.)
2   Train the assistant plant manager. (Diagnose training needs, agree programme for short- and long-term development, implement short-term programme to finish at end of this year.)
3   Keep control over price movements. (Keep prices within inflation figures by negotiation and promote competition among suppliers.)
4   Maintain best quality of supplies. (Institute supplier quality assurance scheme this year, meanwhile fix advance sampling for all deliveries.)
5   Improve computer system – no measure given! (Find reason for late provision of information, institute rectification. Rewrite systems specification for stock ordering system, and implement by end of this year.)

Objectives for improvement

Consider the following statement

MIDDLE MANAGERS ARE NOT THERE
TO RUN SYSTEMS. THEY ARE
THERE TO IMPROVE THEM.

This might be written on stiff card and left on the desk of every manager working in operations. The point is that there should be a constant striving for improvement, even when resources are frozen. The operations manager is not there just to 'produce the numbers', or to preside over a 'holding operation', but to lead the struggle for improvement.

Table 17.5

Accountabilities and objectives (Plant Manager)

Position (role in Department/Unit):
(Title and relationship to other managers.)
Description of contribution to unit results:

PLANT MANAGER

RESPONSIBLE FOR THE MANUFACTURE OF PRODUCTS IN RIGHT
QUANTITY AND QUALITY, MEETING REQUIRED TIMES.

PRINCIPAL ACCOUNTABILITIES (Major areas where my efforts bring greatest returns.)	ANNUAL OBJECTIVES What results are expected of me? Quantify where possible.	Degree of difficulty in reaching these objectives. Why is it difficult? (Do I have enough freedom of decision?)	What can I do about it? – organization changes – role changes – relationship changes
1. Materials flow through plant.	Adequate quantities of raw materials, incidental materials and packages. Running stocks normally are about one week.	Requires continual monitoring. Mechanical breakdown on plant can result in major changes in needs. Suppliers sometimes fail to meet agreed delivery schedules. Yes Plant Manager may alter call-in rates.	Buying Department representative should regularly attend monthly Production/Marketing Liaison meetings.
2. Chemicals and other product specifications.	Product specifications which must be met are laid down in a Product Specification manual. Customers may stipulate additional requirements. Specifications are often those laid down by Statutory bodies, e.g. B.P.C.	Reason for failure to meet a specification may be due to deviation in operating conditions or raw material quality. Cause often elusive. Yes Plant Manager controls operating conditions on plant and is arbiter with regard to raw materials.	
3. Competency and morale of staff.	A correct attitude to work must be cultivated. A plant can only be safely and efficiently operated with properly trained labour. Practices indicated by CAPITB should be followed.	Labour wastage between 20% and 30% per annum. Training programmes make demands on existing operator resources. No Plant Manager selects own labour from applicants screened by Personnel Department, but wage rates, conditions of employment and numbers decided by others.	More resources be allocated to selection and training.

4. Safety of Operators	Operations must be as safe as possible. The criteria laid down in the Health & Safety at Work Act must be met. The target for lost-time accident rate is less than 1.5 accidents per 100,000 hours.	Increasing pressure from Health & Safety Inspectorate for higher safety and environmental standards. No Rate of progress often limited by capital and resources of Engineering Department.	Greater importance be given to safety during modifications and new plant design.
5. Maintenance of Plant	Plant must be properly maintained so that it is safe to operate and also to ensure chemical and services efficiencies are up to the required standard. Standard chemical and services efficiencies vary from process to process, but are specifically set for each process.	Market pressure for product often conflicts with need for plant maintenance. Yes Plant Manager agrees with Engineers when maintenance must be carried out.	Marketing Department formalize policy on finished product stock levels.
6. Data	Stock and usage of raw materials and packages are required for monthly financial accounting reports. These must be submitted within 24 hours of period end. Basic data for new products is required by the Accounting Section when new products are introduced. Basic cost data for existing products reviewed once per year.	Tight time schedules mean that figures must be right first time since there is little or no time for re-checks. Yes By adequate planning and preparation.	Month-end processed data should be fed back to Plant Managers within one week.
7. Development	Improvements of process efficiencies in all respects. Trial runs results from new customer requirements, changes in materials or development section innovation.	Trial runs and modifications have to be fitted in with normal production since no interruption of customer service is a fundamental principle. No Development requirements sometimes overtake events so that crash action is required in attempts to stop share of market being lost to competitors.	Marketing Department give more and earlier information on expected market changes.

Authority/responsibility

One of the most sacred concepts of classical management theory is upheld in the statement 'When a manager is given responsibility then the authority required to carry out the tasks involved should go with it' that is, RESPONSIBILITY = AUTHORITY. Modern operations systems are complex, and modern marketing requirements vary enormously. It is the exception rather than the rule that middle, or indeed senior managers, have control of all the resources and the decision-making which affect their results. How often do we see the profit centre manager who is not in control of his own marketing, but relying on the quality of the decisions of other managers? Frequently the rules of in-company trading allow one part of the organization to make decisions which can have disastrous effects on another part. There must be a careful examination of every manager's job in order to establish the limits of authority and decision-making. These limits must then be equated with the results expected of the manager.

Peter Drucker[2] recognizes the importance of relating a manager's objectives to those of his peers. He insists that the manager's objectives must take account of what other managers can do to assist him in reaching his own objectives. Conversely, they should contain passages describing what he should be doing to help his colleagues with their objectives.

We would now like to consider Table 17.5, which shows the principal accountabilities and annual objectives for a plant manager working for a large chemical company.

Note that, in this real case, not all the annual objectives have been quantified. Some could be more accurately described. However, columns 3 and 4 contain an analysis of the difficulties encountered by this plant manager while trying to achieve these objectives. Column 5 contains his conclusions about action to be taken. Note that the initiative for making these changes lies with the plant manager himself. Note also that, in some cases, the solution will require changes in structure and/or relationships. This analytical document has proved to be very useful for operations managers when they have taken time specifically to examine their own ability to do their job. It needs careful thinking, it forces job-holders to work out the *reality* of their accountabilities and objectives.

Table 17.6
Problems of multiple accountability

ACCOUNTABILITY	OBJECTIVE	PROBLEM
1. Control stocks & WIP to minimize cost of production.	Reduce stockholding by 20% overall.	Sales sell ex-stock, demand pattern difficult to predict.
2. Meet product quality standards.	Reduce customer returns by 50%.	No real control over materials moisture content and flatness.
3. Ensure adequate process material ready for production at all times.	Monitor costs and plant efficiency to achieve 100% service.	No control over resources. Split accountability and lack of senior support.
4. Maintain machines to keep within 10% order delay or disappointment.	Implement preventive maintenance scheme this year.	No good repair shops available. Spare costs rising rapidly.
5. Ensure morale and competency of staff.	Devise & implement training scheme.	No precedent. Training department cooperate but senior managers uncommitted.
6. Ensure efficient plant utilization. (A plant manager)	Hold utilization *and* 75% efficiency.	Very difficult, poor spares availability, poor plant maintenance.
7. Manage production to provide acceptable service at lowest cost.	95% on-time delivery, keep overtime below budget, find ways to reduce costs by 20%.	Delivery planning not under my control. Have no information on stockholding, not under my control.
8. QA department monitor all products. Reduce recalls by 20%.	Find causes, start rectification with marketing & production.	Poor relations with marketing. They don't see need to cooperate.
9. QA policy formulation.	Identify problems, recommend solutions, justify & implement.	No corporate QA policy. No positive support.
10. Organize and motivate laboratory staff.	Achieve 20% higher throughput of testing work.	Staff shared with other managers, sample department too far away.
11. Pollution of environment. (Works chemist)	Achieve nil complaints from residents.	Cannot insist that production change process.
12. Bring forward new products.	X new products to be introduced.	New products hard to find. Evaluation times hard to get. Marketing reluctant to give information.

ACCOUNTABILITY	OBJECTIVE	PROBLEM
13. Project plans for new capital equipment.	Identify problem areas, monitor market, justify expenditure, ensure commissioning.	Lack authority, production managers don't know role. No control over final expenditure.
14. Provide fully trained QA staff.	Achieve primary knowledge of process.	Apathy, production staff against.
15. Develop staff.	Set objectives for each, monitor progress, define training needs.	On my own, senior managers will not be involved.
16. Manage factory costs (manufacturing manager).	Attain budget and develop system for monitoring variances.	No freedom of decision, cannot change pre-set targets.

Multiple accountability and conflicting objectives

One of the most disconcerting problems for the young manager is to realize that he or she is not in control of the decision-making needed to do their job properly. Over a period of years the form of analysis shown in Table 17.5 has been used by the authors to help operations managers to review their jobs in detail. The most frequent problem arising is the inability to make things happen because some other manager is in charge of the people or resources involved. We now add, in Table 17.6, a number of examples of areas of accountability where the manager has encountered problems of this type. They are all real, they have all been considered and discussed with the owners of the problem. In most cases, the manager has returned to the job and been able to find solutions. But it is important for really senior operations managers to take note of the number of times that junior managers feel exposed. Many of the examples show how a young manager does not think that adequate support is being given. In the event this may or may not be true, but it is the feeling of support and back-up which is so important to the effectiveness of such junior managers. There are also examples of multiple accountabilities, where very careful thought is needed to determine where the overlaps occur and how each person is to deal with them. Unfortunately, the evidence shows that not all senior managers understand the advantage to themselves and their staff of spending adequate time clarifying accountabilities.

Personal development task no. 17.1

Think about your own principal accountabilities in the way illustrated in Table 17.1 (p. 314), then record the four or five really vital ones on the left-hand side of a sheet of A4 lined paper. Pick discrete or easily identifiable areas of attention in your job. They should be areas which will always be there as long as your job remains the same, so make sure that they do not have time-scales.

Personal development task no. 17.2.

Take the sheet on which you filled in your accountabilities. On the right-hand side put in this year's annual objectives against each accountability:

1   Do they all have numbers?
2   If not then do they have yes/no completion points?
3   Does each one correctly describe the area for attention?

Personal development task no 17.3

This time we will carry out an analysis of difficulties. Take the sheet containing your accountabilities and objectives. Tape another sheet to the side of it and draw in two columns as in Table 17.5 (p. 320). Now take each objective in turn and consider the difficulties you encounter in trying to fulfil that one. Work across to the last column, finishing with the action you propose to take in order to improve your effectiveness. For column 3 ask the following questions about each objective:

1   Is it realistically attainable?
2   Do you have freedom of decision to effect the results?
3   Do you have to persuade others to do things for you?
4   Will the normal decisions of other people prevent you from reaching your objective?
5   Have you enough resources (material, financial, expertise) to reach this objective?
6   If not then how do you get them?

For column 4 use these questions as a checklist:

1   Do you need a change of reporting relationship in your structure?

2   Do you need to re-negotiate the figures in the objective?
3   Do you need to agree a change of job content for yourself?
4   Or for one of your peers?
5   Do you need to make proposals for new resources?

When each objective has been reviewed in this way your analysis of accountabilities and objectives is complete.

A wider perspective

All this refers to job objectives arising out of areas of accountability – in other words, the job as seen by the organization and the objectives that arise from it. However, this is not the end of the story. We all have personal goals, ways in which we want to influence the job, a style which we bring to our work and these important wants and needs will influence our interpretation of objectives and accountabilities. We will deal with these in the next chapter.

Chapter summary points

- Accountability is an area of attention in our job.
- Attention to a few areas will give maximum results.
- Well thought-out accountabilities often lead to job re-arrangement.
- Objectives are places to get to within a given time limit.
- Objectives always need some kind of quantification.
- Objectives should be for improvement, not maintaining status.

References

1   Humble, J., *Improving Business Results,* New York: McGraw Hill, 1968.
2   Drucker, P., *The Practice of Management,* London: Heinemann, 1955.

Essential reading

Blanchard, K and Johnson, S. *The One-minute Manager,* London: Fontana Books, 1983. This little book quickly became a bestseller when managers realized that the reality of objective-setting and performance appraisal was written into the script of a story about the way a particular manager behaved towards his subordinates.

18 Personal planning and agenda-setting

Resumé

We ended the last chapter with an investigation of the realities of accountability determination and objective-setting. In other words, we have reached the point where the scope and reality of the job have been defined and quantified annual objectives have been set for each major area of accountability. We know what the job is, in detail. However, this is not the end of it. In Chapter 12, where we studied personality, it was emphasized how different people take quite contrasting attitudes to work and how they have expectations and preferences for the way they approach their working life. We must now move on to consider *how* the job is to be done and in particular how *we*, as unique individuals, wish to go about the job. We must then look at our own personal goals and agendas and plan to complete them by 'doing it our way'.

There are many different ways in which to carry out the job of the operations manager. Should the manufacturing manager in a large, multi-purpose assembly plant be seen to have his head inside the machinery? Should the production manager in a major printing works be the technical arbiter on inks, paper quality, and web feeding mechanisms? If he is, then he has almost certainly brought the job with him when he was promoted. How do his very able staff feel about his attention to technical detail and how would they equate that with their own accountabilities?

Personal work style

One way to examine our own work style is to consider the different options open to us, on each of which we take a particular stance, the whole providing a picture or profile of how we approach our job.

Option 1: what we must do ourselves

Here we are faced with decisions about which jobs can only be done by ourselves, (the job-holder) and cannot be ignored, delegated, or passed on. We do not make these decisions on the basis of what we are good at, but because of the position we hold. Discipline is usually one such decision and staffing is another for which the operations manager will not, indeed cannot, delegate. Are there others in your case?

Option 2: what we leave out altogether

Most operations jobs are demanding and stressful, with deadlines, strong competition in the marketplace and little time in which to complete essential daily tasks. So it is important to decide what *not* to do. This may well mean rejecting pleas by subordinates to do things they think we should be doing, such as the details of production planning. It might mean persuading our boss that some time-consuming public relations committee of his should be dropped in favour of more productive work. It may even mean deciding to drop one of our own pet departmental projects after hard and honest thinking. This option allows us to interpret our objectives in such a way that we make our job realistic and the objectives attainable.

Option 3: what we insist that subordinates do

One good rule is to make sure that we delegate repetitive actions, keeping unique ones for ourselves. This way we are always in the position of taking initiatives and improving things. This rule is vital for operations managers, who are usually plagued by repetitive decisions.

Second, subordinates should do things which will help them to develop as managers. So they must be given freedom to make certain decisions rather than refer them upwards; these could include quality decisions, re-order level decisions, change of material decisions – whatever will allow them to think more positively about their job. One manager delegated to a trainee the job of organizing meetings to smell and identify new fragrances, so that he would learn to identify standard fragrances himself.

Option 4: the support we need from our boss

Do we require detailed terms of reference in order to carry out our job properly? The higher the managerial job, the more that manager should demand freedom of manoeuvre, freedom to use personal initiative, albeit with full accountability for the results. How do we ensure support and backing from our boss when making crucial decisions? Does he have the confidence to give us our heads, or do we play it close, and refer back frequently before making nasty decisions? Do we get all the resources we really need? Or do we just go so far and then hand the problem back to him? Mostly we get the support we deserve.

Option 5: what we persuade our peers to do

The chief works chemist in a manufacturing unit who is made responsible for environmental pollution is in an impossible position. In fact, he can only be made responsible for monitoring and reporting. His decision must be how to persuade his peers to accept their own responsibility and to strike up a working relationship which allows sensible cooperation. He has the choice of openly forcing the issue with his superiors, or of settling the issue out of court. Departmental boundaries can become extremely fuzzy, and there are occasions when persuasion and sensible dealing will save untold trouble and inefficiencies. The production/distribution boundary is one difficult area, the product manager system is another. Should the manager of the finishing department of a processing plant persuade his warehousing/distribution manager to take responsibility for the product earlier in the finishing process, so that their respective accountabilities will make more sense? The new product manager who cannot bring forward his products because of inadequate information must decide whether to persuade his marketing peers to spend time and money providing him with appropriate data, or try to justify his own information-gathering unit.

Option 6: where we set the frontiers of our job

The scope of a manager's job is different in the eyes of different parties. The marketing services manager may have a job specification which is vague enough to allow wide differences of interpretation.

He may simply aim to be a service to other managers, in three or four specified subject areas. He may be much more ambitious, extending his sphere of influence until, in practice, he is running an extensive marketing operation. The wise senior manager will get involved as this takes place, defining in detail what he perceives to be the extent and limits of the job. He will also use the situation to stretch his better managers, gradually extending the scope of their work. He will do it openly, defining each new step for other managers to work with and understand.

So we have the option of career advancement when looking at the frontiers of our job. It may be viewed in two ways. First, extend the job, as shown in the examples above. Second, take the job as it stands, and carry it out superbly well, using the experience to make a reputation for good work. Managers, however, do not simply do a new job well or badly. They grow and develop into and through a job, improving themselves, and leaving their personal stamp behind them when they move on.

Demands, constraints, choices

We have taken a purely positive approach to work style in this treatment. Rosemary Stewart[1] conducted a research project into the way in which managers approach their jobs. The work led to a structure for self-examination in which the manager looks at his or her own choices, after considering the demands and constraints on time and decision-making. Consideration of demands and constraints will lead to the elimination of some of them, expanding the area of real choice.

Personal ambition

We have now reached a position where we have:

1 realistically defined our accountabilities;
2 produced annual objectives against each one;
3 examined *how* we go about our own job (our own style).

We now need to think carefully about planning for optimum personal performance – but pause for a moment. Optimum performance means many things to many people. For a single, dedicated, 30-year-old graduate with great ambitions it could mean total immersion, a heavy workload, few hobbies and distractions. For a 35-year-old family man with a nice house and settled to a well-rounded life it may mean a balance between giving good value in an interesting job and carrying on a happy family life as well. Different people achieve different ambitions in life and in their work. However, the reality of present-day managing is:

1 heavy competition;
2 pressure on product or service performance;
3 lean staffing
4 sudden and frequent changes.

Against this background the operations manager is under particular pressure, so it becomes imperative that career and work style choices are carefully thought-out. Perhaps we should have a second card printed and circulated to all operations managers:

THINK AHEAD!
REACTING BRINGS PROBLEMS

Personal planning

So how do we think ahead? What is the formula for personal planning?

Plans, agendas, planning cycles

The raw material procurement planner in the cement industry would be appalled at the shortness of the planning cycles in some financial companies and in the money markets. Each job has its own cycles of activity, and we identify our own quite easily. This time cycle must then become the unit for our own personal planning, certainly in the short and medium term. However, most companies impose arbitrary annual planning cycles for financial planning, for budgeting cost and revenue, salary review and performance review. A major problem in achieving annual plans is the barrage of short-term urgent issues which we suffer daily and weekly, and we must find ways of thinking beyond these items, while not completely ignoring them. This chapter will deal with longer-term plans, while Chapter 19 addresses daily and weekly problems.

Agendas

John P. Kotter[2] uses the word 'agendas' to describe the series of long-term and intermediate intentions, plans, and developing needs, which we carry along during our daily working lives. Some will indeed coincide with our agreed annual plans. Some will be vaguely worded personal intentions, which will gradually harden and formulate as life moves on, until they become important personal or job goals. Others will indeed be short-term expedients, clearing the way for more constructive longer-term actions later on.

In a *Harvard Business Review* article, Kotter describes research into how numbers of effective general managers spent their time. In fact, none of them were immune to daily pressures and distractions, but they all held to certain ideas and intentions for progress, they all had a picture of the 'way ahead' – a sense of purpose which stood out above the daily time-wasters. Now, operations managers are particularly prone to daily pressure and need a formula and a sense of purpose with which to keep working towards some longer-term goal. The concept of agendas provides just such a sense of purpose. Table 18.1 shows an example of a set of agendas for an operations manager.

Table 18.1
Agendas for the operations manager

	This Year	Next Year	Some Time Later
1	Replace Smith. Review Jones' commitment.	Recruit 2 engineers.	Attain a structure which will help ops. objectives, specialize in XYZ technology, provide fast data on techn. changes, and react to market changes.
2	Review job specs. Quantify staff objectives.	Change MIS objectives.	Change organization culture from role to task.
3	Review state of all plant investments. Reassess techn. development systems.	Realign plant investment policy and replacement periods. Engage top process designer.	Attain national notice for best design quality available.
4.	Review every manager.	Set and agree annual objectives for each manager. Install review system.	Attain self-generating review system, based on product excellence.

Opportunism

Effective senior managers are not slaves to short-term pressures. They do have a sense of purpose or grand strategy backing up their daily efforts. So why are so many of them affected by the vicissitudes of managerial life? Clearly, they are often caught out and frustrated by the time-wasters and the interruptions. So why put up with them? Two reasons stand out above all others. First, they are human beings, and they need to communicate with and interrelate with peers, staff, and customers. Second, and perhaps more importantly, they are opportunists.

'I want to keep a finger on the pulse of this operation', said the director of a manufacturing unit.

'I need to know the current problems if I am to be in touch with my job' said the manager of a large distribution region.

They are saying, in another way, that they are quite willing to institute changes on the basis of what they see as actually happening. They are using short-term realities to mould and shape their longer-term intentions and plans. So the whole process of short-term/long-term planning is iterative, a cycle of review and improvement, each depending on the other. The effective manager therefore;

- *is* an opportunist and visionary
- *is not* solely reacting to daily pressures
- *is not* sticking rigidly to long-term plans.

Network of relationships

The director of a management consultancy division had two children, a boy and a girl. As each one approached their majority he gave them a thick, expensive, leatherbound address book. On the fly leaf he wrote: 'Fill this book, it is the key to your future success.'

The 'old boy' network is oft-maligned, in many cases with good reason, but we do all need our networks of friends, relations, colleagues and business contacts, if we are to develop and spread our influence. This network will blossom, change, periodically shrink, but always enable us to find someone who might help us in our careers and our lives. When we think back to the best managers who we have known or worked for, we always remember their ability to find someone to help in a crisis, someone to give good advice, someone to lobby for them in important places.

These networks expand our sphere of influence, help our self-confidence, give other managers confidence in our ability to manage difficult situations and give us a wider platform on which to build our careers.

Period planning

Having taken account of our preferences, our work style, and personal agendas and having produced a set of formal annual plans, we should now pay some attention to breaking down those annual plans into more manageable pieces. The size of the piece depends on the time-scale we adopt, and a convenient period for most people is one month. We can then look at the sequence of planning diagramatically, from accountabilities right through to short-term planning – both the sequence of formal plans and our personal style and preferences (see Table 18.2).

Table 18.2
Personal planning sequence

	Formal	Personal
1.	Accountabilities------------------------Work Style	
2.	Annual Objectives --------------------Options (Demands, Constraints)	
3.	Monthly plans	Networks/Agendas
4.	Diary and Work sheet.	

Monthly plans

These are usually the most difficult plans to produce in such a way that they look convincing or worth carrying out. However, they are the most rewarding in terms of results. They ensure that the important, but non-urgent items in the annual plans actually reach completion. Monthly plans should not simply be moved on to the next month if not completed, but each month the remaining plans for the year should be re-examined and rescheduled.

Table 18.3 shows a monthly planning sheet taken from a personal planning system. It is filled in for the Preparation Plant Superintendent quoted in Chapter 17, Tables 17.1 and 17.3. Note that each annual plan (AP) is broken down into something that can actually be achieved this month (MP). We will not always succeed. There will be times when a particular MP takes three months to achieve. But the reality is that we *are* achieving the APs, even if it is a gradual process. Finally, note the progressing section of the monthly plan, where achievement is recorded against original plans. This becomes the basis for the next month's MP.

Table 18.3
Monthly Plans

Part 1

Item	Plan	Start By	Finish By
1	List every product where departmental processing is inadequate.	1 March	28 March
2.	Create list of all pulps used, with % usage.	3 March	28 March
	Obtain stock list of pulps used with last month's usage of each.	1 March	15 March
3.	Meet engineers with machine register to plan plant downtime schedule.	10 March	—
4.	Obtain current dyestuffs stock list, with last year's usage figures.	5 March	20 March

Part 2: Monthly Progress

Item	Delegate to	Date	Progress and Control
1	J.D.	28 March	Completed.
2.	Yard	28 March	Not yet received
	"	"	"
3.	Self	28 March	Meeting held 20 March. List of inadequate machinery to be produced by engineers by 6 April.
4.	B.D.	28 March	Completed.

Personal development task no. 18.1.

Using the headings shown below, examine your own job for each of the six options described on pages 328–330, listing for each of them your present attitudes and practices, what you feel you ought to be doing and finally what you plan to do about it.

Present Practice Shortcomings	Where You Want to Get to	Actions Needed	By When
Option 1.			
Option 2.			

Personal development task no. 18.2

Put the headings of Table 18.1 (p. 332) on a sheet of A4 paper and start to develop your own set of agendas. Some will be obvious, others will arise out of previously set annual objectives. Some will be personal and private, concerned with your own aspirations in the job and your intentions for your future career. This document will not be completed in one session. You will probably come back to it several times, but when completed it will be your reference point for progressing towards your personal goals in your job.

Personal development task no. 18.3

Buy yourself a thick, expensive, leatherbound address book!

Chapter Summary Points

- Individual managers interpret their jobs differently.
- Managers have options about *what* they do, and *how* they do it.
- Managers who react lose the initiative.
- Personal goals impinge on, and alter, formal objectives.
- Forward thinking plus opportunism equals effective managing.
- Monthly plans are the power house of the operations manager.

References

1 Stewart, R., *Choices for the Manager,* New York; McGraw Hill, 1982.
2 Kotter, John P., 'What the effective general manager really does,' *Havard Business Review,* November–December, 1982

Essential Reading

Stewart, R., *Choices for the Manager,* McGraw Hill, New York, 1982. This book describes the results of research into the way in which managers choose to do their jobs, the demands made on them and the constraints within which they operate. It provides a framework with which to work out a personal strategy in your job.

19 Priority planning and time saving

Introduction

If there is one area of management which has a surfeit of literature it is time management. There are books, there are films, there are videos, audio tapes and complex short-term planning systems. All are seeking to solve the problem of how to squeeze even more work into the time available. They are addressing the increasing pressures for:

1. less manpower;
2. fewer managers;
3. faster reaction time;
4. greater efficiency and product performance.

It is interesting to note the comment of an operations manager while attending a general manager programme at a British management centre. 'How come I've done a time management course, had time management sessions at work, kept a diary and list of time wasters, yet I still feel that I need to go through it all again every year or so?' Most managers have the same feeling. They are really looking for a philosophy, yet find that, without the sense of purpose it promotes in them, the devices and systems are of little use.

That sense of purpose develops from the longer-term objectives, agendas and personal plans discussed in Chapters 17 and 18. It enables us to see through and beyond the daily and weekly urgencies of our jobs. However, the amount of short-term disruption we endure is partly a matter of choice. There are measures we can take to minimize that disruption.

Priority planning

Figure 19.1 shows the various aspects of a personal planning system for planning our priorities. In essence, it allows for our individual personality to dictate the amount of detail we will be happy with in our daily working lives. Some managers are very thorough and follow detailed plans every day. Others prefer a lighter touch, keeping only the essentials on a simple work list.

The inputs to our system include our monthly plans, together with those essential meetings which we must attend, or run ourselves. There will also be a number of routines which we carry out daily or weekly, which we have recognized as being vital to our work. A second category of inputs is whatever planning sheets, work lists or diaries with which we work comfortably, and which help us to work effectively. Finally, we need to do the occasional problem diagnosis, in order to see where we are failing, to spotlight the areas which are non-productive or time-wasting. It is this need to reassess our problems of time management that the operations manager, quoted above, was voicing.

The outputs from priority planning will include the discarding of some jobs which are no longer needed, the delegation of others which we should not be doing personally, and a system of progress checks to keep us up to standard. The result will not be a life free from interruption. It will be a life with which one unique being will be happy, which will allow that person to work with maximum long-term effectiveness. We cannot overemphasize how heavily time management is influenced by personal preference; we must accept the realities of our own personality when devising a system to suit ourselves.

Problem diagnosis

At least once each year – maybe at the time of preparing annual plans – it is useful to look back over the period, in order to see what bad habits have crept in, what new requirements have forced themselves on our time planning, what interruptions have developed. A check list for new problems which have emerged is described in Table 19.1.

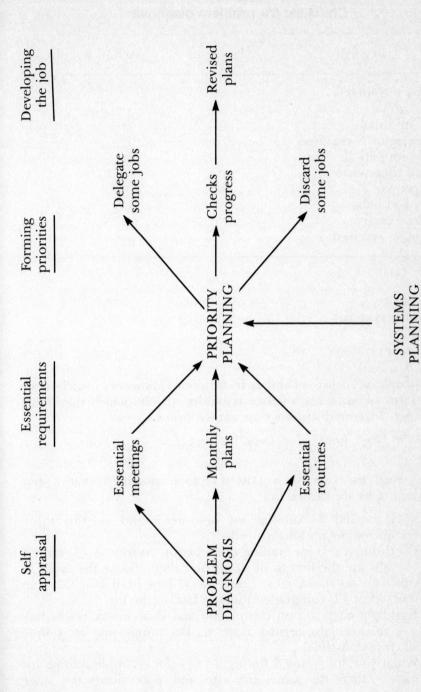

Figure 19.1   The priority planning process

Table 19.1
Checklist for problem diagnosis

Category	Problem	Action Required
1 New meetings – formal – informal New returns required (with period)		
3 New time-wasters people		
4 My bad habits		
5 Unnecessary reports received		

Planning systems

Work list

Most people keep lists of things to be done. Managers usually have some form of work list, often a reminder of jobs which they must not forget. Suggested headings are shown below.

Item No.	Item	Deadline	Progress	Priority (A.B.C.)

The work list can be a powerful tool, provided that a few important tasks are carried out:

1 Start the day by adding any new items and deleting those completed, or no longer needed.
2 Go through the list grading the jobs for priority, A, B, and C. 'A' jobs are the first to be done. You then choose the order in which to do the A jobs. Leave the C jobs until last; they can wait. After all, you graded them as last on the list.
3 Highlight each job on completion and if necessary reschedule any further jobs arising from it. Do things one at a time wherever possible.
4 When you are stopped during a job – for example waiting for data – then do something else and note down the stage reached.

5   When reworking the list each day, remember to plan in specific jobs from your monthly plans. Thus, you will keep moving forward, with the longer-term, very important, strategic jobs which can so easily be left until tomorrow.

Daily planner

While we all keep a diary, there are some days which we know will be very hectic, with meetings, reports to write, places to go to, urgent issues to settle. Some special piece of short-term (daily) planning is required here, and Figure 19.2 shows a document which is useful for this purpose. It is definitely not for use every day, except perhaps by a very small number of people in highly reactive, fast moving jobs. But it can be very comforting for those who hate to have a number of absolutely vital tasks to complete, but not enough time to take them slowly and carefully.

Again, like the work list, the daily planner sheet is completed at the start of the day. Unlike the work list, however, it may begin to collect entries well before the day in question. During the day, as each task is completed, the relevant action points are noted, otherwise one or two of them will be forgotton. It may also help to add to, or amend, the list of special issues/reminders. There can be great satisfaction at the end of a really hectic day, in seeing how well everything fitted in and how much further forward the job has progressed in a very short time.

Other useful planning sheets

Two further planning sheets are offered in Figures 19.3 and 19.4. The monthly planning chart in Figure 19.3 has obvious uses. The second, Figure 19.4, is perhaps not so well known. A single sheet for planning meetings can be invaluable as a way of gathering a meeting together. First, plan the agenda; second, consider the background papers needed, either as pre-reading, or for reference at the meeting. Then, at the meeting itself, use the last column for action points and for the initials of those responsible for that action. Copies of the whole sheet can then be handed out, or circulated, cutting down dramatically on the time and effort needed to mount the meeting efficiently.

	Month	
	Week	
DAILY PLANNER	Day	

Morning Appointments/Plans	Action Notes
8 a.m.	
10 a.m.	

Afternoon	
1 p.m.	
3 p.m.	
5 p.m.	

Evening	
7 p.m.	
9 p.m.	

Special issues/Reminders

Figure 19.2   Daily planner

MONTHLY PLANNER CHART

Month _____   Year _____

Week	Notes	Monday	Tuesday	Wednesday	Thursday	Friday	Saturday	Sunday
1								
2								
3								
4								
5								

Figure 19.3   Monthly planner chart

MEETINGS PLANNER

Month

Week

Topic

Date

Location

Present

Objectives

Personal presentations

Agenda	Documentation		Decisions taken	Follow-up controls	
	Read	Take		By when	By whom

Notes

Figure 19.4   Meetings planner

Discard and delegate

Our priority planning process is now almost complete. As the sequence of problem diagnosis – defining essential requirements and employing planning systems – proceeds, we naturally improve the form and substance of our job. This leads to the discarding of inessential tasks, most of which will have grown up with the system. It is surprising how many procedures, papers and reports can be quietly cancelled, with little complaint from erstwhile recipients.

Delegation needs more thought. At this stage, all the tasks and decisions left in our job are seen to be essential. So which do we do ourselves and which do we delegate? First, we should list the jobs which none of our subordinates can do:

1 because they are not capable or experienced enough; or
2 because only we ourselves have the authority to do them.

In the first case, we have the option of training and testing them, then gradually handing the jobs over to them as part of their own development. This is the normal, if time-consuming, part of any manager's job, and the operations manager needs to give time and thought to how this is best accomplished. In case (2) above, there are some tasks – never more than two or three – which cannot be delegated. The list would include personnel development, discipline and departmental policy-making. Each is critical to our success, and each is carried out with the mark of our own personal style. They are all time-consuming, but if we discard and delegate effectively, we will have time to concentrate on these vital tasks and dramatically raise our level of management performance.

Personal development task no. 19

Using the format shown in Table 19.1 (page 340), identify your own problem areas which have arisen during the last year, paying close attention to the cause. Then work out plans to rectify them, bearing in mind that any of them may be the signals of a change of emphasis elsewhere which will require new initiatives by yourself.

Having filled in this form, and there may only be two or three items on it, the action required may well go into the next monthly plan, or in extreme cases need a re-examination of accountabilities and objectives. Whichever way, we now have a periodic reappraisal mechanism for our priority-setting process. The area of time-wasters might be large enough to treat separately. If so, use the following headings to identify them, noting what action is necessary.

My Major Time-wasters	Rating 1-5	What to do about the Three Worst Offenders

Chapter summary points

- Saving time is a continual challenge.
- Priority planning is a sense of purpose, not a device.
- The priority planning process is continuous.
- Problem diagnosis is needed regularly – at least annually.
- Short-term priorities should originate from long-term plans.
- Planning devices depend for their success on personal preference.

Essential reading

Your own accountability statement and this year's annual plans. You cannot plan for priorities properly until longer-term intentions and agendas have been worked out.

Other reading

Garratt, S., *Manage Your Time,* London: Fontana/Collins, 1985.

Mintzberg, H., *The Nature of Managerial Work,* New York: Harper and Row, 1974.

Part VI
THE FUTURE: A VISION

20 The future for the operations manager

Introduction

The world of operations has changed out of all recognition in recent times; it is changing while this work is being written and will continue to change inexorably as the world continues to alter and develop. If operations managers are to remain in tune with that world and be equipped to meet the challenges emanating from these changes, then they will require a good working knowledge of the state of the operations world. That world consists of an external and an internal environment, and operations managers live in both of them. Not only will they need to understand what is happening in both spheres, but they will have the essential role of recognizing the symptoms of change and of managing the consequences. This throws a heavy burden on their professionalism, technical expertise, managerial wisdom and intellectual capacity. So there will be dramatic changes in the job specification, and also in the person specification for the typical operations manager. We should now explore all those changes in order to complete our task in this book.

The external environment

In looking at the future for operations managers, and in order to evaluate how the job will change, we must look at how the environment is changing. The following sections introduce a range of potential change areas and examine the effects of each one.

Markets

The key element in market changes during recent years has been their increasingly international scale. No longer can home markets be relied upon to provide a comfortable turnover. The European Economic Community, despite many attempts by member countries to protect their politically sensitive industries, has opened up trade within its membership to a considerable extent. Because home markets are freely accessible to other member countries, home-made products are more easily compared with the competition. At the same time, customers are conscious of the wider choice available to them and of their own need for cost-effective buying. They are developing much greater product knowledge and cannot be sidetracked with eye-catching accessories. The scale of operations brought about by these market movements has also increased dramatically, so that there is much more to aim for and a great deal more competition in doing so. In addition, large areas of the rest of the world have now opened up for trading. This has a twofold effect. First, although these areas provide larger markets for imported products and services, they are also building up their own expertise in manufacturing and providing services and are exporting them to the traditional trading countries. There is often a considerable difference in labour costs, leading to very keen prices and competitive products.

A second unsettling aspect of international trading is the volatile nature of many markets. Political and economic activities frequently lead to fluctuating exchange rates and the need to be able to switch rapidly from product to product and from country to country. International companies will move their manufacturing facilities to areas of competitive advantage, either coming nearer to the end customer or to areas of lower labour cost. All these factors in international trading militate against stability, long production runs and an easy life for the operations manager.

Products/services

Given the market characteristics outlined above, the products and services offered in those markets will themselves create special requirements for the producer. Life cycles are becoming shorter as the pace of technological change increases, and many more companies are entering the marketplace. This means that a constant stream of new offerings are appearing, that designers are creating infinitely more variety in their products, and that buyers are frequently spoilt for choice. The problem for the producer then becomes one of creating a competitive edge over other manufacturers; and two alternatives are being exploited more frequently. The first is to offer a more tailored product, making special versions for individual customers, focusing on their unique requirements, helping to keep their business through specialized customer service. The second alternative is to compete through ever higher quality of design, always endeavouring to offer a better standard of product and ensuring that the quality of conformance is also excellent.

Competition

Competition is now worldwide; there are fewer barriers than hitherto and the environment is itself more competitive. This situation has great dangers for those who think in defensive terms, who will always be reacting to others' initiatives, and so will always, by definition, be coming from behind. But for the more imaginative – the positive corporate thinkers, the inventive product developers – there are enormous opportunities. While the marketing activity is always seeking to exploit opportunities, the really imaginative managers will be gearing up their operations units to compete through superb operations skills, flexibility, consistency and quality standards.

Resources

The pressures brought to bear on resources are conflicting and will test operations managers' technical and problem-solving skills. On the one hand there is the pressure for greater utilization of plant, equipment and other resources, including manpower, the satisfaction of which requires long runs of standard products. The same requirements are demanded when calls are made for the most efficient use of money, which not only entails the use of inherently efficient plant, but also suggests long-running, standardized, single-purpose operations, with staff capable of extracting the utmost in output and consistency from that plant. Unfortunately, set against these are conflicting requirements – born of the volatility and speed of reaction of modern markets – for the employment of flexible facilities. The call is for the ability to change at will from high to low volume operations and, at the same time, to be capable of producing a wide variety of products or services. The operations managers who solve these dilemmas successfully are the ones who will give their companies a competitive advantage which will be hard to beat.

Technology

Processes are becoming more sophisticated, and the attention paid to instrumentation and computer controls mean that greater accuracy is available. This in turn enables closer specifications to be accepted and followed, with the certainty that good products will be produced. The consequence of this is that process research and development will be – indeed already is – concentrating on the development of plant and facilities which are extremely accurate, yet capable of high volume operations without loss of accuracy. Tall order that this may sometimes be, technological advances in the fields of electronics, computing, miniaturization, and the use of new materials have allowed extraordinary improvements in the performance, reliability and flexibility of operational processes.

Legislation

As outlined in Chapter 16, there has been a significant increase in the volume of collective labour law, although individual employment law has decreased. There will be periodic changes in this form of law, and it is complex, sometimes confusing, for managers. The demands on the operations manager are to decide how expert to become, whether to manage by the law, or to use it as a shield. A further trend might be the move towards greater individual accountability in the workplace, so that more care should be taken to manage people, to define their accountabilities more formally and to ensure that they operate and manage individually within the law.

Trade unions

There have been great changes in the power and attitudes of the trade unions. The economic downturn, together with the change in management attitude and the legislation introduced by successive Conservative administrations in the United Kingdom, have served to cause a major re-think in the role of trade unions. No longer do they dictate the terms under which they will allow companies to manage. The future role may well be a more balanced one, where managers regain the initiative in managing their workforces, and where unions guard the rights of their members in carrying out their jobs. When managers are creating an atmosphere in which people want to work and there is a collective will for companies to succeed, then trade unions will have the opportunity to take a more positive stance in the creation of wealth for their members. Whether they actually reach this situation depends to a great extent on how managers in general, and operations managers in particular, seize their current opportunities to manage. If they do not, then the chances of survival in international competition will be negligible. Few other nations will permit the paralysis that has frequently resulted from British management–union relationships during the past thirty years.

Individual aspirations

One of the most dramatic changes in workplace relationships has been the awakening of workers to the partnership which manager and worker should share. Modern workers are not satisfied with being told what to do, or how to do it. They expect more dialogue, they expect not just to be consulted about their jobs but to have more say in how they are organized, what should be done when, and what the job scope should be. They are moving more towards the responsibility and authority which managers expect for their own positions. All the pressures listed above lead to a responsible, highly technically trained and intelligent workforce, whose individual contribution towards company success is far in excess of previous expectations. They will be highly critical of any job which does not allow them full expression of their capabilities, and they will be equally critical of managers who do not manage them professionally.

The internal environment

Having examined developments in the external environment we must now look at the internal world which the operations manager occupies. This world is itself influenced, if not controlled, by the business environment in which it operates. So a number of the issues already addressed will have a bearing on the present discussion. In this rather more micro system, the interests of individuals and work groups will predominate, rather than markets or countries or economic alliances.

Attitudes towards operations

The need to be efficient and yet flexible, to combine low cost with high quality, to react quickly to product and market movements must change traditional impressions of both the importance of operations and of the contribution which they make to the effectiveness of the whole company. The operations activity can only fulfil these requirements by being more visible on the corporate stage. No longer can product–market decisions be made elsewhere and then passed on for operations to fathom out and do the best they can with them. Their whole attitude must be one of pro-active decision-making, of taking initiatives for new process design, for new product investigation, for joint development teams with marketers and technologists. The ability to leapfrog the technology of other companies is only achieved by continual cross-functional teamwork. In this respect, the activity with the most to offer is usually operations/production/manufacturing. So often in the past the thinking has been: 'If we can get into this market quick enough we could do very well. So we will put the money aside for marketing, and by the way we had better give production warning of what we want them to do.'

There will also be a requirement for realistic measures of successful performance. Traditional costing methods will not be sufficient by themselves. There will need to be a positive encouragement for actions which lead to competitive advantage, for the development of better methods and processes and for cooperative ventures between production units. There is thus the need for more involvement with other functions, a greater visibility at corporate level, and more imaginative methods of measuring performance.

Organization structure

Functional structures have always been preferred for one-product companies and, so long as changes are minimal, this form of structure works well. However, it does not provide the linkages required when the essence of success is rapid reaction and frequent product update. The project organization required of NASA contractors was designed to concentrate on one project or product, and was always cross-functional. This form of structure is much preferred for transient activities, those with a predictable completion date, and there will be many such projects in the future pattern of operations.

It will be common for operations units to have a number of time-related projects in action, using experts from other functions, while at the same time operating production units on normal products. The pattern of structure will have one enormous advantage over classical functions. Many managers and technologists from other functions will be exposed to the problems and realities of operations. They will begin to recognize the scope of operations and the opportunities for corporate initiative available to that activity. In the same way, the operations managers will have great opportunities for job rotation, either temporarily, or on a more permanent basis, as the chances arise. Those chances must be made to arise if operations managers are in turn to be inculcated with a truly commercial approach to their job.

Adopting new technology

Another effect of the changing pattern of business will be the importance of changing technology when the need arises. If an operations unit has made no changes for a long time, and the same products are being produced with little alteration, then a technology change will be a traumatic experience for all personnel involved. There is already more frequent change and its pace is accelerating. Obviously many changes will be incremental rather than substantial, but the structure will need to be designed in such a way that technology change can take place without pulling out the heart of the operations system as well as the machinery. Technology life cycles are getting shorter, so that every part of operations – the equipment and plant, the personnel, the planning systems and the interdepartmental relationships – must be arranged in such a way that they will take these changes in their stride. This may well prove to be one of the most complex challenges for operations managers. Not least among their responses will be the multiskilling of personnel, in order to cope with flexible manufacturing equipment.

Communication and involvement

Large companies making a few standard products in a seller's market develop an atmosphere of self-satisfaction, where standardization is paramount and change strongly resisted. The lean years of the early 1980s destroyed this culture in all but the most obtuse of managements and an atmosphere of change, of opportunity accepted, and of personal challenge is developing. Perceptive operations managers recognize the need to encourage individuals to think about change, and to accept the responsibility for designing it as well as for implementing it. This amounts to an attitude of continual improvement, of personal achievement built around change objectives rather than performance objectives. At the beginning of the 1980s this scenario was merely a dream for the future, but the intervening years have turned the dream into approaching reality for many organizations, while the leading ones have already arrived there. Only the present front-runners and those who follow the same trail, will succeed in the environment portrayed in earlier sections.

Planning for such fundamental transformations requires skills in communication and motivation of a high order. Cultures do not change overnight any more than managing directors change their leadership style, so the efforts must be made over periods of time, using every opportunity to relate actions to the changing circumstances, and to convince workforces of the commitment and good intentions of the management.

The changing job of the operations manager

All the external and internal factors described above will have an impact on the operations manager's job, and indeed much of the transformation has already been inferred. The operations manager has begun to change and will need to change further as cultures alter and expectations are upgraded. The job itself will expand in scope and outlook, moving towards a more commercial approach by operations, focusing on those factors which win business and create customer satisfaction.

The job

The prime movement will be for operations managers to think in strategic terms: first, in assessing the position and responsibility of operations and, second, in using strategically-oriented criteria to evaluate performance. In thinking strategically they will become pro-active, because the one must lead to the other. Following from this they will take a more outward-looking approach, searching for ways in which operations can help other parts of their own business, while themselves gaining an edge on the operations ability of their competitors.

The person

By now, it will be evident that the job is no sinecure and that the people who will carry out the job successfully will be of high calibre. They will see through and beyond the daily detail, and will be those who . . . 'can keep their head when all about them' . . . (to paraphrase the Kipling poem), not being distracted by sudden crises.

While detailing the job requirements one is impressed increasingly by the general management aspects of the position: the strategic approach, the cross-functional project teams, the recognition and initiation of change and the reviews of culture and philosophy. This leads us to a summary of the skills and characteristics embodied in the successful operations manager:

1 To be articulate, to explain well, to communicate effectively.
2 To be of substantial intellect. The ability to think through complex situations rationally and logically and to visualize the wider potential offered by a strategic approach to operations.
3 To have the skills of persuasion in all their variety, to be able to cajole, to convince, to argue logically and with conviction. To be able to convince people of the ultimate success of their proposals.
4 To have the presence and personal authority needed to lead people through difficult periods of change.
5 To have a wide enough technical knowledge in order to be able to understand the problems and viewpoints of all peer managers in the company and to take a more businesslike approach.
6 To be able to define and agree objectives for all subordinates so that they will want to achieve them; to monitor and change them when the occasion arises.
7 To be mentally and physically capable of withstanding the pressures which will arise periodically.

Final comment

The seven items listed above might seem to be less appropriate to a human being than to an archangel! The challenges are great. The consequences of failure amount to no less than corporate extinction commercially and economic decline nationally. But the opportunities are enormous, for personal advancement, for corporate success, for economic resurgence. It's up to you!

Name index

NAME INDEX

Stewart, R. 330, 336

Taylor, S.G. 119

Vollman, T.E. 96, 119

Warr, P. 292
Whybark, D.C. 96, 119

Subject index